Microsoft® Office Word 2003

ILLUSTRATED

ADVANCED

(3 of 3)

Carol M. Cram

THOMSON
COURSE TECHNOLOGY

Australia • Canada • Mexico • Singapore • Spain • United Kingdom • United States

THOMSON
COURSE TECHNOLOGY

Microsoft® Office Word 2003 - Illustrated Advanced

Carol M. Cram

Executive Editor: Nicole Jones Pinard	**Product Managers:** Christina Kling Garrett, Jane Hosie-Bounar, Jeanne Herring	**Associate Product Manager:** Emilie Perreault
Production Editors: Melissa Panagos, Kelly Robinson		**Editorial Assistant:** Abbey Reider
	Developmental Editor: Pamela Conrad	**Composition House:** GEX Publishing Services
QA Manuscript Reviewers: John Freitas, Holly Schabowski	**Text Designer:** Joseph Lee, Black Fish Design	

Trademarks
Some of the product names and company names used in this book have been used for identification purposes only and may be trademarks or registered trademarks of their respective manufacturers and sellers.

Microsoft and the Office logo are either registered trademarks or trademarks of Microsoft Corporation in the United States and/or other countries. Course Technology is an independent entity from Microsoft Corporation, and not affiliated with Microsoft in any manner.

This text may be used in assisting students to prepare for a Microsoft Office Specialist Exam. Neither Microsoft Corporation, its designated review company, nor Course Technology warrants that use of this text will ensure passing the relevant exam.

Use of the Microsoft Office Specialist Approved Courseware Logo on this product signifies that it has been independently reviewed and approved in complying with the following standards: "Includes acceptable coverage of all content related to the Microsoft Office Exam entitled Microsoft Office Word 2003 and sufficient performance-based exercises that relate closely to all required content, based on sampling of text."

ISBN 0-619-05771-8

The Illustrated Series Vision

Teaching and writing about computer applications can be extremely rewarding and challenging. How do we engage students and keep their interest? How do we teach them skills that they can easily apply on the job? As we set out to write this book, our goals were to develop a textbook that:

- works for a beginning student
- provides varied, flexible, and meaningful exercises and projects to reinforce skills
- serves as a reference tool
- makes your job as an educator easier, by providing resources above and beyond the textbook to help you teach your course

Our popular, streamlined format is based on advice from instructional designers and customers. This flexible design presents each lesson on a two-page spread, with step-by-step instructions on the left, and screen illustrations on the right. This signature style, coupled with high-caliber content, provides a comprehensive yet manageable introduction to Microsoft Office Word 2003—it is a teaching package for the instructor and a learning experience for the student.

Acknowledgments

I wish to thank Pam Conrad, who provided so much encouragement, support, and intelligence throughout the editorial process. She is truly beyond compare! I also wish to thank my husband, Gregg Simpson, for his ongoing support and encouragement, and our daughter Julia for her enthusiastic help. Finally, I'd like to thank my students at Capilano College in North Vancouver. They are what it's all about.

Carol M. Cram
and the Illustrated Team

Preface

Welcome to *Microsoft® Office Word 2003–Illustrated Advanced*. Each lesson in this book contains elements pictured to the right.

How is the book organized?

This book is organized into six units and an appendix on Word, covering integrating Word with other programs, building forms, working with charts and diagrams, collaborating with others on documents, and working with XML.

What kinds of assignments are included in the book? At what level of difficulty?

The lessons use MediaLoft, a fictional chain of bookstores, as the case study. The assignments on the light purple pages at the end of each unit increase in difficulty. Data Files and case studies, with many international examples, provide a great variety of interesting and relevant business applications. Assignments include:

- **Concepts Reviews** include multiple choice, matching, and screen identification questions.

- **Skills Reviews** provide additional hands-on, step-by-step reinforcement.

- **Independent Challenges** are case projects requiring critical thinking and application of the unit skills. The Independent Challenges increase in difficulty, with the first one in each unit being the easiest (most step-by-step with detailed instructions). Independent Challenges 2 and 3 become increasingly more open-ended, requiring more independent problem solving.

- **E-Quest Independent Challenges** are case projects with a Web focus. E-Quests require the use of the World Wide Web to conduct research to complete the project.

- **Advanced Challenge Exercises** set within the Independent Challenges provide optional steps for more advanced students.

- **Visual Workshops** are practical, self-graded capstone projects that require independent problem solving.

Each 2-page spread focuses on a single skill.

Concise text introduces the basic principles in the lesson and integrates a real-world case study.

UNIT M
Word 2003

Adding and Modifying Text Form Fields

Once you have created a structure for your form, you need to designate form fields where users enter information. You insert **text form fields** in the table cells where users will enter text information, such as their names or the current date. A text form field allows you to control the kind of information users can enter. For example, you can specify that a text form field accepts only a numeric value, limits the number of characters entered, or requires dates to be entered in a specified format. You insert text form fields in the table cells where you need users to enter text or numbers. You then work in the Text Form Field Options dialog box to specify the kind of information required for each text form field.

STEPS

1. Click **View** on the menu bar, point to **Toolbars**, then click **Forms**
   The Forms toolbar contains the buttons used to create and modify the various elements of a form. Table M-1 describes each button on the Forms toolbar.

   TROUBLE
   If dots do not appear in the shaded rectangle, click the Show/Hide ¶ button on the Formatting toolbar.

2. Click after **Name:**, press **[Spacebar]** one time, then click the **Text Form Field button** on the Forms toolbar
   A gray shaded rectangle with five dots appears following Name. When completing the form, the user will be able to enter text into this form field.

3. Press **[Tab]**, click after **Date:**, press **[Spacebar]** one time, then click

4. Repeat step 3 to insert a text form field after **Extension:** and after **Other (please specify):**
   Figure M-4 shows the form with text form fields inserted in four table cells. You want each user who completes the form to enter a date in a specific format in the text form field following the Date label.

5. Click the **text form field** next to **Date:**, then click the **Form Field Options button** on the Forms toolbar
   The Text Form Field Options dialog box opens. In this dialog box, you specify options related to the format and content of the selected text form field.

   QUICK TIP
   If the user types 03/03/06, the date entered will appear as March 3, 2006.

6. Click the **Type list arrow**, click **Date**, click the **Date format list arrow**, click **MMMM d, yyyy** as shown in Figure M-5, then click **OK**
   The text form field looks the same. In a later lesson, you will add a Help message to inform users how to enter the date.

7. Click the **text form field** next to **Extension:**, then click

8. Click the **Maximum length up arrow** until **4** appears, then click **OK**
   You specify the number of characters a field can contain when you want to restrict the length of an entry. For example, a user completing this form can enter a phone extension of no more than four digits.

9. Click the **Save button** on the Standard toolbar to save the template

Clues to Use

Locking form fields

When you protect a form using the Protect Form button on the Forms toolbar, the form information, such as field labels, is protected or locked. A user can input information only in form fields and the input information must match the type specified by the person who originated the form. Sometimes, however, instead of protecting an entire form, you might want to lock certain form fields. For example,

if you are entering numbers in a form for a budget and you want to be sure that the numbers do not inadvertently get changed, you can lock the form field after you enter the numbers. To lock a form field, and prevent changes to the current field results, click the field, then press [Ctrl][F11]. If you need to unlock a field to update the field results, click the field, then press [Ctrl][Shift][F11].

WORD M-4 BUILDING FORMS

Tips, as well as troubleshooting advice, are located right where you need them—next to the step itself.

Clues to Use boxes provide concise information that either expands on the major lesson skill or describes an independent task that in some way relates to the major lesson skill.

Every lesson features large, full-color representations of what the screen should look like as students complete the numbered steps.

Brightly colored tabs indicate which section of the book you are in.

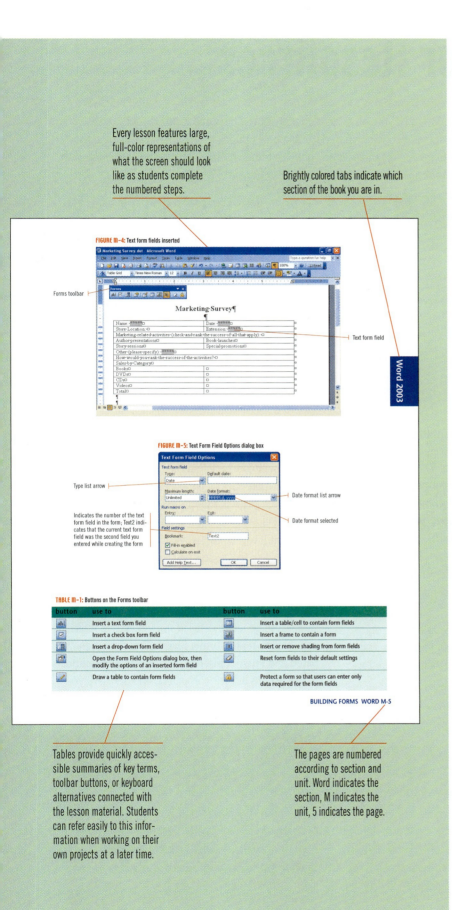

Forms toolbar

FIGURE M-4: Text form fields inserted

Text form field

Word 2003

FIGURE M-5: Text Form Field Options dialog box

Type list arrow

Date format list arrow

Date format selected

Indicates the number of the text form field in the form; Text2 indicates that the current text form field was the second field you entered while creating the form

TABLE M-1: Buttons on the Forms toolbar

button	use to	button	use to
	Insert a text form field		Insert a table/cell to contain form fields
	Insert a check box form field		Insert a frame to contain a form
	Insert a drop-down form field		Insert or remove shading from form fields
	Open the Form Field Options dialog box, then modify the options of an inserted form field		Reset form fields to their default settings
	Draw a table to contain form fields		Protect a form so that users can enter only data required for the form fields

BUILDING FORMS WORD M-5

Tables provide quickly accessible summaries of key terms, toolbar buttons, or keyboard alternatives connected with the lesson material. Students can refer easily to this information when working on their own projects at a later time.

The pages are numbered according to section and unit. Word indicates the section, M indicates the unit, 5 indicates the page.

What online content solutions are available to accompany this book?

Visit www.course.com for more information on our online content for Illustrated titles. Options include:

MyCourse 2.0

Need a quick, simple tool to help you manage your course? Try MyCourse 2.0, the most flexible syllabus and content management tool available. MyCourse 2.0 offers you brand new content, including Topic Reviews, Extra Case Projects, and Quizzes to accompany this book.

WebCT

Course Technology and WebCT have partnered to provide you with the highest quality online resources and Web-based tools for your class. Course Technology offers content for this book to help you create your WebCT class, such as a suggested Syllabus, Lecture Notes, Practice Test questions, and more.

Blackboard

Course Technology and Blackboard have also partnered to provide you with the highest quality online resources and Web-based tools for your class. Course Technology offers content for this book to help you create your Blackboard class, such as a suggested Syllabus, Lecture Notes, Practice Test questions, and more.

Is this book Microsoft Office Specialist Certified?

When used in conjunction with *Microsoft Office Word 2003–Illustrated Basic* and *Microsoft Office Word 2003–Illustrated Intermediate*, this book covers the objectives for Microsoft Office Word 2003 and Microsoft Office Word 2003 Expert. When used in this sequence, these titles have received certification approval as courseware for the Microsoft Office Specialist program. See the inside front cover for more information on other Illustrated titles meeting Microsoft Office Specialist certification.

The first page of each unit indicates which objectives in the unit are Microsoft Office Specialist skills. If an objective is set in red, it meets a Microsoft Office Specialist skill. A document on the CD accompanying this book cross-references the skills with the lessons and exercises.

v

Instructor Resources

The Instructor Resources CD is Course Technology's way of putting the resources and information needed to teach and learn effectively into your hands. With an integrated array of teaching and learning tools, the CD offers you and your students a broad range of technology-based instructional options—the highest quality and most cutting–edge resources available to instructors today. Many of these resources are available at www.course.com. The resources available with this book are:

- **Data Files for Students**—To complete most of the units in this book, your students will need the Data Files on the CD in the back of this book. The Data Files are also available on the Instructor Resources CD and can be downloaded from www.course.com. Direct students to use the **Data Files List** located on the CD. This list provides instructions on copying and organizing files.

- **Solutions to Exercises**—Solutions to Exercises contains every file students are asked to create or modify in the lessons and End-of-Unit material. A Help file on the Instructor Resources CD includes information for using the Solution Files. There is also a document outlining the solutions for the End-of-Unit Concepts Review, Skills Review, and Independent Challenges.

- **PowerPoint Presentations**—Each unit has a corresponding PowerPoint presentation that you can use in a lecture, distribute to your students, or customize to suit your course.

- **Instructor's Manual**—Available as an electronic file, the Instructor's Manual is quality-assurance tested and includes unit overviews and detailed lecture topics with teaching tips for each unit.

- **Sample Syllabus**—Prepare and customize your course easily using this sample course outline.

- **Figure Files**—The figures in the text are provided on the Instructor Resources CD to help you illustrate key topics or concepts. You can create traditional overhead transparencies by printing the figure files, or you can create electronic slide shows by using the figures in a presentation program such as PowerPoint.

- **ExamView**—ExamView is a powerful testing software package that allows you to create and administer printed, computer (LAN-based), and Internet exams. ExamView includes hundreds of questions that correspond to the topics covered in this text, enabling students to generate detailed study guides that include page references for further review. The computer-based and Internet testing components allow students to take exams at their computers, and also save you time by grading each exam automatically.

SAM 2003 Assessment & Training

SAM 2003 helps you energize your class exams and training assignments by allowing students to learn and test important computer skills in an active, hands-on environment.

With SAM 2003 Assessment, you create powerful interactive exams on critical applications such as Word, Outlook, PowerPoint, Windows, the Internet, and much more. The exams simulate the application environment, allowing your students to demonstrate their knowledge and think through the skills by performing real-world tasks.

Designed to be used with the Illustrated series, SAM 2003 Assessment & Training includes built-in page references so students can create study guides that match the Illustrated textbooks you use in class. Powerful administrative options allow you to schedule exams and assignments, secure your tests, and run reports with almost limitless flexibility.

Contents

Read This Before You Begin

Software Information and Required Installation

This book was written and tested using Microsoft Office 2003 - Professional Edition (which includes Microsoft Office Word 2003), with a typical installation on Microsoft Windows XP, including installation of the most recent Windows XP Service Pack, and with Internet Explorer 6.0 or higher. Some of the exercises in this book assume that your computer is connected to the Internet. If you are not connected to the Internet, see your instructor.

Tips for Students

What are Data Files?

To complete many of the units in this book, you need to use Data Files from the CD in the back of this book. A Data File contains a partially completed document, so that you don't have to type all the information in the document yourself. Your instructor can give you instructions on how to organize your files, as well as a complete file listing, or you can find the list and the instructions for organizing your files on the CD. If you are saving your work on floppy disks as you complete the exercises in this book, then you may need to use multiple disks to complete all of the work in Unit K, depending on the size of graphics files that you use.

Why is my screen different from the book?

Your desktop components and some dialog box options might be different if you are using an operating system other than Windows XP.

Depending on your computer hardware and the Display settings on your computer, you may notice the following differences:

- Your screen may look larger or smaller because of your screen resolution (the height and width of your screen).

- Your title bars and dialog boxes may not display file extensions. To display file extensions, click Start on the taskbar, click Control Panel, click Appearance and Themes, then click Folder Options. Click the View tab if necessary, click Hide extensions for known file types to deselect it, then click OK. Your Office dialog boxes and title bars should now display file extensions.

- Depending on your Office settings, your Standard and Formatting toolbars may be displayed on a single row and your menus may display a shortened list of frequently used commands. Office menus and toolbars can modify themselves to your working style by displaying only the most frequently used buttons and menu commands. To view buttons not currently displayed, click a Toolbar Options button at the right end of either the Standard or Formatting toolbar. To view the full list of menu commands, click the double arrow at the bottom of the menu.

TOOLBARS ON ONE ROW

TOOLBARS ON TWO ROWS

This book assumes you are displaying toolbars in two rows and displaying full menus. In order to have your toolbars displayed on two rows, showing all buttons, and to have the full menus displayed, you must turn off the personalized menus and toolbars feature. Click Tools on the menu bar, click Customize, select the show Standard and Formatting toolbars on two rows and Always show full menus check boxes on the Options tab, and then click Close.

Integrating Word with Other Programs

OBJECTIVES

Explore integration methods

Embed an Excel worksheet

Link an Excel chart

Embed a PowerPoint slide

Insert a Word file

Import a table from Access

Manage document links

Merge with an Access data source

If you have a SAM user profile, you may have access to hands-on instruction, practice, and assessment of the skills covered in this unit. Log in to your SAM account and go to your assignments page to see what your instructor has assigned.

The Office suite includes several programs, each with its own unique purpose and characteristics. Sometimes information you want to include in a Word document is stored in files created with other Office programs such as PowerPoint or Excel. For example, the report you are writing in Word might need to include a pie chart from a worksheet created in Excel. You can embed information from other programs in a Word document or you can create links between programs. Nazila Sharif in the Marketing Department has started a report on how to market Media-Loft.com, MediaLoft's home on the World Wide Web. She asks you to supplement the report with information contained in another Word file and in files she created in Excel, PowerPoint, and Access. You then need to merge an Access data source with the cover letter you'll send along with the report to all the MediaLoft store managers.

Exploring Integration Methods

You can integrate information created with other Office programs into a Word document in a variety of ways. Figure K-1 shows a six-page Word document containing shared information from PowerPoint, Excel, Access, and another Word document. The methods available for sharing information between programs include copy and paste, drag and drop, Object Linking and Embedding, and inserting files. Table K-1 describes each Office program and includes its associated file extension and icon. Each program uses a unique **file extension**, the three letters that follow the period in a filename.  Before you integrate information created in other programs into the report contained in a Word document, you review the various ways in which information is shared between programs.

DETAILS

You can share information in the following ways:

- **Copy and paste**
  You use the Copy and Paste commands to copy information from one program and paste it into another program, usually when you need to copy a small amount of text.

- **Drag and drop**
  You can position documents created in two programs side by side in separate windows and then use drag and drop to copy or move selected text or objects from one document (the source file) into another document (the destination file).

- **Insert a Word file**
  You can use the File command on the Insert menu to insert an entire file. The file types you can insert include Word documents (.doc) or templates (.dot), documents saved in rich text format (.rtf), and documents created as .mht or .htm files for Web pages.

- **Object Linking and Embedding**
  The ability to share information with other programs is called **Object Linking and Embedding (OLE)**. Two programs are involved in the OLE process. The **source program** is the program in which information is originally created, and the **destination program** is the program to which the information is copied. With OLE, you use the source program to create a **source file** and you use the destination program to create a **destination file**.

- **Objects**
  An **object** is defined as self-contained information that can be in the form of text, spreadsheet data, graphics, charts, tables, or even sound and video clips. Objects provide a means of sharing information between programs. You can create objects by selecting Object on the Insert menu or by selecting Paste Special on the Edit menu.

- **Embedded objects**
  An **embedded object** is created within the destination file or copied from the source file. You can edit an embedded object within the destination program using the editing features of the source program. Any changes you make to an embedded object appear only in the destination file; the changes are *not* made to the information in the source file.

- **Linked objects**
  A **linked object** is created in a source file, then inserted into a destination file and linked to the source file. When you link an object, changes made to the data in the source file are reflected in the destination file. In a linked object, the connection between the source file and the destination file is called a **Dynamic Data Exchange (DDE)** link.

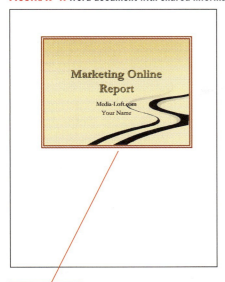

PowerPoint slide
created as an
embedded object
in Word

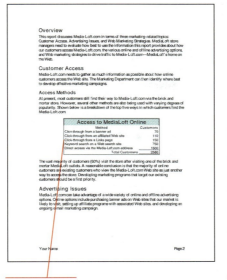

Excel worksheet
inserted as an
embedded object
into Word

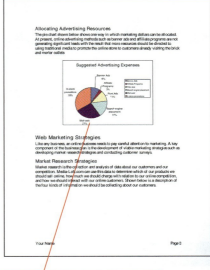

Excel pie chart inserted into Word as a
linked object; the linked chart in Word
can be updated to reflect changes
made to the chart in Excel

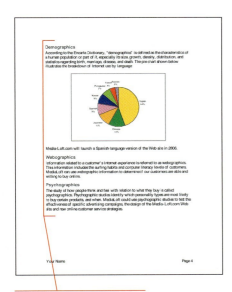

Word file inserted into the Word
document with formatting and
chart image intact

Access table copied
from Access and
then formatted

Word 2003

TABLE K-1: Office programs

icon	program	extension	purpose
W	Word	.doc	To create documents and share information in print, e-mail, and on the Web
X	Excel	.xls	To create, analyze, and share spreadsheets and to analyze data with charts, PivotTable dynamic views, and graphs
P	PowerPoint	.ppt	To organize, illustrate, and deliver materials in an easy-to-understand graphics format for delivery in a presentation or over the Internet
A	Access	.mdb	To store, organize, and share database information
F	FrontPage	.htm or .html	To create and manage the files required for a Web site

UNIT K
Word 2003

Embedding an Excel Worksheet

An embedded object uses the features of another program such as Excel, but is stored as part of the Word document. You embed an object, such as an Excel worksheet or a PowerPoint slide, in Word when you do *not* need changes made in the source file to be updated in the embedded Word object. You edit an embedded object directly in Word using the source program toolbars. For example, you can embed a worksheet created in Excel into a Word document, double-click the embedded worksheet object to enter edit mode and show the Excel toolbars, and then edit the embedded object using the Excel toolbars. The Online Marketing Report that Nazila created in Word contains placeholder text and bookmarks to designate where information created in other programs should be inserted. Your first task is to embed an Excel worksheet that contains data related to the top five methods customers use to find Media-Loft.com.

STEPS

TROUBLE

This unit assumes your system settings are set to display file extensions. If you do not see .doc after the filename, change your system settings or ask your instructor or technical support person for help.

1. Start Word, open the file **WD K-1.doc** from the drive and folder where your Data Files are located, save it as **Online Marketing Report**, click the Show/Hide ¶ button ¶ to select it, then scroll through the report to note where you will insert content from other programs

2. Click **Edit** on the menu bar, click **Go To**, click **Bookmark** in the Go to what list box, verify that **Customers** appears in the Enter bookmark name text box, click **Go To**, click **Close**, then delete the placeholder text **Excel Worksheet Here** but *not* the ¶ mark following Here

3. Click **Insert** on the menu bar, then click **Object**

   You use the Object dialog box to create a new object using the tools of a program other than Word or to insert an object created in another program.

4. Click the **Create from File tab**, click the **Browse button**, navigate to the drive and folder where your Data Files are located, click **WD K-2.xls**, then click **Insert**

   The Object dialog box opens. Because you want to create an embedded object, you leave the Link to file check box blank, as shown in Figure K-2.

5. Click **OK**

   The Excel worksheet is inserted as an embedded object in Word.

QUICK TIP

Any changes you make to the file in Word, even those using the Excel toolbars, are not reflected in the original Excel file.

6. **Double-click the embedded worksheet object**

   The embedded object opens in an Excel object window and the Excel toolbars appear under the Word menu bar. You can use the Excel toolbars to format the cells or change the data in the Excel worksheet object.

7. Click the **value** in cell B3 as shown in Figure K-3, type **70**, click the **value** in cell B8, then click the **Bold button** B on the Excel Formatting toolbar

   The total number of customers shown in cell B8 increases by 32 from 2548 to 2580.

8. **Click to the right of the embedded Excel worksheet object**

   The Excel toolbars close and the Word toolbars open.

9. Click the worksheet object again to select it, click the **Center button** ☰ on the Formatting toolbar, click the **Outside Border button** ⊞ on the Formatting toolbar, click below the worksheet object, then save the document

   The modified embedded Excel worksheet object appears in the Word document, as shown in Figure K-4.

FIGURE K-2: Object dialog box

Use this tab to create a new object

Object embedded in Word will be based on this Excel file

Description of current action

Click to navigate to location (the drive and folder) of the file to insert

Link to file is *not* selected when embedding the file in Word

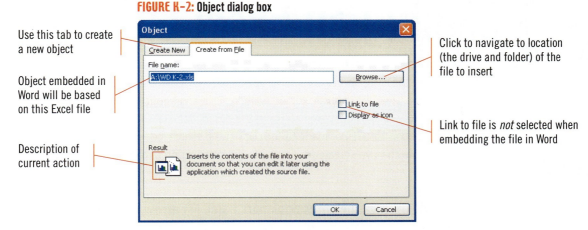

FIGURE K-3: Editing the embedded worksheet object

Microsoft Word title bar

Excel Standard and Formatting toolbars

Embedded work-sheet appears in an Excel object window

Bold button

Cell B3

Cell B8

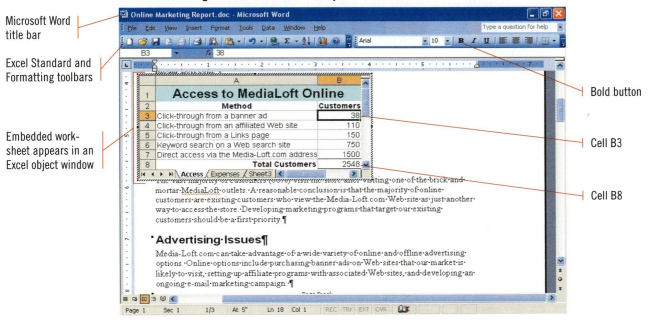

FIGURE K-4: Modified embedded worksheet object

Word toolbars

Excel worksheet embedded in Word document; formatted using Word toolbars

Outside Border button

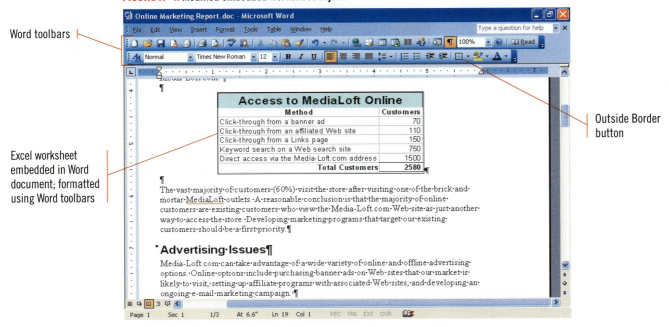

Linking an Excel Chart

You can use the Paste Special command on the Edit menu to integrate data from a source file into a destination file. When you use the Paste Special command, you create a linked object by copying data from the source file in one program and pasting the data into the destination file in another program. If you make a change to the data in the source file, the data in the linked object in the destination file is updated. Any changes you make to the data in the destination file are *not* made to the data in the source file. You use the Paste Special command to insert a pie chart you created in Excel into the Word report as a linked object.

STEPS

QUICK TIP

The data in cell B3 is outdated because of the change you made in the previous lesson. You do not need to update the data.

1. Press [Ctrl][G], click the Enter bookmark name list arrow, select Resources, click Go To, click Close, then delete the text Excel Pie Chart Here but *not* the ¶ mark following Here

2. Click Start on the taskbar, click Microsoft Office Excel 2003 to start Microsoft Excel, open the file WD K-2.xls from the drive and folder where your Data Files are located, then save it as Online Marketing Data

   Two programs are currently open, as indicated by the program buttons on your taskbar.

TROUBLE

Be sure a border with sizing handles surrounds the pie chart and all its related components. If only one component is selected, click outside the chart area, then repeat Step 3.

3. Click the Expenses tab at the bottom of the Excel worksheet, click the white space in the lower-right corner of the chart area to select the pie chart and all its components, then click the Copy button 🖺 on the Standard toolbar

4. Click the Microsoft Word program button on the taskbar to return to Word, click Edit on the menu bar, then click Paste Special

   You use the Paste Special dialog box, shown in Figure K-5, to identify whether the data you want to paste will be inserted as an embedded object or a linked object.

5. Click the Paste link option button, then click OK

   The pie chart is inserted. Notice that Banner Ads account for 2% of suggested advertising expenses.

6. Click the Microsoft Excel program button on the taskbar to return to Excel, scroll up to see the top of the worksheet, click cell B2, type 9000, then press [Enter]

   The Banner Ads slice increases to 9%, as shown in Figure K-6.

TROUBLE

If your link did not update automatically, you can right-click the chart, then click Update Link on the shortcut menu.

7. Click Online Marketing Report on the taskbar to return to Word, then verify that the Banner Ads slice now shows 9%

8. Right-click the pie chart object, click Format Object, click the Size tab in the Format Object dialog box, select the contents of the Width text box in the Size and rotate section, type 3.8, then click OK

   You use the Format Object dialog box to format embedded and linked objects.

9. Click the Center button ☰ on the Formatting toolbar, click away from the pie chart object to deselect it, scroll up to view the heading Allocating Advertising Resources, compare the pie chart object to Figure K-7, then save the document

10. Click the Microsoft Excel program button on the taskbar to return to Excel, click File on the menu bar, click Exit, then click Yes to save the updated worksheet

    The Online Marketing Report in Word is again the active document.

FIGURE K-5: Paste Special dialog box

Use the Paste option button to create an embedded object

Use the Paste link option button to create a linked object

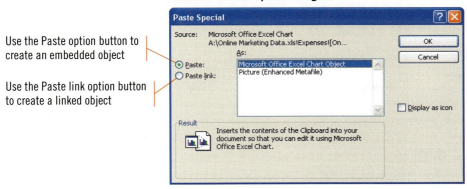

FIGURE K-6: Modified pie chart in Excel

Microsoft Excel title bar

Banner Ads slice increased to 9%

Word file open

Cell B2

Excel file active window

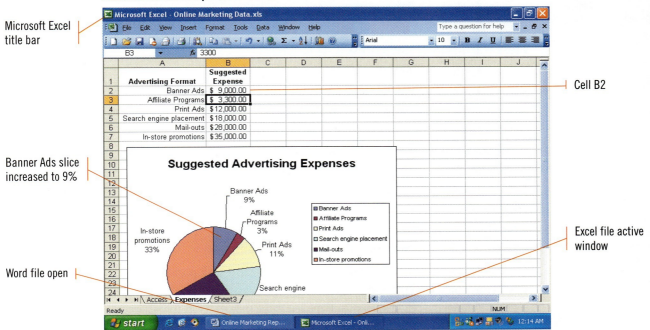

FIGURE K-7: Updated pie chart in Word

Banner Ads slice increased to 9%

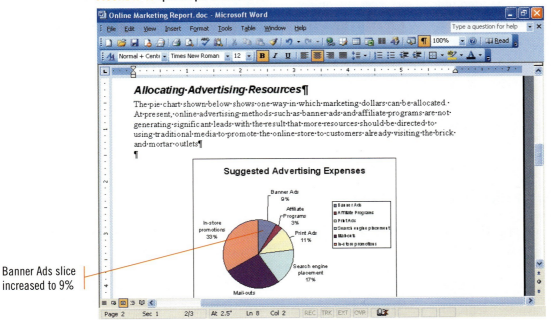

INTEGRATING WORD WITH OTHER PROGRAMS WORD K-7

Embedding a PowerPoint Slide

You can share information between Word and PowerPoint in a variety of ways. You can use the Paste Special command to insert a slide as a linked or an embedded object into a Word document. You can use Create New to create a PowerPoint slide as an embedded object in Word, and then use PowerPoint tools to modify the slide in Word. ▰▰▰▰ You plan to distribute the Online Marketing Report at a conference where you will also deliver a PowerPoint presentation. You decide to use the theme you've chosen for the PowerPoint presentation on the title page of the report. You create a new PowerPoint slide and embed it in the title page, then you use PowerPoint tools to format the embedded object.

STEPS

1. **Press [Ctrl][Home], then press [Ctrl][Enter]**
   A page break appears. You want to embed a PowerPoint slide on the new blank page.

2. **Press [Ctrl][Home], click Insert on the menu bar, then click Object**
   The Object dialog box opens. The types of objects that you can create new in Word are listed in the Object type list box.

3. **Scroll down, select Microsoft PowerPoint Slide in the Object type list box, then click OK**
   A blank PowerPoint slide appears along with the PowerPoint toolbars.

4. **Click in the Click to add title text box, type Marketing Online Report, click in the Click to add subtitle text box, type Media-Loft.com, press [Enter], then type your name**

TROUBLE
If the slide design is not applied to the slide, double-click Stream.pot in the Available for Use list box.

5. **Click the Slide Design button** 🖼 Design **on the PowerPoint Formatting toolbar, then scroll down and click the Stream.pot design (see Figure K-8)**

6. **Click Color Schemes at the top of the Slide Design task pane, then scroll down and click the beige color scheme (see Figure K-9)**
   Figure K-9 shows the beige color scheme applied to the slide. You can apply new color schemes to any of the slide designs included with PowerPoint.

7. **Click the Zoom list arrow on the Standard toolbar, click Whole Page, click below the embedded slide object, click the object to select it if necessary, click Format on the menu bar, click Object, click the Size tab, type 6 in the Width text box in the Size and rotate section, then click OK**

8. **Click Format on the menu bar, click Borders and Shading, click Box on the Borders tab, select the double border style, the Brown color, and the 3 pt width, then click OK**

9. **Click to the right of the slide object to deselect it, then save the document**
   The embedded PowerPoint slide appears in a Word document, as shown in Figure K-10.

Clues to Use

Creating a PowerPoint presentation from a Word outline

When you create a PowerPoint presentation from a Word outline, the Word document is the source file and the PowerPoint document is the destination file. In the Word source file, headings formatted with heading styles are converted to PowerPoint headings in the PowerPoint destination file. For example, each Level 1 heading becomes its own slide. To create a PowerPoint presentation from a Word outline, create the outline in Word, click File on the menu bar, point to Send To, then click Microsoft Office PowerPoint. In a few moments the Word outline is converted to a PowerPoint presentation, where you can modify it just like any PowerPoint presentation. Any changes you make to the presentation in PowerPoint are *not* reflected in the original Word document.

FIGURE K-8: Stream.pot design applied to slide

Microsoft Word title bar

PowerPoint Standard and Formatting toolbars

Slide Design button on the PowerPoint Formatting toolbar

Stream.pot selected; list arrow appears when pointer moves over slide design

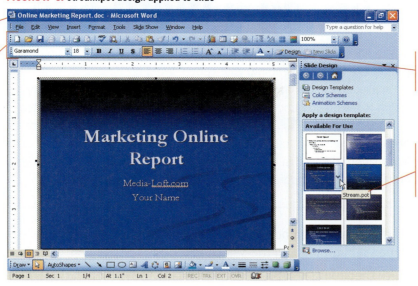

FIGURE K-9: Beige color scheme applied to slide

Beige color scheme

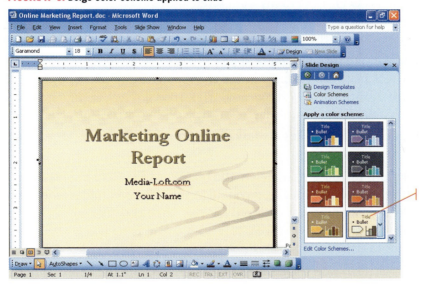

FIGURE K-10: Completed embedded PowerPoint slide object in Word

Microsoft Word title bar

Word Standard and Formatting toolbars

PowerPoint Stream.pot design applied to embedded PowerPoint slide using PowerPoint toolbars in Word

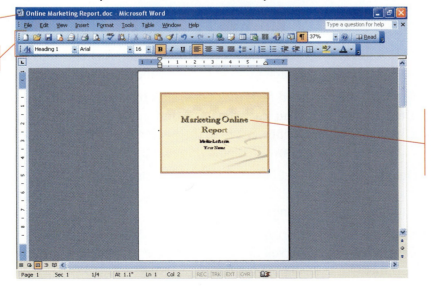

Inserting a Word File

When you need the contents of an entire Word document, you can insert an entire Word file rather than copy and paste the document into your current Word document. The formatting of the current document can be applied to the text in the inserted file. When you insert a Word file into a Word document, you cannot return to the original document from the inserted file; instead, the inserted file becomes an integral part of the Word document. 🎨 You previously created a Word document that contains information about methods used to conduct market research. You use the File Search function to find the Word file containing the information you need to include in the report and then you use the Research function to look up a definition of the word "Demographics."

1. Click **File** on the menu bar, click **File Search** to open the Basic File Search task pane, then type **Webographics** in the Search text box

2. Click the **Results should be list arrow**, click the **Anything check box**, click the **Search in list arrow**, click the **Expand button** ⊞ next to Everywhere to expand the menu if necessary, then click ⊞ next to My Computer

    By default, the Search function looks for the search text in several locations, including your computer's hard drive and any network drives. You want to search the contents of your Data Files only.

> **TROUBLE**
> If your Data Files are *not* located in drive A, select the check box next to the drive where your Data Files are located.

3. Make sure no check mark appears in the check box next to My Computer, make sure a **check mark** does appear in the check box next to 3½ Floppy (A:), then click **Go** two times

    The filename for the Word document (WD K-3.doc) that contains the search text "Webographics" appears. You can click a filename listed in the Search Results task pane to open that file in its associated program.

4. Close the Search Results task pane, press **[Ctrl][G]**, select the **Research** bookmark, click **Go To**, then click **Close**

5. Return to 100% view, delete the text **Word File Here** but leave the ¶ mark, click **Insert** on the menu bar, click **File**, navigate to the drive and folder where your Data Files are located if necessary, click **WD K-3.doc**, then click **Insert**

    The contents of the WD K-3.doc file appear in your current document. If you make changes to the text you inserted in this destination file, the changes will *not* be reflected in the WD K-3.doc source file.

6. Scroll up to view the Demographics heading, click the **Research button** 📖 on the Standard toolbar, click in the **Search for text box**, type **Demographics**, then click the **list arrow** next to All Reference Books

    A selection of the references you can search appears. You can find word definitions and synonyms or search various research sites for information about specific topics.

> **TROUBLE**
> This lesson assumes you have an active Internet connection. If you do not, you will need to type the definition shown in Figure K-11.

7. Click **Encarta Dictionary: English (North America)**, click the **Start searching button** ➡, scroll down the Research task pane, then select the definition as shown in Figure K-11

8. Right-click the selected text, click **Copy**, click to the left of the first line of text under the Demographics heading, click the **Paste button** 📋 on the Standard toolbar, type a **period** (.), press **[Spacebar]** once, move to the beginning of the sentence and add the text **According to the Encarta Dictionary, "demographics" is defined as**, then press **[Spacebar]**

9. Delete the title **Market Research Methods** including the ¶, select the **Demographics** heading, apply the **Heading 3 style**, then apply the **Heading 3 style** to the **Webographics** and **Psychographics** headings

10. Scroll up and insert a page break to the left of the **Demographics** heading, close the Research task pane, scroll down and compare the document to Figure K-12, then save the document

FIGURE K-11: Selecting a definition in the Research task pane

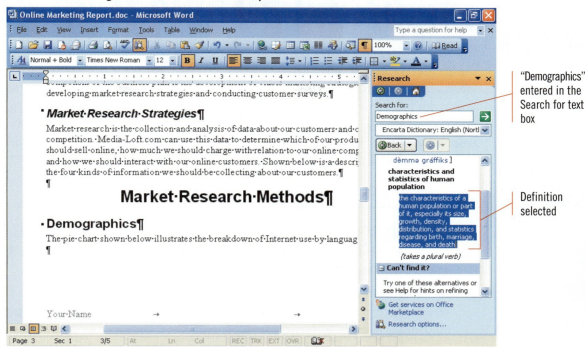

"Demographics" entered in the Search for text box

Definition selected

FIGURE K-12: Word file inserted into a Word document and formatted

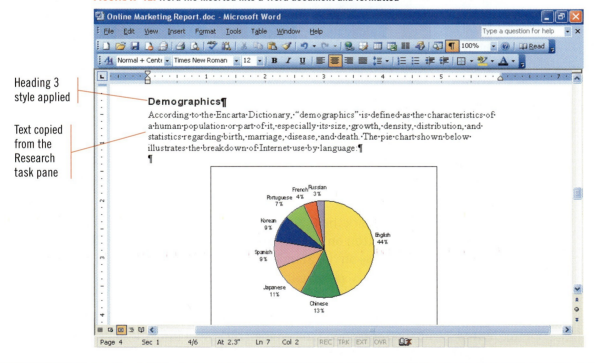

Heading 3 style applied

Text copied from the Research task pane

Clues to Use

Conducting a search

Using the File Search command on the File menu opens the Basic Search task pane, where you can search for specific text in files located on your computer hard drive, your local network, your Microsoft Outlook mailbox, and your network places. When you conduct a search from the Basic Search task pane, all the files that contain the search text you specified are displayed according to their location. For example, a search for the text "book club" yields a list of all the files that contain the text "book club" in the filename, contents, or properties in the locations you specified. When you find the file you want, you can open and edit the file in its program, you can create a new document based on the file, you can copy a link to the file to the Office Clipboard, or you can view the file's properties.

Importing a Table from Access

You can share information between Access and Word in a variety of ways. The most common method is to use the Access Publish It with Microsoft Office Word command, which publishes an Access table into Word. When you publish an Access table, Access launches Word and then copies the Access table to a Word window in rich text format (.rtf). Once the Access table is published to Word, you can use Word's table features to format it. 🎨 You have already created an Access database that contains information related to online survey results. You open the Access database, then use the Publish It command in Access to publish one of the Access database tables into Word. You format it with one of Word's preset Table AutoFormats, and then copy the Word table into the Marketing Online Report.

STEPS

1. Press [Ctrl][G], select the Survey bookmark, go to and then delete the placeholder text Access Table Here but *not* the ¶ mark, click Start on the taskbar, point to All Programs, point to Microsoft Office, then click Microsoft Office Access 2003

   TROUBLE
   If warning messages appear, click Yes, then click Open.

2. Click the Open button 📂 on the Standard toolbar in Access, navigate to the drive and folder where your Data Files are located, click WD K-4.mdb, then click Open

   The database file opens in Microsoft Access. You publish the Online Survey table in a Word document.

3. Click Online Survey in the Tables window as shown in Figure K-13, click the OfficeLinks list arrow 📊▾ on the Access Standard toolbar, then click Publish It with Microsoft Office Word

   In a few moments, a Word window opens with a new document named Online Survey.rtf, as shown in Figure K-14. The "rtf" extension stands for "rich text format." Notice that the taskbar indicates you have two Word documents open. You may see one Word button with the number 2 (as shown in Figure K-14), or you may see two Word buttons. When you use the Publish It with Microsoft Office Word command in Access, the Access data is always copied into a new Word window.

4. Click the table move handle ⊞ in the upper-left corner of the table to select the entire table, click Table on the menu bar, click Table AutoFormat, click Table List 7, then click Apply

   The Online Survey table is formatted with the Table List 7 style.

5. With the entire table still selected, move the pointer over any column border in the gray area of the first row to show the +‖+ pointer, then double-click to automatically resize the columns to fit the data

6. With the table still selected, click the Copy button 📋 on the Standard toolbar, click the Microsoft Word program button on the taskbar, select Online Marketing Report.doc, then click the Paste button 📋 on the Standard toolbar

   The Word table is copied into your Word document. The Word table is just that—a Word table; it is *not* an embedded object or a linked object.

7. Scroll up to see the first row of the table, click ⊞ to select the entire table, click the Center button ▤ on the Formatting toolbar, then click away from the table to deselect it

   Figure K-15 shows the formatted table in Word.

8. Save the Word Online Marketing Report document, click the Microsoft Word button on the taskbar, select Online Survey.rtf, then close the document without saving it

   You don't need to save the Online Survey.rtf file because you've already copied the table.

9. Click the Microsoft Access button on the taskbar, click File on the menu bar, then click Exit

   The Online Marketing Report is the active document.

FIGURE K-13: Online Survey table selected in Access

Microsoft Access title bar

Access toolbar

Open button

Tables selected

OfficeLinks list arrow

Online Survey table selected

Tables window

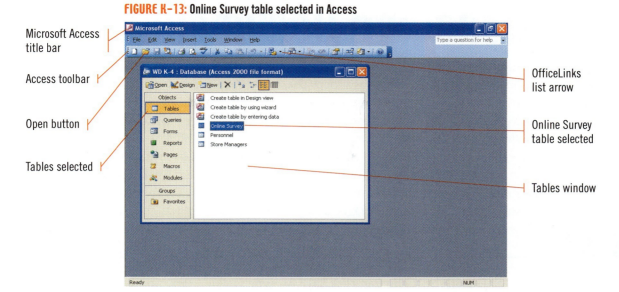

FIGURE K-14: Online Survey.rtf file published in Word

Microsoft Word Online Survey.rtf

Click to show menu that includes Microsoft Word Online Marketing Report.doc

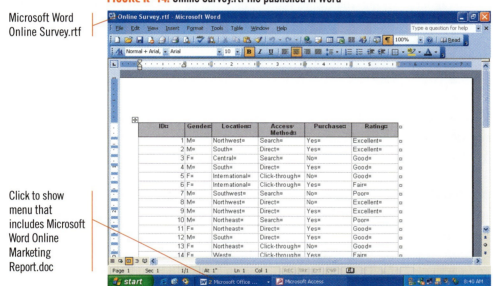

FIGURE K-15: Access table published to Word, then formatted and copied to a Word document

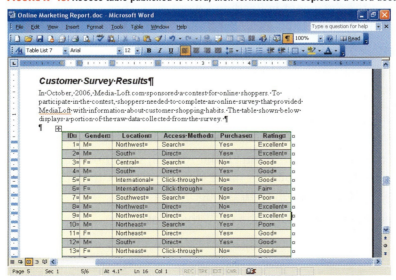

Managing Document Links

When you create a document that contains linked objects, you must include all source files when you copy the document to a new location, such as a floppy disk, or when you e-mail the document to a colleague. If you do *not* include source files, you (or your colleague) will receive error messages when trying to open the destination file. If you do *not* want to include source files when you move or e-mail a document containing links, then you should break the links before moving or e-mailing the document. After you break the links, the Update Links command cannot be used to update information in your destination file. Any changes you make to the source files after breaking the links will *not* be reflected in the destination file. The objects in the destination file will appear as they do at the time the links are broken. ▨▨▨▨▨ You need to distribute the Word report to all the MediaLoft store managers. You keep a copy of the original report with the links intact and then you save the report with a new name and break the links. You also view the entire report in Reading Layout view.

STEPS

1. **Click File on the menu bar, click Save As, type Online Marketing Report_Managers, then click Save**

   Now you can break the link you created between the Excel pie chart in the Word destination file and the Excel pie chart in the Excel source file.

2. **Click Edit on the menu bar, then click Links**

   The Links dialog box opens, as shown in Figure K-16. You can use the Links dialog box to update links, open source files, change source files, and break existing links. Notice that only one source file is listed in the Links dialog box—the Excel file called "Online Marketing Data.xls."

3. **With the Excel file selected, click Break Link**

   A message appears asking if you are sure you want to break the selected link.

4. **Click Yes**

   The link between the Excel source file and the pie chart in the Word destination file is broken. Now if you make a change to the pie chart in the Excel source file, the pie chart in Word will *not* change.

5. **Scroll up until the Suggested Advertising Expenses pie chart is visible, then double-click the pie chart**

   The Format Picture dialog box opens. When you broke the link to the source file, Word converted the pie chart from a linked object to a picture object. You can format the picture object using the Format Picture dialog box, but you cannot change the content of the pie chart.

6. **Click Cancel, click the Reading Layout button 📖 to the left of the horizontal scroll bar to open the document in Reading Layout view, then click the Thumbnails button ⬛ Thumbnails on the Reading Layout toolbar if the Thumbnails pane is not open**

TROUBLE

Your total number of pages may differ depending on your monitor and printer settings.

7. **Scroll up the Thumbnails pane, then click page 3**

   Screen 3 of 16 and 4 of 16 appear in Reading Layout view as shown in Figure K-17. In Reading Layout view, you can comfortably read the document text and scroll from page to page by clicking thumbnails or using the Document Map. As you scroll through the report in Reading Layout view, you notice that some elements, such as the Access table on screen 12, appear less attractively formatted then they did in Print Layout view. Page breaks also appear in different places.

8. **Click Close on the Reading Layout toolbar, scroll down to view the footer, double-click in the footer area, type your name where indicated, then click Close on the Header and Footer toolbar to return to the document**

9. **Save the document, print a copy, then close it**

FIGURE K-16: Links dialog box

Excel file

Source information
for the selected link;
information changes
to reflect link
selected in list

Break Link button

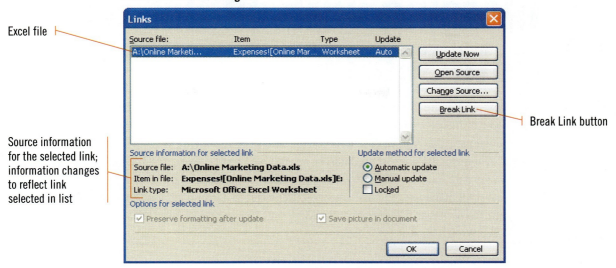

FIGURE K-17: Completed report in Reading Layout view

Reading
Layout toolbar

Thumbnails
button

Page 3
selected in the
Thumbnails
pane; text
placement on
your thumb-
nails and
pages may
differ

Total number
of pages; yours
may differ

Page number

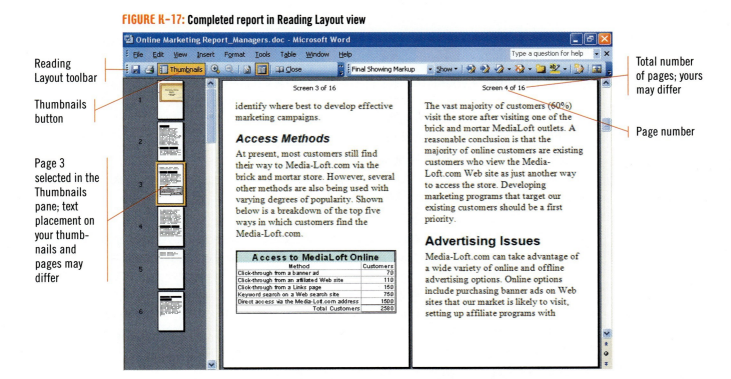

Merging with an Access Data Source

Many businesses store the names and addresses of contacts, employees, and customers in an Access database. You can merge information contained in an Access database with a letter, a sheet of labels, or any merge document that you've created in Word. The data you merge with the destination file is the **data source**. When you use an existing database as your data source, you save time because you do *not* need to create a new data source.  You need to mail a printed copy of the Online Marketing Report to all the MediaLoft store managers. You first create a cover letter to accompany the report and then you merge the letter with the names and addresses of the MediaLoft store managers that are stored in an Access database.

STEPS

1. Open the file WD K-5.doc from the drive and folder where your Data Files are located, save it as Online Marketing Cover Letter, replace Current Date with today's date, scroll down, then type your name in the complimentary closing

2. Click Tools on the menu bar, point to Letters and Mailings, then click Mail Merge
   The Mail Merge task pane opens at Step 3 of 6.

   > **TROUBLE**
   > If the Mail Merge task pane does not open at Step 3 of 6, click Next two times.

3. Click Browse, navigate to the drive and folder where your Data Files are located, select the Access database called WD K-4.mdb, then click Open
   The Select Table window lists the tables available in the WD K-4.mdb Access database.

4. Click Store Managers in the Select Table window, click OK to open the Mail Merge Recipients dialog box, then click OK

5. Click Next: Write your letter in the Mail Merge task pane to move to Step 4 of 6, show the paragraph marks, if necessary, click at the second paragraph mark below the current date in the cover letter, then click Address block in the Mail Merge task pane
   A preview of the default address block appears in the Preview area in the Insert Address Block dialog box.

6. Click OK to accept the default settings, click to the left of the second paragraph mark below the address block, click Greeting line in the Mail Merge task pane, select Joshua as shown in Figure K-18, then click OK
   The field code for the Address block and the field code for the Greeting Line are inserted in your letter.

7. Click Next: Preview your letters in the Mail Merge task pane to move to Step 5 of 6, then click >> to view the letters containing the name and address of each store manager
   You've successfully merged the cover letter with the names and addresses of the store managers. Now you can print just a selection of the letters.

8. Click Next: Complete the merge to move to Step 6 of 6, click Print, click the From option button, enter 1 in the From text box and 2 in the To text box, click OK, then click OK
   The letters to Harriet Gray and Sandra Barradas print, as shown in Figure K-19.

9. Save the document in Word, close it, then exit Word

FIGURE K-18: Greeting Line dialog box

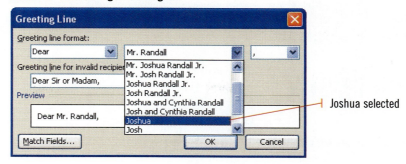

Joshua selected

FIGURE K-19: Merged cover letters

Practice

▼ CONCEPTS REVIEW

Refer to Figure K-20 to answer the following questions.

FIGURE K-20

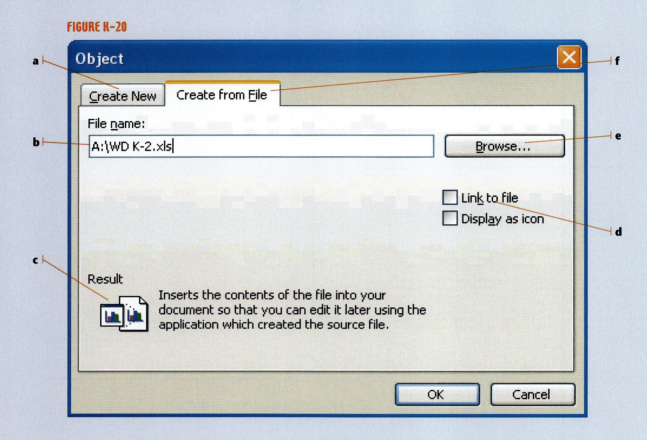

1. **Which element do you click to insert a file created in another program?**
2. **Which element do you click to create an Excel worksheet or PowerPoint slide directly in Word?**
3. **Which element describes the action being taken?**
4. **Which element points to the name of the file that will be inserted?**
5. **Which element do you click to link the inserted file to its source program?**
6. **Which element do you click to find the file you want to insert?**

Match each term with the statement that best describes it.

7. **OLE**
8. **Object**
9. **DDE**
10. **Embedded object**
11. **Source program**
12. **Destination program**

    a. Describes the connection between linked objects
    b. Program to which information is copied
    c. Doesn't change if the source document is edited
    d. Self-contained information that can be in the form of text, graphics, and so on
    e. Program from which information is copied
    f. Provides a means of exchanging information between programs

Select the best answer from the list of choices.

13. What is the destination program?
- **a.** The program from which the information is copied
- **b.** The program to which the information is copied
- **c.** The program in which the information is created
- **d.** The program containing new information

14. What is the source program?
- **a.** The program from which the information is copied
- **b.** The program to which the information is copied
- **c.** The program containing new information
- **d.** None of the above

15. What does DDE stand for?
- **a.** Dedicated Data Exchange
- **b.** Dynamic Data Extension
- **c.** Dynamic Data Exchange
- **d.** Dynamic Data Enhancements

16. Which of the following statements is *not* true about an embedded object?
- **a.** An embedded object can be created in a source file and inserted into a destination file.
- **b.** An embedded object becomes part of the destination file.
- **c.** Changes you make to an embedded object are reflected in the destination file.
- **d.** Changes you make to an embedded object are reflected in the source file.

17. Which of the following statements is *not* true about a linked object?
- **a.** A linked object is created in a source file and inserted into a destination file, while maintaining a connection between the two files.
- **b.** Source files must accompany destination files with linked objects when the destination files are moved.
- **c.** Changes made to a linked object in the destination file are also reflected in the source file.
- **d.** The linked object can be updated in the destination file by right-clicking it, then clicking Update Link.

18. Which command can be used to insert a linked object?
- **a.** Paste
- **b.** Paste Special
- **c.** Link Paste
- **d.** Insert Link

19. Which command do you use in Access to create a Word version of a selected table?
- **a.** Publish It with Access
- **b.** Publish It with Microsoft Office Word
- **c.** Publish It
- **d.** Insert

20. Which view do you access to scroll through a document screen by screen so you can easily read the text?
- **a.** Window view
- **b.** Screen view
- **c.** Thumbnails view
- **d.** Reading Layout view

▼ SKILLS REVIEW

1. Embed an Excel worksheet.
- **a.** Start Word, open the file WD K-6.doc from the drive and folder where your Data Files are located, then save it as **Untamed Tours Report**.
- **b.** Use the Go To command to find the Categories bookmark, then delete the placeholder text **Insert Excel Worksheet Here** but do *not* delete the ¶ mark.
- **c.** Click Insert on the menu bar, then click Object.
- **d.** Click the Create from File tab, then use the Browse feature to insert the file WD K-7.xls from the drive and folder where your Data Files are located into the Word document.
- **e.** Edit the worksheet object. Change the value in cell B7 from 1500 to **2400**, then enhance the value in cell B8 with Bold.
- **f.** In Word, center the worksheet object, apply an outside border, then save the document. (*Hint*: You may need to change the border style to a single black line.)

2. Link an Excel chart.
- **a.** Use the Go To command to find the Popularity bookmark, then delete the placeholder text **Insert Excel Chart Here**, but do *not* delete the ¶ mark.
- **b.** Start Microsoft Office Excel, open the file WD K-7.xls from the drive and folder where your Data Files are located, then save it as **Untamed Tours Data**.

▼ SKILLS REVIEW (CONTINUED)

c. Show the Popularity worksheet, copy the column chart, switch to Word, then use the Paste Special command in Word to paste the column chart as a link in the Word document.

d. Switch to Excel, scroll up to view the data used to create the column chart, then change the value in cell C2 from 1800 to **3400**.

e. Save the worksheet in Excel, then exit Excel.

f. In Word, right-click the chart, then click Update Link.

g. Reduce the width of the chart in Word to **5"**, center the chart, then save the document.

3. Embed a PowerPoint slide.

a. Insert a blank page at the top of the document, then insert a PowerPoint slide as an embedded object on the new blank page.

b. Enter the text **Untamed Tours** as the slide title, then enter **your name** as the subtitle.

c. Apply the Mountain Top.pot slide design to the embedded slide object.

d. Select the turquoise color scheme.

e. Switch to Whole Page view, click below the embedded slide object, then change the width of the object to **6"**.

f. Save the document.

4. Insert a Word file.

a. Use the File Search command to find the Data File that contains the text **Queen Charlotte Islands**.

b. Make note of the Data File filename, close the Search Results task pane, then use the Go To command to find the Tours bookmark in the Untamed Tours Report Word document.

c. Return to 100% view, remove the placeholder text but not the ¶, then insert the file WDK-8.doc from the drive and folder where your Data Files are located.

d. Scroll up, click the second paragraph mark below the paragraph describing sea kayaking tours, then open the Research task pane.

e. Enter the text Queen Charlotte Islands in the Search for text box, click the list arrow to the right of All Reference Books, then select Encarta Encyclopedia: English (North America) as the reference source to search. (*Note*: You must be connected to the Internet to complete this step and the following two steps.)

f. When a description of the Queen Charlotte Islands appears in the Research task pane, scroll down the Research task pane and click the link called Dynamic Map-Encarta Encyclopedia. In a few moments a map of the Queen Charlotte Islands will open in your Web browser.

g. Right-click the map in the Web browser, click Save Picture As, navigate to the drive and folder where your Data Files are located, then click Save.

h. Close the Web browser, then in Word, close the Research task pane.

i. Click Insert on the menu bar, point to Picture, click From File, select the MapImg file, click Insert, be sure the heading Backpacking is on a line by itself, then reduce the width of the map to 3.5" and center it between the left and right margins of the page.

j. Scroll up, delete the centered title, **Untamed Tours**, then remove the extra ¶ above Sea Kayaking.

k. Apply the Heading 3 style to the five headings: Sea Kayaking, Backpacking, Wildlife Photography, Wilderness Canoeing, and Mountain Biking.

l. Save the document.

5. Import a table from Access.

a. Use the Go To command to find the Profile bookmark, then remove the placeholder text **Insert Access Table Here**.

b. Start Microsoft Access, then open the file WD K-9.mdb from the drive and folder where your Data Files are located.

c. Publish the Customer Profile table to Word.

d. Apply the Table Columns 3 AutoFormat to the table in Word, then automatically reduce the column widths to fit the column content.

e. Copy the formatted table to the Untamed Tours Report Word document.

f. Save the Untamed Tours Report Word document, switch to and close the Customer Profile.rtf file without saving it, then switch to and exit Access.

▼ SKILLS REVIEW (CONTINUED)

6. Manage document links.

  a. Open the Links dialog box, then break the link to the Untamed Tours Data.xls file.

  b. Insert a page break to the left of the Tour Popularity heading.

  c. Insert a page break to the left of the Sea Kayaking heading.

  d. Enter your name where indicated at the end of the document.

  e. Switch to Reading Layout view, show the thumbnails, then scroll through the screens.

  f. Save the document, print a copy, then close it.

7. Merge with an Access data source.

  a. Open the file WD K-10.doc from the drive and folder where your Data Files are located, save it as **Untamed Tours Cover Letter**, then replace the placeholder text **Current Date** and **Your Name** with the appropriate information.

  b. Open the Mail Merge task pane, then move to Step 3 of 6, if necessary.

  c. Browse to the drive and folder where your Data Files are located, then select the Access file WD K-9.mdb.

  d. Select the Tour Guides table from the Access database, click OK, then click OK to select all the tour guides listed in the Mail Merge Recipients dialog box.

  e. Move to Step 4 of 6, insert the Address block at the second paragraph mark below the date, use the default format, then insert the Greeting line with the first name selected to follow **Dear** at the second paragraph mark below the Address block. Insert blank paragraphs as needed to ensure proper letter format.

  f. Move to Step 5 of 6, then preview each letter.

  g. Move to Step 6 of 6, print a copy of letters 2 and 3, save and close the document, then exit Word.

▼ INDEPENDENT CHALLENGE 1

As a member of the Rainforest Recreation Commission in the Great Bear Rainforest in British Columbia, you are responsible for compiling the minutes of the monthly meetings. You have already written most of the text required for the minutes. Now you need to insert information from two sources. First, you insert a worksheet from an Excel file that shows the monies raised from various fundraising activities and then you insert a Word file that the director of the commission has sent you for inclusion in the minutes.

  a. Start Word, open the file WD K-11.doc from the drive and folder where your Data Files are located, then save it as **Recreation Commission Minutes**.

  b. Go to the Fundraising bookmark, then insert the Data File WD K-12.xls from the drive and folder where your Data Files are located as an embedded object. (*Hint*: Click the Create from File tab in the Object dialog box.)

  c. Edit the worksheet object by changing the value in cell D5 from 800 to **700**, and then by using the Excel Formatting toolbar to enhance the contents of cells A5 and A6 with Bold.

  d. Center the worksheet in Word, then enclose it with a border.

  e. Press [Ctrl][End], then insert the file WD K-13.doc from the drive and folder where your Data Files are located.

  f. Use Format Painter to apply the formatting of the current headings to the text **Director's Report**, then delete the paragraph mark above **Director's Report**.

  g. Type **Prepared by** followed by your name at the bottom of the document.

Advanced Challenge Exercise

  ■ Double-click the embedded Excel worksheet, click cell A1, change the shading color to Light Turquoise, then change the shading color of cells B4 to F4 to Tan.

  ■ Click cell A6, then press [↓] once to view another row in the worksheet.

  ■ Click cell A7, type **Per Person**, click cell B7, enter the formula **=B6/B5**, then press [Enter].

  ■ Drag the lower-right corner of cell B7 across to cell F7 to fill cells C7 to F7 with the formula, then with the cells still selected, click the Currency Style button on the Formatting toolbar.

  ■ Bold and right-align the label in cell A7, use the vertical scroll bar at the right edge of the worksheet object to scroll up to view cell A1, then drag the lower-right corner of the worksheet object down slightly so that the new row 7 is visible.

  ■ Click outside the worksheet object.

  h. Print, save, and close the document, then exit Word.

▼ INDEPENDENT CHALLENGE 2

You run a summer camp in Grand Canyon National Park in Arizona for teenagers interested in taking on leadership roles at their schools and in their communities. You need to create a report in Word and a presentation in PowerPoint that describes the camp for potential investors. You start by creating an outline of the report in Word, then sending it to PowerPoint as a presentation.

a. Start Word, open the file WD K-14.doc from the drive and folder where your Data Files are located, then save it as **Grand Canyon Camp Report**.

b. Send the outline to PowerPoint as a presentation. (*Hint*: Click File on the menu bar, point to Send To, then click Microsoft Office PowerPoint.)

c. In PowerPoint, apply the Capsules.pot design template and select the maroon color scheme (last selection in the first column).

d. Save the PowerPoint presentation as **Grand Canyon Camp Presentation**, close it, then exit PowerPoint.

e. In Word, insert a new page above the first page in the document, then insert an embedded PowerPoint slide formatted with the Capsules design and the maroon color scheme. Include **Grand Canyon Camp Report** as the title and **your name** as the subtitle.

FIGURE K-21

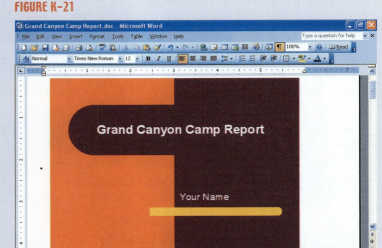

f. In Whole Page view, center and resize the slide object to fit the space. See Figure K-21.

g. Press [Ctrl][End], scroll up to the Student Enrollment heading, click after the subheading that begins **The chart shows**, then press [Enter] twice.

h. Insert the Excel file WD K-15.xls from the drive and folder where your Data Files are located as an embedded object.

i. Double-click the worksheet object, then change the value in cell B3 from 1500 to **1900**.

j. Exit the worksheet object, then center it.

Advanced Challenge Exercise

- Go to the beginning of the document, then double-click about 1" below the embedded slide on page 1.
- Open the Research task pane, be sure your Internet connection is active, then search the Encarta Encyclopedia using the search text "Grand Canyon."
- When the search results appear, scroll to the Media section, click any of the links that appear, then find and save a picture of your choice.
- Insert the picture you've selected below the embedded PowerPoint slide in the Word report.
- Center the picture, resize the picture if necessary, then add a note under the picture with information about the source of the picture.

k. View the document in Print Preview, save the document, print a copy, close the document, then exit Word.

▼ INDEPENDENT CHALLENGE 3

You own a small Web-based business that sells art materials online. The business is growing—thanks in large part to the help you're receiving from several art stores in your area. The store managers are promoting your Web site in exchange for commissions paid to them when a customer from their target market purchases art materials from your Web site. You've decided to send a memo to the store managers every few months to keep them informed about the growth of the Web site. The memo will include a linked Excel worksheet and a table published to Word from Access. Once you have completed the memo, you will merge it with a database containing the names of all the store managers who are helping to promote the Web site.

a. Start Word, open the file WD K-16.doc from the drive and folder where your Data Files are located and save it as **Arts Online Memo**.

▼ INDEPENDENT CHALLENGE 3 (CONTINUED)

b. Start Access, then open the file WD K-17.mdb from the drive and folder where your Data Files are located.

c. Publish the Access table called May 1 Sales to Word.

d. In Word, apply the table AutoFormat of your choice, automatically adjust the column widths, copy the formatted table, then paste it to the second paragraph mark below the paragraph The table illustrated below in the Arts Online Memo Word document. Center the table.

e. Start Excel and open the file WD K-18.xls from the drive and folder where your Data Files are located, then save the Excel file as **Arts Online Data**.

f. Scroll down the worksheet, click the pie chart to select it, copy the pie chart, switch to the Arts Online Memo file in Word, then paste the worksheet as a link at the second paragraph mark below the paragraph **The pie chart shown below**.

g. In Excel, click cell F4, change the sale generated by the Delaware customer from 240.62 to **320.15**, press [Enter], then save and close the worksheet.

h. Switch to the Arts Online Memo Word document, then update the link to the pie chart. Change the width of the chart to **3"**, then center it and add a border.

i. Scroll to the top of the document, then replace the placeholder text with your name and today's date in the Memo heading.

j. Click after the **To:** → in the Memo heading, open the Mail Merge task pane, navigate to Step 3 of 6 in the Mail Merge task pane, browse to the drive and folder where your Data Files are located, select the file WD K-17.mdb, then select the Retail Outlets table and all the recipients listed in the table.

k. Insert an Address Block following To: that contains only the recipient's name. (*Hint*: Deselect the Insert postal address check box and the Insert company name check box in the Insert Address Block dialog box.)

l. View the recipients, then print copies of the memos from Tara Winston through Richard Harwood.

m. Save and close the document in Word, close the published table without saving it, then exit all open applications.

▼ INDEPENDENT CHALLENGE 4

The Internet is a great resource for gathering information about products and services. If you are starting a new business or even if you run an established business, you can always gain new ideas by checking out the ways competing businesses use the Internet to advertise and sell products and services. You decide to evaluate the contents of a Web site that sells a product or service of your choice and write a report. You plan to integrate information from the Web site into your report. To integrate the information, you will use Copy and Paste commands or the drag-and-drop method to copy excerpts from the Web site you've selected so that you can comment on them.

a. Select a product or service that interests you and that you might even want to sell as part of your own business. For example, if you are interested in mountain biking, you could decide to find a Web site that sells mountain bikes and related equipment.

b. Open your Web browser and conduct a search for a company that sells the product or service that interests you. You can try entering related keywords such as **mountain biking**, **cycling**, and **mountain bikes** into your favorite search engine, or you can try entering generic domain names such as www.bikes.com or www.mountainbiking.com in the Address box of your Web browser.

c. Open the file WD K-19.doc from the drive and folder where your Data Files are located, then save it as **Competition Research**. This document contains questions about the Web site you've selected.

d. Complete the Competition Research document with the information requested. Follow the directions in the document. Note that you will be directed to integrate information from the Web site into your document. You might need to modify the formatting of the copied information. Be sure to always cite your source.

e. Type your name at the bottom of the document, print a copy, save and close it, then exit Word.

▼ VISUAL WORKSHOP

In Word, enter the headings and text for the document shown in Figure K-22. Start Excel, open the file WD K-20.xls from the drive and folder where your Data Files are located, then save it as **Cell Phone Data**. Copy the pie chart, then paste it as a link to the Word document. Center the pie chart in Word. In Excel, change the value in cell B2 to **180**, then save the worksheet. In Word, verify that the pie chart appears as shown in Figure K-22, update the pie chart in Word as needed, then break the link to the Excel file. Save the document as **Missouri Arts Cell Phone Report**, type your name under the chart, print a copy, then close the document and exit Word. Close the worksheet in Excel, then exit Excel.

FIGURE K-22

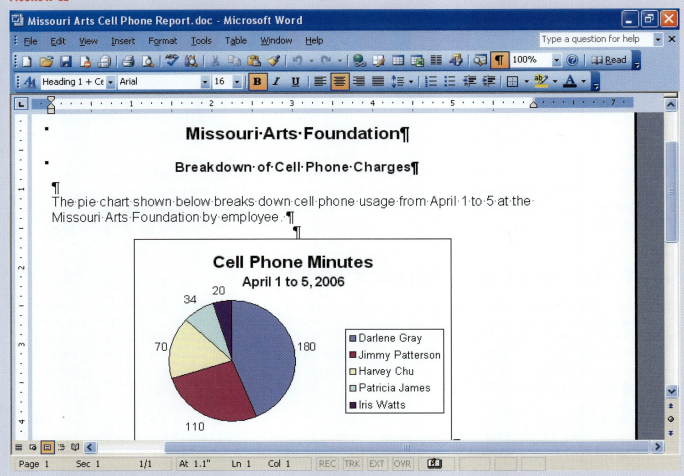

Exploring Advanced Graphics

OBJECTIVES

Insert drop caps
Edit clip art
Work with the drawing canvas
Use layering options
Align, distribute, and rotate graphics
Use advanced positioning options
Adjust shadow and 3-D settings
Insert a watermark and a page border

If you have a SAM user profile, you may have access to hands-on instruction, practice, and assessment of the skills covered in this unit. Log in to your SAM account and go to your assignments page to see what your instructor has assigned.

Word includes features you can use to create and modify pictures and other objects such as shapes and text boxes. In addition, you can enhance a document with drop caps, a watermark, and a page border. You can use shadow and 3-D effects to add pizzazz to all kinds of graphics objects. You can also create your own pictures in the drawing canvas by modifying clip art pictures and combining them with other pictures and drawn objects. The Seattle MediaLoft is excited about holding a series of Mystery Book Nights featuring authors who will sign their books and meet readers. You work in the Marketing Department at MediaLoft and have offered to provide the Seattle MediaLoft store with sample posters for advertising the events. You have already written the text for the posters. Now you will enhance the posters with a variety of graphics objects.

Inserting Drop Caps

A **drop cap** is a large dropped character that appears as the first character in a paragraph. By default, a drop cap that you insert from the Format menu is three lines high and appears in its own text box. You can modify the size of a drop cap and its position relative to the paragraph of text. You can also select a font style for the drop cap that differs from the font style of the surrounding text.  The poster you created to advertise the first Mystery Book Night featuring Emily Chow includes a description of three of Ms. Chow's novels. You decide to make the first letter of each novel title a drop cap. You experiment with different looks for the drop caps, decide on the best drop cap format, and then edit the drop caps so that they all contain the same formatting.

STEPS

QUICK TIP
This unit assumes Show/Hide ¶ is on.

1. **Start Word, open the file WD L-1.doc from the drive and folder where your Data Files are located, then save the file as Mystery Book Night Poster_Emily Chow**
   A WordArt object appears at the top of the poster and two clip art pictures (also called clip art objects) appear at the bottom. You will use these pictures in later lessons.

2. **Click in the paragraph that starts with the book title *On the Wharf***
   Word automatically assigns the drop cap to the first letter of the paragraph containing the insertion point.

QUICK TIP
If your document is formatted in columns, the In margin option is not available.

3. **Click Format on the menu bar, then click Drop Cap**
   The Drop Cap dialog box opens. You use this dialog box to insert a drop cap in the margin or as part of the current paragraph. You can also use it to select a font style for the drop cap and to specify the number of lines to drop.

4. **Click Dropped, click the Font list arrow, select Arial Black, click the Lines to drop down arrow once to reduce the lines to drop to 2 as shown in Figure L-1, then click OK**
   The letter *O* in *On the Wharf* appears as a drop cap in its own text box, as shown in Figure L-2. The drop cap looks good, but you format the next drop cap differently so you can decide which effect you prefer.

5. **Click in the paragraph that begins *Silicon Sleuth*, click Format, click Drop Cap, click Dropped, click the Font list arrow, select Arial Black, click the Lines to drop list arrow two times to reduce the lines to drop to 1, then click OK**
   The letter *S* in *Silicon* is a drop cap that drops 1 line. You decide that dropping 1 line is not enough. You format the next drop cap as 2 lines dropped and experiment with the distance from text option.

6. **Click in the paragraph that begins *Dragon Swindle*, click Format, click Drop Cap, click Dropped, select the Arial Black font, select 2 for the lines to drop, click the Distance from text up arrow one time to set the distance from the text at 0.1", then click OK**
   The *D* in *Dragon Swindle* is a drop cap and exactly what you want. You modify the other two drop caps.

QUICK TIP
The black handles that appear around the border indicate that the drop cap is selected.

7. **Click the drop cap O, then click the shaded border**

8. **Right-click the drop cap, click Drop Cap, change the distance from text to 0.1", click OK, then revise the drop cap for Silicon Sleuth to drop 2 lines and appear 0.1" from the text**

9. **Click away from the selected drop cap, scroll up slightly so that the poster appears as shown in Figure L-3, then save the document**
   Notice that a portion of the paragraph mark appears next to each drop cap because the Show/Hide ¶ button on the Standard toolbar is selected. Remember that the ¶ marks do not print.

FIGURE L-1: Drop Cap dialog box

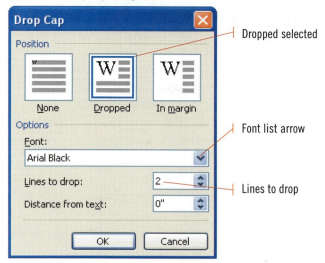

Dropped selected

Font list arrow

Lines to drop

FIGURE L-2: Drop cap inserted

Text box containing the drop cap

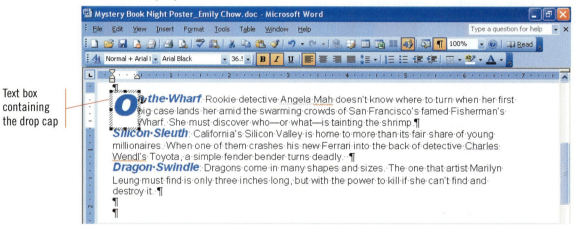

FIGURE L-3: Paragraphs with drop caps

Paragraph marks will not print

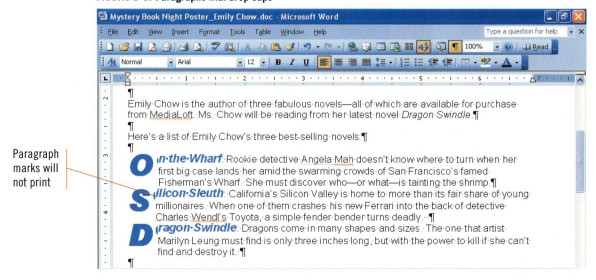

Editing Clip Art

UNIT

L

Word 2003

The pictures included in the poster document are all clip art pictures obtained from the Clip Organizer. When you first import a clip art picture into a document, all of the objects that make up the clip art picture are grouped together into one picture. When you edit a clip art picture, you are really editing the objects that make up the picture. Because clip art pictures are composed of many objects, you work with the Group and Ungroup commands. ▓▓▓ You have already inserted two clip art pictures from the Clip Organizer into the poster. You decide to combine them with some drawn objects to create a new picture.

STEPS

TROUBLE

If the Drawing Canvas toolbar does not appear, right-click the selected picture, then click Show Drawing Canvas Toolbar.

1. **Scroll to the bottom of the poster, right-click the picture of the bridge, then click Edit Picture**

    The picture is contained in a drawing canvas. A shaded border encloses the edge of the drawing canvas and the Drawing Canvas toolbar appears. The **drawing canvas** is an area upon which you can draw multiple shapes and insert clip art.

2. **Click the blue shape that represents the sky as shown in Figure L-4, then press [Delete]**

3. **Click the Expand Drawing button 🔲 Expand on the Drawing Canvas toolbar three times**

    Each time you click, the drawing canvas enlarges, creating more white space around the picture.

4. **Click View on the menu bar, point to Toolbars, click Drawing, then click the Select Objects button � on the Drawing toolbar**

5. **Point ⌖ at the upper-left corner of the drawing canvas, then click and drag to select all the objects that make up the bridge as shown in Figure L-5**

6. **Click the Draw button Draw ▾ on the Drawing toolbar, then click Group**

    The Group command combines all the objects that make up the bridge into one object.

TROUBLE

If you see Format Drawing Canvas, click outside the drawing canvas to deselect it, click the bridge to select it, and then repeat Step 7.

7. **With the bridge still selected, click the right mouse button, click Format Object, click the Size tab, enter 2.5 in the Height text box, enter 4 in the Width text box, then click OK**

    The bridge is resized. Notice that the area under the bridge consists of two objects: one black object that represents the skyline of San Francisco and one turquoise object that represents the frigid waters of San Francisco Bay.

8. **Right-click the bridge, point to Grouping, click Ungroup, click outside the drawing canvas to deselect all the objects, click just the skyline object to select it, then press [Delete]**

9. **Right-click a blank area of the drawing canvas, point to Grouping, click Regroup, then save the document**

    The bridge picture appears, as shown in Figure L-6. While you can spend many hours using the tools on the Drawing toolbar to modify a clip art picture, the key concept is that every clip art picture is composed of two or more drawn objects—all of which can be modified or removed.

Clues to Use

Converting clip art pictures

You can use two methods to convert a clip art picture into a drawing object. First, you can right-click a clip art picture and select Edit Picture from the menu. You used this method to convert the clip art picture of the bridge into a clip art object. Second, you can change a clip art picture from an inline graphic to a floating graphic. In the next lesson you will use this second method to convert a clip art picture of a dragon into a clip art object that you can ungroup and modify. Which method you choose depends on how you wish to modify the graphic. If your main purpose is to change components of a graphic (for example, change the fill color of one of the elements), then use the Edit Picture method. If your main purpose is to change the layout of the graphic so that you can wrap text around it or use your mouse to move the graphic to another location in the document, then use the Layout dialog box to change the graphic from an inline graphic to a floating graphic.

FIGURE L-4: Sky object selected

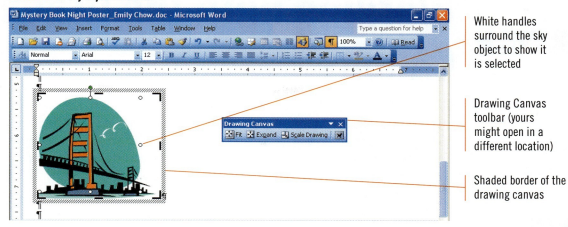

White handles surround the sky object to show it is selected

Drawing Canvas toolbar (yours might open in a different location)

Shaded border of the drawing canvas

FIGURE L-5: Selecting the bridge objects

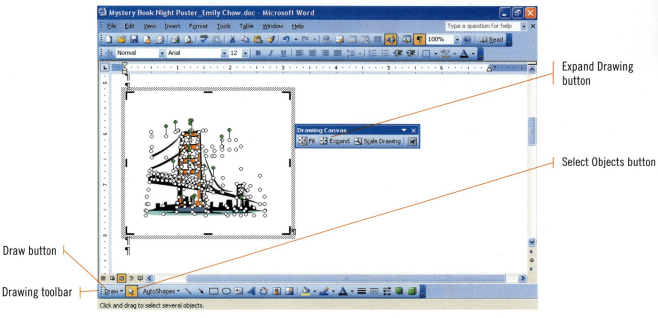

Expand Drawing button

Select Objects button

Draw button

Drawing toolbar

FIGURE L-6: Modified bridge picture

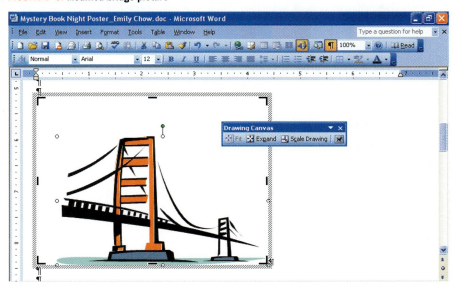

Working with the Drawing Canvas

The drawing canvas appears when you right-click a clip art picture and select Edit Picture or when you draw an AutoShape. You can add new objects such as clip art pictures or shapes you draw yourself to an existing drawing canvas. You also can change the size of the drawing canvas, move it anywhere in the document, and format it with an attractive fill color and border, just as you would any graphics object. When you move the drawing canvas, all the pictures and objects contained within it also move. You want to include a picture of a dragon next to the Golden Gate Bridge, draw a lightning bolt shape, and change the size and fill color of the drawing canvas.

STEPS

1. **With the bridge picture still selected, click the Expand Drawing button** Expand **on the Drawing Canvas toolbar three times, then drag the bridge picture down and to the lower-left corner of the drawing canvas**

2. **Scroll down the document to the top of page 2, click the dragon to select it, right-click the dragon, click Format Picture, click the Layout tab in the Format Picture dialog box, click the Square wrapping style, then click OK**

3. **Click the Zoom list arrow on the Standard toolbar, click Two pages, drag the dragon onto the bridge, click the Zoom list arrow and select Page Width, then position the dragon as shown in Figure L-7**

4. **Make sure the dragon picture is selected, click the More Brightness button** ☀ **on the Picture toolbar three times, then click a blank area in the drawing canvas to deselect the dragon**

   You can add objects that you draw yourself to the drawing canvas.

5. **Click the AutoShapes button** AutoShapes ▾ **on the Drawing toolbar, point to Basic Shapes, select the Lightning Bolt shape, then draw a lightning bolt that appears as shown in Figure L-8**

6. **Right-click the lightning bolt, click Format AutoShape, click the Size tab, change the Height to 1.3" and the Width to 0.8", then click OK**

7. **With the lightning bolt selected, click the Fill Color list arrow** ◇ ▾ **on the Drawing toolbar, click the Yellow color in the second row from the bottom, position the lightning bolt relative to the bridge as shown in Figure L-9, then click a blank area of the drawing canvas**

8. **Right-click a white area of the drawing canvas, click Format Drawing Canvas, click the Colors and Lines tab in the Format Drawing Canvas dialog box, click the Color list arrow in the Fill section, then click Fill Effects**

9. **In the Gradient tab, click the Preset option button, click the Preset colors list arrow, select Fog, click the upper-left square in the Variants section, click OK to exit the Fill Effects dialog box, click OK to exit the Format Drawing Canvas dialog box, then save the document**

   The picture appears in the poster, as shown in Figure L-10.

FIGURE L-7: Dragon and bridge pictures positioned

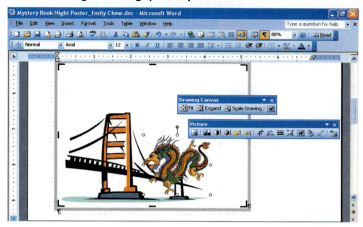

FIGURE L-8: Lightning bolt drawn

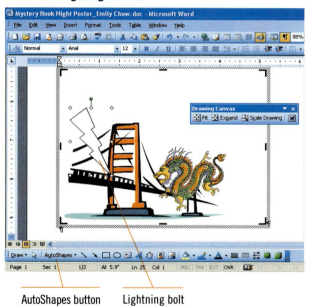

AutoShapes button   Lightning bolt

FIGURE L-9: Lightning bolt sized and positioned

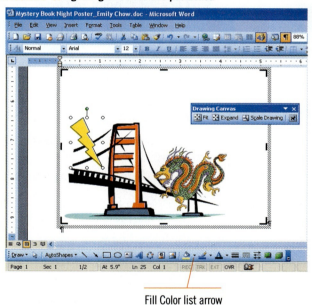

Fill Color list arrow

FIGURE L-10: Formatted drawing canvas

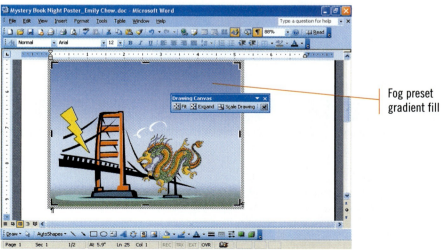

Fog preset gradient fill

Using Layering Options

The Draw menu includes the Order command, which in turn includes several options for specifying how objects should appear in relation to each other. For example, you can choose to show one object partially on top of another object. By using layering commands in combination with the group and ungroup commands, you can achieve some interesting effects. The layering options available in Word are explained in Table L-1. ███ You want the lightning bolt to strike between the two suspension cables of the bridge and the dragon to slither up behind the bridge roadbed. Your first task is to use the Ungroup command to separate the bridge into its various objects.

STEPS

1. **Click the bridge to select it, click the Draw button** Draw ▾ **on the Drawing toolbar, click Ungroup, then click a blank area in the drawing canvas to deselect the bridge objects**

2. **Click the lower of the two suspension cables as shown in Figure L-11 to select it**
   You want this lower cable to appear in front of the lightning bolt.

3. **Click** Draw ▾ **, point to Order, click Bring to Front, then click a blank area in the drawing canvas to deselect the suspension bridge**
   The lightning bolt appears to be striking between the suspension cables.

4. **Click the Zoom list arrow on the Standard toolbar, click 200%, then scroll down to view the bridge roadbed**
   The bridge roadbed consists of numerous black objects. You want just the solid black line that represents the roadbed and one of the suspension cables to appear in front of the dragon.

5. **Press and hold [Ctrl], then click the solid black roadbed object and the suspension cable nearest the dragon**
   Figure L-12 shows the two objects selected.

6. **Click** Draw ▾ **, point to Order, click Bring to Front**
   Notice that the dragon appears to slither up behind the bridge roadbed.

7. **Click the Zoom list arrow, click 100%, then use your pointer to position the dragon as shown in Figure L-13**

8. **Click away from the dragon to deselect it, click the Fit Drawing to Contents button** ⊞ Fit **on the Drawing Canvas toolbar, then save the document**
   The contents of the drawing canvas now fit the drawing canvas.

TABLE L-1: Layering options in Word

command	function	command	function
Bring to Front	Places the object in front of all other objects	Send Backward	Moves the object backward one layer at a time
Send to Back	Places the object behind all other objects	Bring in Front of Text	Moves the object on top of text
Bring Forward	Moves the object forward one layer at a time; use to show an object overlapping one object and then being overlapped by another object	Send Behind Text	Moves the object behind text; often used to show a lightly shaded picture behind relevant text

FIGURE L-11: Lower suspension cable selected

Click here to select the correct cable

Handles appear just around the lower suspension cable

FIGURE L-12: Roadbed and suspension cable objects selected

Two sets of sizing handles are visible, which indicate that both the roadbed object and the suspension cable closest to the dragon are selected

FIGURE L-13: Dragon positioned

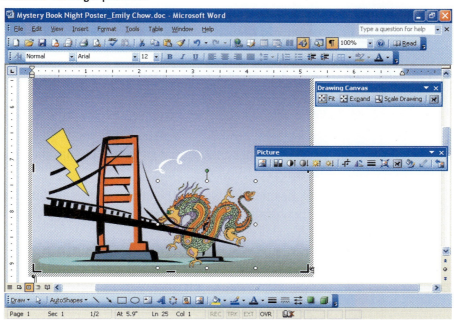

UNIT

L

Word 2003

Aligning, Distributing, and Rotating Graphics

The Align or Distribute option on the Draw menu includes commands you can use to change the relative positioning of two or more objects. For example, you can use the Left Align command to align several drawn objects along their left sides. You can use the Distribute Vertically or the Distribute Horizontally command to display three or more objects so that the same amount of space appears between each object. The Rotate or Flip option on the Draw menu includes commands you can use to rotate or flip an object. For example, suppose you insert a clip art picture of a cat stalking to the right. You can use the Flip Horizontal command to flip the cat so that it stalks to the left, or you can use the Rotate option to make the cat stalk uphill or downhill. You decide to include a series of stars that are aligned and distributed vertically above the dragon along the right side of the drawing canvas. You also want to rotate the dragon by 30 degrees.

STEPS

1. **Click the drawing canvas to select it, click the AutoShapes button** AutoShapes ▾ **on the Drawing toolbar, point to Stars and Banners, click 5-Point Star, then draw a star similar to the star shown in Figure L-14**

2. **With the star selected, click the Fill Color list arrow** 🎨 ▾ **on the Drawing toolbar, select Red, click the Line Color list arrow** ✏ ▾ **on the Drawing toolbar, then click No Line**
   The star is filled with the color red and is no longer outlined in black.

> **QUICK TIP**
>
> If you want to specify both a height and a width that are not necessarily proportional, then clear the Lock aspect ratio check box.

3. **Right-click the star, click Format AutoShape, click the Size tab, click the Lock aspect ratio check box to select it, set the Height at 0.3", press [Tab] to set the Width automatically, then click OK to exit the Format AutoShape dialog box**
   By selecting the Lock aspect ratio check box, you make sure that the Width is calculated in proportion to the Height you enter (or vice versa).

4. **Drag the star to the left so it appears above the dragon's head and towards the top of the drawing canvas, press [Ctrl][C], press [Ctrl][V] three times, then drag the bottom star right so that it appears just above the dragon's tail**
   Four red stars are visible.

5. **Press and hold [Ctrl], then click each star until all four stars are selected, click the Draw button** Draw ▾ **on the Drawing toolbar, point to Align or Distribute, then click Align Right**
   The four stars are aligned along the right side of the drawing canvas.

6. **With all four stars still selected, click** Draw ▾ **, point to Align or Distribute, then click Distribute Vertically**
   The aligned and distributed stars appear, as shown in Figure L-15. The Distribute Vertically command places the stars so that the distance between each star is equal.

7. **Click the dragon to select it, click Draw, point to Rotate or Flip, then click Free Rotate**
   Green dots appear at each corner of the selected picture.

8. **Press and hold [Shift], position the 🔄 over the upper-left green dot, drag to the right so the dragon rotates, then drag to the right again**
   Each time you drag the dragon, a dotted box shows the new position. Holding the [Shift] key rotates the dragon 15 degrees each time you drag, in this case, to the right. The dragon is rotated 30 degrees to the right, as shown in Figure L-16.

9. **Click away from the dragon to deselect it, then save the document**

FIGURE L-14: Star drawn in the drawing canvas

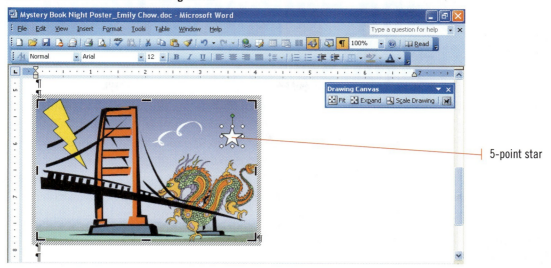

5-point star

FIGURE L-15: Aligned and distributed stars

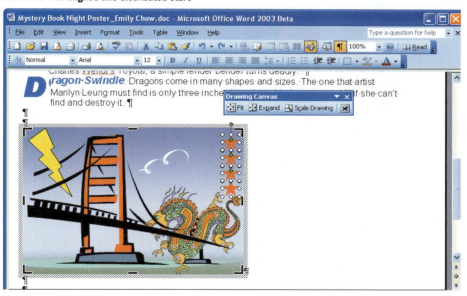

FIGURE L-16: Rotated dragon

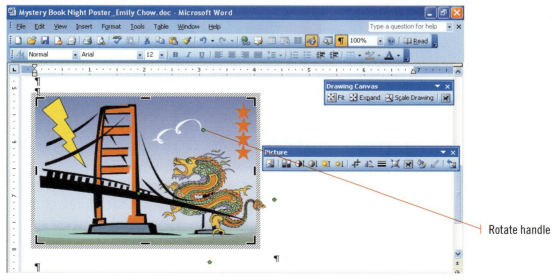

Rotate handle

Using Advanced Positioning Options

Word offers a variety of ways to position objects. You can use your pointer to position an object anywhere on the page in a Word document, including on the drawing canvas, or you can use the Nudge command on the Draw menu to move an object by very small increments. You can also use the Layout tab in the Format Object dialog box to position an object precisely in relation to the page, margin, column, paragraph, or line in a Word document. Finally, you can use the Advanced Layout dialog box in the Format Drawing Canvas dialog box to position an object precisely on the drawing canvas. You decide to group the stars into one object and then position the object precisely in relation to the upper-right corner of the drawing canvas. You then use the Nudge option to position the dragon in relation to the bridge.

STEPS

1. **Use [Ctrl] to select each of the four stars, click the Draw button** `Draw ▾` **on the Drawing toolbar, then click Group**

   You group the stars into one object so that you can position the group of stars easily.

2. **Right-click the grouped object, click Format Object, then click the Layout tab**

   The Layout tab in the Format Object dialog box appears. In this dialog box you can set an exact horizontal and vertical position for the selected object in relation to either the upper-left corner or the center of the drawing canvas.

3. **Set the Horizontal position at 3.6, set the Vertical position at .1 as shown in Figure L-17, then click OK**

   The star object is positioned precisely, based on the measurements you entered.

4. **Click the dragon to select it, click** `Draw ▾`**, point to Nudge, then click Left**

   The dragon moves 1 pixel to the left. The Nudge command moves an object one pixel at a time. You can also use the arrow keys to nudge an object up, down, left, or right.

5. **With the dragon still selected, use the arrow keys to move it up, down, left, or right so that its final position appears similar to Figure L-18**

6. **Right-click the border of the drawing canvas, click Format Drawing Canvas, click the Square wrapping style, then click the Center option button in the Horizontal alignment section**

   You select the Square wrapping style to transform the drawing canvas from an inline graphic to a floating graphic. Now you can apply advanced positioning options.

7. **Click the Advanced button**

   The Advanced Layout dialog box opens.

8. **Click the Absolute Position option button in the Vertical section of the dialog box to select it, enter 6 in the text box, click the below list arrow, click Page, click OK to exit the Advanced Layout dialog box, then click OK**

   The Format Drawing Canvas dialog box closes. The drawing canvas is centered horizontally and positioned exactly six inches from the top of the page. You can use the Click and Type feature to position the insertion point below the drawing canvas.

9. **Scroll down, double-click below the drawing canvas, click the Center button** `≡` **on the Formatting toolbar if necessary, then type and format the address of the Seattle MediaLoft as shown in Figure L-19**

10. **Save the document**

FIGURE L-17: Format Object dialog box

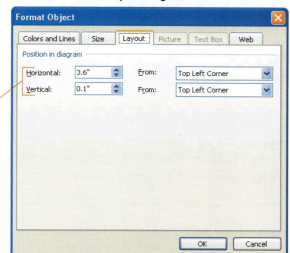

Use to set exact horizontal and vertical placement of an object in relation to a diagram or a drawing canvas

FIGURE L-18: Dragon nudged into position

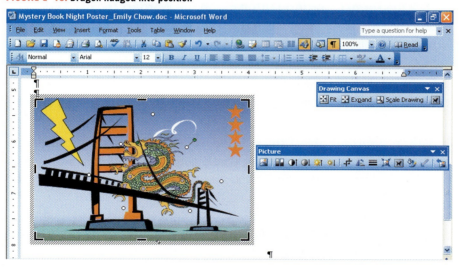

FIGURE L-19: Address information entered

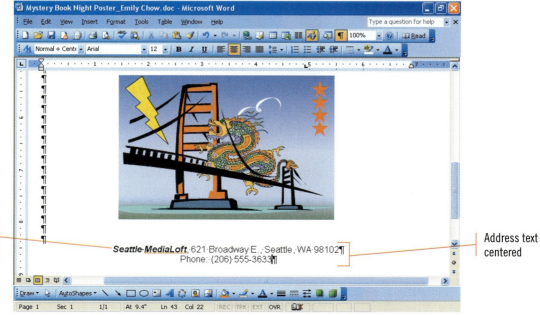

Enhance Seattle MediaLoft with bold and italic

Address text centered

Adjusting Shadow and 3-D Settings

The Drawing toolbar includes the Shadow and 3-D buttons that you can use to enhance a graphics object. You can change a flat object to a 3-D object and you can add a shadow effect to an object. You can also modify the appearance of the shadow and 3-D effects you apply. 🎨 The poster includes a WordArt object that you want to enhance with a textured fill and a 3-D effect. You also want to add a blue shadow to the lightning bolt in the drawing canvas.

STEPS

TROUBLE

Click toward the top of the "B" in "Book" to select the WordArt object.

1. **Scroll to the top of the document, then click the WordArt object to select it**

   When you select the WordArt object, the WordArt toolbar opens. If the WordArt toolbar does not appear, right-click the WordArt object, then click Show WordArt Toolbar.

2. **Click the Format WordArt button 🖼 on the WordArt toolbar, click the Colors and Lines tab, click the Color list arrow in the Fill section, click Fill Effects, click the Texture tab, select Blue tissue paper as shown in Figure L-20, click OK to exit the Fill Effects dialog box, then click OK**

   The Format WordArt dialog box closes and the WordArt object is formatted with the Blue tissue paper texture.

QUICK TIP

As you move the pointer over the 3-D styles, the style name appears in a ScreenTip.

3. **With the WordArt object selected, click the 3-D Style button 🔲 on the Drawing toolbar, then select 3-D Style 2**

4. **With the WordArt object still selected, click 🔲, then click 3-D Settings**

   The 3-D Settings toolbar appears. Table L-2 describes the buttons on the 3-D Settings toolbar. These buttons are used to change the appearance of the 3-D effect. For example, you can change the depth and lighting of the 3-D effect.

5. **Click the Depth button 🖼 on the 3-D Settings toolbar, select 36.00 pt in the Custom text box, type 18, press [Enter], click the Lighting button 🔶 on the 3-D Settings toolbar, then click the Lighting Direction button in the lower-left corner**

   The WordArt is modified based on the style, depth, and shadow settings you set.

6. **Scroll down to view the drawing canvas, click the lightning bolt in the drawing canvas to select it, click the Shadow Style button 🔲 on the Drawing toolbar, then click Shadow Style 1**

   One way to enhance a shadow effect is to change the shadow color.

7. **Click 🔲, click Shadow Settings, click the Shadow Color list arrow 🔲, verify that Semitransparent Shadow is selected, then select Dark Red**

8. **Click the Nudge Shadow Left button 🔲 on the Shadow Settings toolbar three times to move the shadow slightly to the left**

   Your poster is completed.

9. **Close the Shadow Settings, 3-D Settings, and Drawing Canvas toolbars, double-click below the address at the bottom of the document, then type Contact Your Name for assistance.**

10. **Save the document, print a copy, then close the document**

    The completed poster is shown in Figure L-21.

FIGURE L-20: Blue tissue paper texture selected

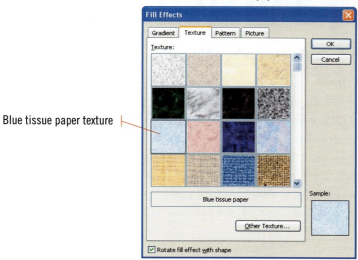

Blue tissue paper texture

FIGURE L-21: Completed poster

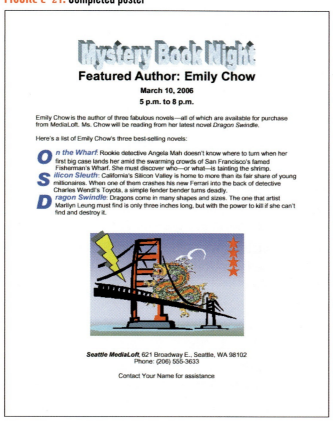

TABLE L-2: The 3-D Settings toolbar

button	use to	button	use to
	Turn the 3-D effect on or off		Change the depth of the 3-D effect
	Tilt the 3-D effect down		Change the direction of the 3-D effect
	Tilt the 3-D effect up		Select a lighting direction
	Tilt the 3-D effect to the left		Select a surface texture for the 3-D effect
	Tilt the 3-D effect to the right		Select a 3-D color

Inserting a Watermark and a Page Border

You can enhance a document with a watermark and a page border. A **watermark** is a picture or other type of graphics object that appears lightly shaded behind text in a document. For example, you could include a company logo as a watermark on every page of a company report, or you could create "Confidential" as a WordArt object that appears in a very light gray behind the text of an important letter or memo. A **page border** encloses one or more pages of a document. You can create a box border using a variety of line styles and colors, or you can insert one of Word's preset art borders. You have promised to supply two poster designs. To finish the poster advertising Jonathon Grant's appearance, you need to add a watermark and a page border.

STEPS

1. Open the file WD L-2.doc from the drive and folder where your Data Files are located, then save it as Mystery Book Night Poster_Jonathon Grant

   The picture that you want to make into a watermark appears at the bottom of the document.

2. Scroll to the end of the document, then click the picture of the magnifying glass and pipe to select it

3. Click the Color button 🖼 on the Picture toolbar, then click Washout

   The colors of the picture now appear very lightly tinted. You can use the More Brightness, Less Brightness, More Contrast, and Less Contrast buttons on the Picture toolbar to further modify the appearance of the picture. However, you are pleased with the default settings.

4. Click the Text Wrapping button 🖼 on the Picture toolbar, then click Behind Text

5. Use the Zoom list arrow to select Whole Page, click the Format Picture button 🖼 on the Picture toolbar, click the Size tab, click the Lock aspect ratio check box to clear it, change the Height to 6" and the Width to 4", click OK, then use the pointer to position the picture behind the text as shown in Figure L-22

6. Click away from the picture to deselect it, click Format on the menu bar, click Borders and Shading, then click the Page Border tab

   In the Page Border tab of the Borders and Shading dialog box you can add a simple box border, a shadow border, or a 3-D border.

7. Click Box, scroll down the Style list box, then select the Thick-Thin border style, the Teal border color, and the 4½ pt border width (see Figure L-23)

8. Click OK to exit the Borders and Shading dialog box, return to 100% view, then type your name in place of Your Name at the bottom of the document

9. Save the document, print a copy, close the document, then exit Word

   The completed poster appears as shown in Figure L-24.

TROUBLE
If your page border does not appear as expected, read the Clues to Use on the next page.

Clues to Use

Printing a page border

Sometimes a document formatted with a page border will not print correctly on certain printers because the page border falls outside the print area recognized by the printer. For example, the bottom border or one of the side borders might not print. To correct this problem, open the Borders and Shading dialog box, click Options on the Page Border tab, then increase the point size of the top, bottom, left, or right margins. Or, you can specify that the border be measured from the text, not from the edge of the page, and set the points to measure from the text. Experiment until you find the settings that work with your printer.

FIGURE L-22: Watermark sized and positioned

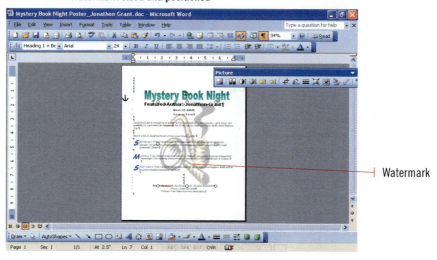

Watermark

FIGURE L-23: Borders and Shading dialog box

Line style selected

Color selected

Width selected

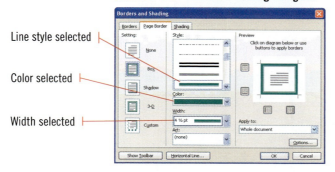

FIGURE L-24: Completed poster

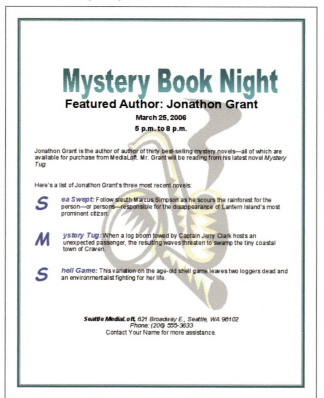

Practice

▼ CONCEPTS REVIEW

Refer to the pictures in the drawing canvas shown in Figure L-25, then answer the following questions.

FIGURE L-25

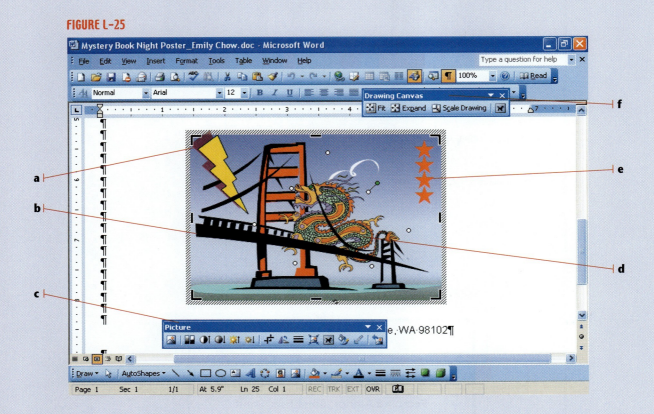

1. Which items are vertically distributed?
2. Which item is enhanced with a shadow?
3. A layering option was applied to which item?
4. Which item is currently ready to rotate?
5. Which item contains the tools used to modify a picture?
6. Which item contains the button used to expand the drawing canvas?

Match each term with the statement that best describes it.

7. **Drawing canvas**	**a.** Large single letter that appears at the beginning of a paragraph
8. **Drop cap**	**b.** Color shading that ranges from light to dark in various patterns
9. **Ungroup**	**c.** Evenly spaces three or more objects
10. **Distribute Vertically**	**d.** Used to separate a clip art picture into its component objects
11. **Align Left**	**e.** Arrange two or more objects along the same plane
12. **Gradient Fill Effect**	**f.** Enclosed box that contains a variety of graphics objects

Select the best answer from the list of choices.

13. **Which of the following options is *not* available in the Drop Cap dialog box?**
    - **a.** Distance from text
    - **b.** Vertical alignment
    - **c.** Lines to drop
    - **d.** Font style

14. **What is the purpose of the Expand button on the Drawing Canvas toolbar?**
    - **a.** To increase the size of the drawing canvas, but not the contents of the drawing canvas
    - **b.** To increase the size of the drawing canvas and its contents
    - **c.** To increase only the contents of the drawing canvas
    - **d.** To expand the contents to fit the drawing canvas

15. **Which of the following fill effects is *not* available in the Fill Effects dialog box?**
    - **a.** Texture
    - **b.** Gradient
    - **c.** Picture
    - **d.** Color

16. **How do you select two or more objects?**
    - **a.** Press and hold [Ctrl], then click each object in turn.
    - **b.** Click each object in turn.
    - **c.** Press and hold [Alt], then click each object in turn.
    - **d.** Click Edit on the menu bar, then click Select.

17. **Which option from the Draw menu do you select to modify how two or more objects appear in relation to each other?**
    - **a.** Align or Distribute
    - **b.** Nudge
    - **c.** Edit AutoShape
    - **d.** Distribute

18. **How far does a Nudge button move an object?**
    - **a.** 2 pixels
    - **b.** 1 inch
    - **c.** 1 pixel
    - **d.** 10 pixels

19. **Which option in the Color button on the Picture toolbar do you select to turn an object into a watermark?**
    - **a.** Washout
    - **b.** Grayscale
    - **c.** Watermark
    - **d.** More Brightness

▼ SKILLS REVIEW

1. **Insert drop caps.**
   - **a.** Start Word. Open the file WD L-3.doc from the drive and folder where your Data Files are located, then save it as **Story Time Poster_Joanne**.
   - **b.** Click in the paragraph that begins with the text **Joanne Preston has been delighting....**
   - **c.** Insert a drop cap that is dropped three lines and uses the Britannic Bold font (or an alternate font if this one is not available).
   - **d.** Insert a drop cap at the beginning of the next paragraph that is dropped two lines and uses the Britannic Bold font.
   - **e.** Insert a drop cap at the beginning of the next paragraph that is dropped two lines, uses the Britannic Bold font, and is positioned 0.1" from the text.
   - **f.** Modify the **J** drop cap and the **M** drop cap to match the **A** drop cap, then save the document.

2. **Edit clip art.**
   - **a.** Scroll to the bottom of the poster, right-click the picture of the Eiffel Tower, then click Edit Picture.
   - **b.** Ungroup the picture.
   - **c.** Delete all the objects that make up the sky, including the pink object behind the bridge toward the bottom of the picture. (*Hint*: You will need to delete quite a few objects so that the tower appears against a white background.)
   - **d.** Use the Drawing Canvas toolbar to expand the drawing canvas four times, then change to 75% zoom or whatever zoom setting allows you to see the entire drawing canvas.
   - **e.** Use the Select Objects tool on the Drawing toolbar to select all the objects that make up the Eiffel Tower picture.
   - **f.** Group the picture into one object.
   - **g.** With the object selected, open the Format Object dialog box, click the Size tab if necessary, then change the Height of the object to 2.5" and the width to 3.5".

3. Work with the drawing canvas.

   a. Drag the Eiffel Tower picture down so that its lower-left sizing handle is even with the lower-left corner of the drawing canvas. (*Note*: If the entire picture does not move, use the Select Objects tool to select and group the picture again.)

   b. Use the Zoom list arrow to view Two Pages, click the picture of the bicycle, then change it to an object with the Square wrapping style.

   c. Ungroup the bicycle, answer Yes if prompted, delete the blue background object, then select all the elements of the bicycle and group them into one object.

   d. Drag the bicycle picture into the drawing canvas, then switch to a zoom setting that allows you to see the entire drawing canvas. (*Note*: If the wheels on the bike are black, you did not group all of the objects successfully in Step 3c. Undo the move object command, and then regroup all the elements of the bike.)

   e. Position the bicycle so the back wheel is even with the right side of the Eiffel Tower picture and the front wheel is on the bridge. You don't need to be exact at this stage.

   f. Draw a crescent moon AutoShape that is 0.8" high with the lock aspect ratio check box selected. Position the moon in the sky to the left of the Eiffel Tower.

   g. Fill the moon shape with a light yellow color and delete the black outline.

   h. Fill the drawing canvas with the Daybreak preset gradient, using the top-right variant (light pink at the top). Save the document.

4. Use layering options.

   a. Use the Send Backward command to position the bicycle behind the Eiffel Tower picture so that part of the wheels are hidden.

   b. Use the Fit button on the Drawing Canvas toolbar to fit the picture inside the drawing canvas.

   c. Save the document.

5. Align, distribute, and rotate graphics.

   a. Make sure the drawing canvas is selected, draw a heart AutoShape that is 0.3" wide and 0.3" in height, then fill it with pink.

   b. Copy the heart twice so that you have a total of three hearts, then move the selected heart near the right edge of the picture.

   c. Align the hearts along their bottom edges.

   d. Use the Distribute Horizontally feature to distribute the hearts, then position them so that they appear about an inch above the bicycle. You do not have to position them precisely yet.

   e. Select the bicycle, then flip it horizontally. (*Hint*: Click Draw, point to Rotate or Flip, then click Flip Horizontal.)

6. Use advanced positioning options.

   a. Group the hearts into one object.

   b. Position the grouped hearts in the drawing canvas so that the horizontal position is 1.8" from the top left corner and the vertical position is 0.5" from the top left corner. (*Note*: If a warning appears, enter the measurements suggested.) Refer to the picture of the completed drawing in Figure L-26.

   c. Position the moon so that the horizontal position is .38" from the top left corner and the vertical position is 0.24" from the top left corner.

   d. Nudge the bike so it appears as shown in the completed drawing in Figure L-26.

   e. Change the layout of the drawing canvas to select the Square wrapping style and Center horizontal alignment.

   f. In the Advanced Layout dialog box, set the Absolute Vertical position of the drawing canvas to 5.8" below the page.

   g. Double-click below the drawing canvas, then type with center alignment the following text:

      MediaLoft Houston, 2118 Westheimer Road, Houston, TX 77098

      Phone: (281) 555-8233

      Contact Your Name for assistance.

   h. Enhance **MediaLoft Houston** with bold, then save the document.

▼ SKILLS REVIEW (CONTINUED)

7. Adjust Shadow and 3-D settings.

   a. Click the WordArt object at the top of the document to select it.

   b. Fill the WordArt object with the Papyrus texture.

   c. Add the 3-D Style 3 to the WordArt object.

   d. Change the 3-D settings so that the depth is 18 points and change the lighting so it comes from the center right.

   e. Scroll down, click the crescent moon in the drawing canvas to select it, then add the Shadow Style 5.

   f. Make the shadow semitransparent and light orange. The completed drawing appears as shown in Figure L-26.

   g. Save the document, view it in Print Preview, print a copy, then close the document.

8. Insert a watermark and a page border.

   a. Open the file WD L-4.doc from the drive and folder where your Data Files are located, then save it as **Story Time Poster_Hayley**.

   b. Click the picture at the top of the document, then use the Color button on the Picture toolbar to change its color to the Washout setting.

   c. Click the More Brightness button twice to further increase the washed out effect.

   d. Change the text wrapping of the picture to Behind Text.

   e. Use the Zoom list arrow to view the Whole Page, change the Height of the picture to 5" with the Lock Aspect ratio check box selected so that the Width is calculated automatically.

   f. Center the picture and position it 4" below the top of the page.

   g. Add a green page border in the 3 pt, double-line box style.

   h. In 100% view, replace Your Name at the bottom of the document with your name.

   i. Save the document, print a copy, close the document, then exit Word.

FIGURE L-26

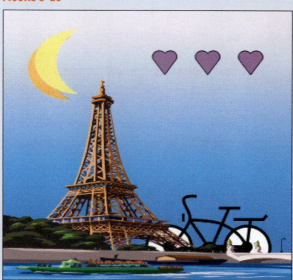

▼ INDEPENDENT CHALLENGE 1

You work as a teacher's aide at an elementary school. Your supervisor has asked you to create an attractive picture that includes a variety of elements that children can color, according to the labels. You've already downloaded the clip art pictures you plan to use to create the picture. Now you need to work in the drawing canvas to modify the pictures you've downloaded, draw some AutoShapes, then add some text objects.

   a. Start Word, open the file WD L-5.doc from the drive and folder where your Data Files are located, and save it as **Learning Colors Picture**.

   b. Edit the picture of the balloons, then expand the drawing canvas eight times. (*Note*: Change the zoom setting as needed to meet your needs as you work.)

   c. Remove the colored shape from each balloon, then group the balloons into one object.

   d. Increase the Height of the balloons to 5" with the Lock aspect ratio check box selected.

   e. Scroll down the page to find the picture of the hat and balloon, edit the picture, then remove all the objects that make up the single balloon.

   f. Expand the drawing canvas containing the hat two times, then group all the objects that make up the hat into one object.

   g. Drag the grouped hat picture into the drawing canvas that contains the three balloons. Position the hat picture in the lower-left corner of the drawing canvas, then increase its Height to 3" with the Lock aspect ratio check box selected so the Width is calculated automatically.

▼ INDEPENDENT CHALLENGE 1 (CONTINUED)

h. Rotate the hat picture by 15 degrees to the left. (*Hint*: Press and hold [Shift] while dragging a rotate handle to constrain the rotation to 15-degree increments.)

i. Nudge the hat to position it as shown in the completed drawing in Figure L-27.

Advanced Challenge Exercise

■ Refer to Figure L-27 to complete the picture, according to the following instructions.

■ Add the Sun AutoShape, then use rotate and layering options to show the sun just behind the two balloons on the right.

■ Position all the objects so they are placed similarly to how they are shown in Figure L-27. Use the pointer, as well as the order, rotate, and size commands as needed.

■ Add text boxes and draw lines. Type text in the text boxes and format it in 16 pt, Arial, and Bold. (*Note*: Remove the border around each text box and move text boxes as needed to ensure they do not block other parts of the picture.)

FIGURE L-27

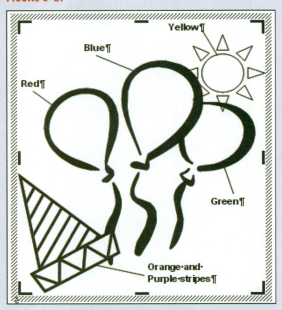

j. Click the Fit button to fit the canvas to the objects, then create a page border that is a dark red single line.

k. Change the layout of the drawing canvas to a Square floating graphic, then center the drawing canvas.

l. Use Click and Type to enter **Prepared by** followed by your name centered below the Drawing canvas.

m. View the document in Whole Page view, delete the blank drawing canvas below the picture, save the document, print a copy, close the document, then exit Word.

▼ INDEPENDENT CHALLENGE 2

You have just been hired to create a series of templates for the menus and other documents produced by Grains & Greens—a new vegetarian café in your neighborhood. Your first task is to create the logo for Grains & Greens that appears as shown in Figure L-28. Refer to this figure as you work.

FIGURE L-28

a. Start Word. Open a new blank Word document, show the Drawing toolbar, if necessary, click the Insert WordArt button on the Drawing toolbar, select the upper-left WordArt style (the default style), then enter the text G & G. Select the Bauhaus 93 font style (or alternate font if this one is not available).

b. Change the WordArt object to a floating graphic with the Square wrapping style and left-aligned. (*Hint*: Right-click the WordArt object, then click Format WordArt to open the Format WordArt dialog box.)

c. Set the Width of the WordArt object to 2" with the Lock aspect ratio check box unselected, then fill the object with the Green marble texture.

d. Apply the Shadow Style 1 to the WordArt object, then add a semitransparent lime to the shadow.

e. Refer to Figure L-28 to insert and modify the pea pod clip art picture. (*Hint*: Click the Insert Clip Art button on the Drawing toolbar, then enter the search term **pea pod** to find the clip art picture). You need to change the layout of the drawing canvas with the pea pod picture to square and right, then ungroup the pea pod and change the background color to bright green. Use your mouse to resize, rotate, and reposition the pea pod so that it appears as shown in Figure L-28.

▼ INDEPENDENT CHALLENGE 2 (CONTINUED)

Advanced Challenge Exercise

- ■ Insert a horizontal line graphic below the WordArt object and pea pod picture as follows:
- ■ Position the insertion point below the logo, then open the Page Border tab in the Borders and Shading dialog box.
- ■ Click Horizontal Line, select the middle line style in the second row of the line style selections, then click OK.
- ■ Right-click the horizontal line, click Format Horizontal Line, change the height to 10 pt, then click OK.

f. Type your name right-aligned below the logo, save the document as **Grains and Greens Logo** to the drive and folder where your Data Files are located, print a copy, save and close the document, then exit Word.

▼ INDEPENDENT CHALLENGE 3

You are the owner of a small home-based business in Halifax, Nova Scotia. You determine the kinds of products and services you sell. For example, you could operate a small catering business that specializes in company parties, or you could operate a Web site design service for other home-based businesses. You use Word's graphics features to create an attractive flyer to advertise your business.

a. On a piece of paper, plan the contents of your flyer. Your flyer must include four of the following five elements: WordArt object containing the name of the company or a slogan, clip art picture that has been modified in some way, three or more AutoShapes that are aligned and distributed, a formatted drawing canvas containing the modified clip art picture and AutoShapes, along with additional graphics if appropriate, and two or more drop caps used appropriately.

b. Start Word. Open a new blank Word document, show the Drawing toolbar if necessary, then create the text for your flyer. You should include the following information: company name, company address and contact information, including the URL of a Web site, and two or three short paragraphs describing the products or services offered.

c. Add the graphics objects required. Use Drawing tools as you create and edit the graphics. Experiment with some of the tools you did not use in this unit. Make sure you use at least five of the following Drawing tools: align and distribute; group and ungroup; fill colors, textures, or gradients—use at least one fill effect somewhere in your document; advanced positioning to set the position of an object within the drawing canvas; layering options; rotate; and 3-D and Shadow effect.

d. Enter your name in an appropriate location on your flyer.

e. View the flyer in Whole Page view, then make any final spacing and sizing adjustments to ensure all the text and graphics elements appear attractively on the page.

f. Save your flyer as **My Company Flyer** to the drive and folder where your Data Files are located.

g. Print a copy of the flyer, close the document, then exit Word.

▼ INDEPENDENT CHALLENGE 4

Many of the Web pages on the World Wide Web are beautifully designed with attractive graphics that entice the Web surfer to explore further. Other Web pages are less well designed, and sometimes have clashing colors, unattractive graphics, and hard-to-read text. To increase your understanding of the role graphics play in enhancing—or detracting from—the effectiveness of a document, you decide to evaluate design elements on the home pages of two Web sites that sell similar products or services.

a. Open your Web browser and search for two companies that sell a product or service of interest to you. You can try entering product-related keywords, such as **art supplies**, **pastels**, and **watercolors**, or you can try entering generic domain names, such as www.art.com or www.artsupplies.com, in the Address box of your Web browser.

b. Open the file WD L-6.doc from the drive and folder where your Data Files are located, then save it as **Web Page Design Evaluations**. This document contains criteria for ranking the design elements on the Web pages you've chosen.

c. As directed in the Web Page Design Evaluations document, enter the company name and copy the URL of each Web site to the spaces provided.

d. Assign a ranking to each site as directed, then complete the two questions at the bottom of the document.

e. Type your name at the bottom of the document, print a copy, save and close it, then exit Word.

▼ VISUAL WORKSHOP

You have been hired by Fur and Feathers, a local pet store, to design an attractive letterhead. The graphics you need to create the letterhead are already included in a Word file. Open the file WD L-7.doc from the drive and folder where your Data Files are located, then save it as **Fur and Feathers Letterhead**. Use the graphics to create the letterhead shown in Figure L-29. Note that you need to fill the WordArt object with the Woven Mat texture and then add the 3-D Style 3 with a depth of 18 pt and brown as the 3-D color. To modify the pictures, start by editing the parrot and changing the color of the blue feathers on the parrot to red. Change the layout of the puppy to Square, then drag the puppy into the same drawing canvas inhabited by the parrot. Modify, size, and position the puppy and parrot, then fit the drawing canvas to the two pictures and position the drawing canvas so that the completed letterhead appears as shown in Figure L-29. Use Click and Type to enter the contact information. Save the document, then print a copy.

FIGURE L-29

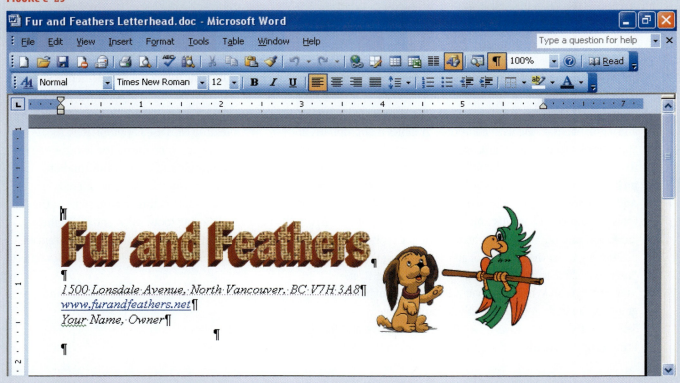

Building Forms

OBJECTIVES

Construct a form template
Add and modify text form fields
Add drop-down and check box form fields
Use calculations in a form
Add Help to a form
Insert form controls
Format and protect forms
Fill in a form as a user

If you have a SAM user profile, you may have access to hands-on instruction, practice, and assessment of the skills covered in this unit. Log in to your SAM account and go to your assignments page to see what your instructor has assigned.

Word provides the tools you need to build forms that users can complete within a Word document. A **form** is a structured document with spaces reserved for entering information. You create a form as a template that includes labeled spaces—called **form fields**—into which users type information. The form template can include check boxes, drop-down lists, formulas used to perform calculations, Help messages, and other form controls to make the form interactive. Finally, you can protect a form so that users can enter information into the form, but they cannot change the structure of the form itself. Alice Wegman in the Marketing Department wants to create a form to survey MediaLoft store managers. You start by creating the form template.

Constructing a Form Template

A Word form is created as a **form template**, which contains all the components of the form. As you learned in an earlier unit, a template is a file that contains the basic structure of a document, such as the page layout, headers and footers, and graphic elements. In the case of a form template, the structure usually consists of a table form that contains field labels and form fields. Figure M-1 shows a completed form template containing several different types of form fields. A **field label** is a word or phrase such as "Date" or "Location" that tells users the kind of information required for a given field. A **form field** is the location where the data associated with a field label is stored. Information that can be stored in a form field includes text, an X in a check box, a number, or a selection in a drop-down list. 🎨 You need to create the basic structure of the form in Word and then save the document as a template. You start by creating the form in Word, then saving it as a template to a new folder that you create in the drive and folder where your Data Files are located.

STEPS

1. **Start Word, click File on the menu bar, then click New to open the New Document task pane**

2. **Click On my computer in the Templates section of the New Document task pane**
   The Templates dialog box opens.

3. **Verify Blank Document is selected, click the Template option button in the Create New section, then click OK**
   A new document appears in the document window and Template1 appears on the title bar.

4. **Type Marketing Survey, center the text, enhance it with Bold and the 18 pt font size, press [Enter] twice, then clear the formatting**

5. **Click Table on the menu bar, point to Insert, click Table, enter 2 for the number of columns and 13 for the number of rows, then click OK**

6. **Type Name:, press [Tab], type Date:, press [Tab], then enter the remaining field labels and merge selected cells as shown in Figure M-2**
   Once you have created the structure for your form, you can save it as a template. First, you create a new folder to contain the template and then you specify this folder as the location of user templates so that Word can find it.

   > **TROUBLE**
   > To merge cells, click to the left of the row to select it, click Table on the menu bar, then click Merge Cells.

7. **Minimize Word, right-click My Computer on your computer desktop, click Explore to open Windows Explorer, navigate to the drive and folder where your Data Files are located, click File, point to New, click Folder, type Your Name Form Templates as the folder name, then press [Enter]**
   In order to have your templates stored in the same location, you set this new folder as the default location for user templates. A **user template** is any template that you create yourself.

8. **Close Windows Explorer, click Template1 on the taskbar, click Tools on the menu bar, click Options, click File Locations, click User templates in the list of File types, click Modify, click the Look in list arrow, select the location where you created the Your Name Form Templates folder, click the folder to select it, click OK, then click OK**

9. **Click the Save button 🖫 on the Standard toolbar, verify that "Marketing Survey.dot" appears in the File name text box as shown in Figure M-3, then click Save**
   Word saves the template to the new folder you created.

FIGURE M-1: Form construction

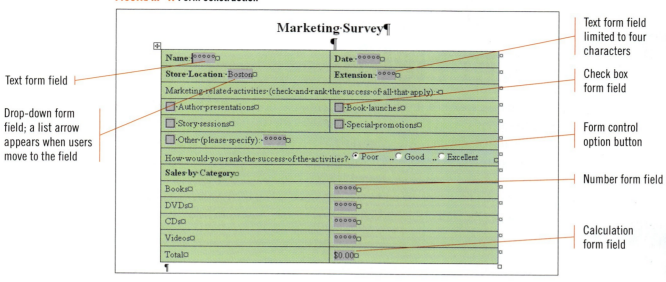

Text form field

Drop-down form field; a list arrow appears when users move to the field

Text form field limited to four characters

Check box form field

Form control option button

Number form field

Calculation form field

FIGURE M-2: Table form

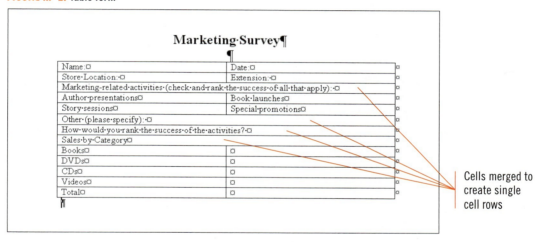

Cells merged to create single cell rows

FIGURE M-3: Saving a user template

Save location is the folder you identified as the default location for template files

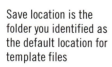
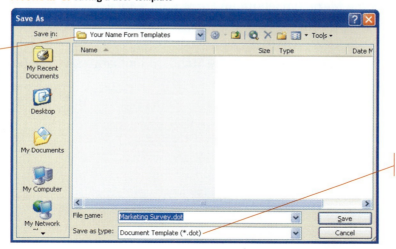

.dot extension identifies the file as a template

Adding and Modifying Text Form Fields

Once you have created a structure for your form, you need to designate form fields where users enter information. You insert **text form fields** in the table cells where users will enter text information, such as their names or the current date. A text form field allows you to control the kind of information users can enter. For example, you can specify that a text form field accepts only a numeric value, limits the number of characters entered, or requires dates to be entered in a specified format. You insert text form fields in the table cells where you need users to enter text or numbers. You then work in the Text Form Field Options dialog box to specify the kind of information required for each text form field.

STEPS

1. **Click View on the menu bar, point to Toolbars, then click Forms**

   The Forms toolbar contains the buttons used to create and modify the various elements of a form. Table M-1 describes each button on the Forms toolbar.

TROUBLE

If dots do not appear in the shaded rectangle, click the Show/Hide ¶ button on the Formatting toolbar.

2. **Click after Name:, press [Spacebar] one time, then click the Text Form Field button 🔲 on the Forms toolbar**

   A gray shaded rectangle with five dots appears following Name. When completing the form, the user will be able to enter text into this form field.

3. **Press [Tab], click after Date:, press [Spacebar] one time, then click 🔲**

4. **Repeat step 3 to insert a text form field after Extension: and after Other (please specify):**

   Figure M-4 shows the form with text form fields inserted in four table cells. You want each user who completes the form to enter a date in a specific format in the text form field following the Date label.

5. **Click the text form field next to Date:, then click the Form Field Options button 📝 on the Forms toolbar**

   The Text Form Field Options dialog box opens. In this dialog box, you specify options related to the format and content of the selected text form field.

QUICK TIP

If the user types 03/03/06, the date entered will appear as March 3, 2006.

6. **Click the Type list arrow, click Date, click the Date format list arrow, click MMMM d, yyyy as shown in Figure M-5, then click OK**

   The text form field looks the same. In a later lesson, you will add a Help message to inform users how to enter the date.

7. **Click the text form field next to Extension:, then click 📝**

8. **Click the Maximum length up arrow until 4 appears, then click OK**

   You specify the number of characters a field can contain when you want to restrict the length of an entry. For example, a user completing this form can enter a phone extension of no more than four digits.

9. **Click the Save button 🔲 on the Standard toolbar to save the template**

FIGURE M-4: Text form fields inserted

Forms toolbar

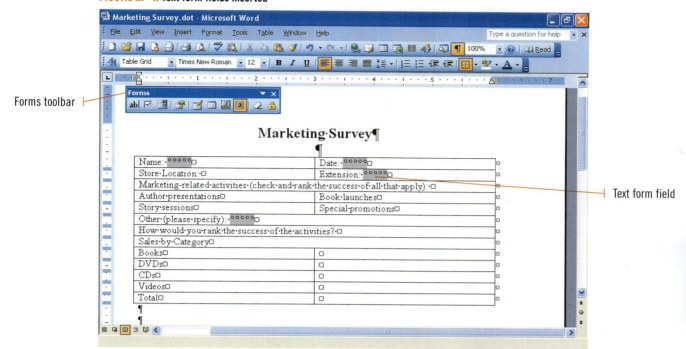

Text form field

FIGURE M-5: Text Form Field Options dialog box

Type list arrow

Indicates the number of the text form field in the form; Text2 indicates that the current text form field was the second field you entered while creating the form

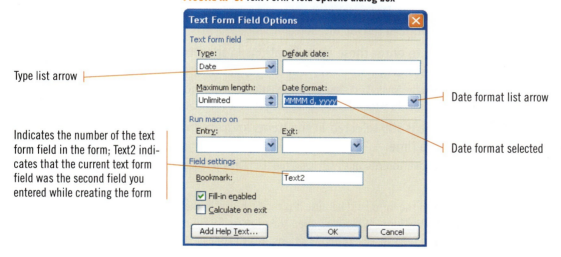

Date format list arrow

Date format selected

TABLE M-1: Buttons on the Forms toolbar

button	use to	button	use to
ab|	Insert a text form field	⊞	Insert a table/cell to contain form fields
☑	Insert a check box form field	🗐	Insert a frame to contain a form
🗐	Insert a drop-down form field	a	Insert or remove shading from form fields
🖳	Open the Form Field Options dialog box, then modify the options of an inserted form field	✐	Reset form fields to their default settings
✎	Draw a table to contain form fields	🔒	Protect a form so that users can enter only data required for the form fields

Word 2003

Adding Drop-Down and Check Box Form Fields

In addition to text form fields, Word forms can include check box form fields and drop-down form fields. Users can use the pointer to make selections in check box or drop-down form fields. For example, users can click a check box to select it or they can select an item from a drop-down list. You want to provide store managers an easy way to select the location of their MediaLoft store. You decide to provide a drop-down list of the MediaLoft store locations so that store managers can select the location of their MediaLoft store. You also want the store managers to identify which marketing-related activities listed in the form they engaged in during the past month. You provide check boxes next to the activities so store managers can quickly make their selections.

STEPS

1. **Click after Store Location:, press [Spacebar] one time, then click the Drop-Down Form Field button on the Forms toolbar**

   A gray shaded rectangle without dots appears, indicating that the field is a drop-down form field and not a text form field.

2. **Click the Form Field Options button on the Forms toolbar**

   The Drop-Down Form Field Options dialog box opens. In this dialog box, you enter the selections you want to appear in the drop-down list.

3. **Type Boston in the Drop-down item text box, then click Add**

   Boston becomes the first entry in the drop-down list.

   > **QUICK TIP**
   > You can press [Enter] after typing each entry, or you can click Add.

4. **Repeat Step 3 to enter these store locations in the Drop-down item text box: Chicago, Houston, Kansas City, New York, San Diego, San Francisco, Toronto, and Seattle**

   Figure M-6 shows the MediaLoft store locations entered in the Drop-Down Form Field Options dialog box. You can change the order in which the locations are presented so that the entire list appears in alphabetical order.

5. **Be sure Seattle is still selected in the Items in drop-down list box, then click the Move up button one time**

   Seattle moves above Toronto in the list and the list is in alphabetical order.

6. **Click OK**

   Boston appears in the form field because it is the first item in the drop-down form field list. In a later lesson, you will protect the form. When you open the protected form to complete it as a user, a list arrow appears next to Boston to indicate that other selections are available.

7. **Click to the left of Author presentations, click the Check Box Form Field button on the Forms toolbar, then press [Spacebar] one time to insert a space between the check box and the text**

   A gray shaded box appears before the text "Author presentations." After the form is protected, an X will appear in the box when a user selects it.

8. **Repeat Step 7 to insert check boxes next to Book launches, Story sessions, Special promotions, and Other (please specify):**

   Figure M-7 shows the form with the text form fields, a drop-down form field, and check box form fields.

9. **Save the template**

FIGURE M-6: Drop-Down Form Field Options dialog box

Drop-down item text box

Boston and Chicago appear above Houston

Move up button

Move down button

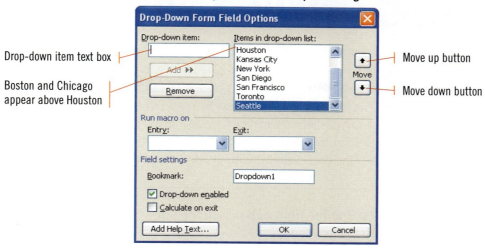

FIGURE M-7: Form fields inserted in a Word form

Text form field

Check box form fields

Drop-down form field

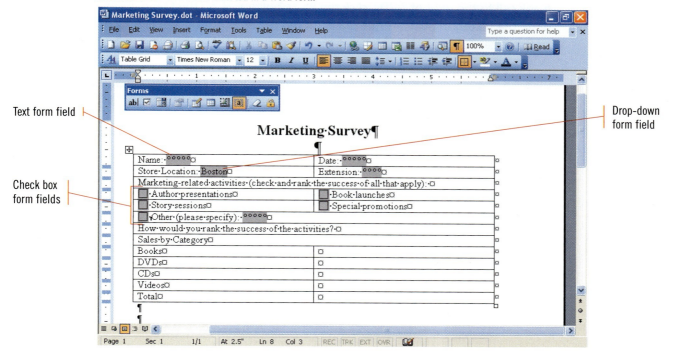

Using Calculations in a Form

A Word form can be designed to perform calculations. For example, you can specify that a text form field should add a series of numbers. To perform calculations in a form, you must follow two steps. First, you specify each text form field that will be used to perform the calculation as Number type so that a user can only enter numbers. Second, you specify the text form field that contains the result of the calculation as Calculation type and you type the mathematical formula that will perform the calculation.  You want the store managers to enter the dollar amounts generated in the current month from the sale of books, DVDs, CDs, and videos. Then you want the form to calculate the total sales automatically.

STEPS

1. **Click the blank cell to the right of Books in the table form, then click the Text Form Field button abl on the Forms toolbar**

2. **Click the Form Field Options button 🖳 on the Forms toolbar, click the Type list arrow, then select Number**

   You change the text form field type to Number because you want users to be able to enter only a number.

3. **Click the Number format list arrow, select the number format shown in Figure M-8, click the Calculate on exit check box, then click OK**

   You select the Calculate on exit check box because you want the number that users enter into the text form field to be included as part of a calculation. The three table cells under the current cell require the same text form field as the one you just created. You can save time by copying and pasting the text form field you just created.

4. **With the form field selected, click the Copy button 🖺 on the Standard toolbar, click the blank cell to the right of DVDs, click the Paste button 🖺 on the Standard toolbar, then paste the text form field into the blank cells to the right of CDs and Videos**

   You want the cell to the right of Total to display the total of the values users enter in the four cells immediately above it.

5. **Click the blank cell to the right of Total, click 🖺, click 🖳 to open the Text Form Field Options dialog box, click the Type list arrow, then click Calculation**

6. **Click in the Expression text box to the right of the = sign, type SUM(ABOVE), then compare the Text Form Field Options dialog box to Figure M-9**

   The formula =SUM(ABOVE) is a standard calculation expression that is recognized by programs such as Word and Excel. The =SUM(ABOVE) calculation expression calculates all the values entered in the designated text form fields. The designated text form fields must be above the text form field that contains the calculation expression, and the text form fields must use a Number format.

7. **Click OK**

   The $0.00 entered next to Total indicates that the cell contains a calculation form field.

8. **Compare your form to Figure M-10, then save the template**

FIGURE M-8: Number format selected

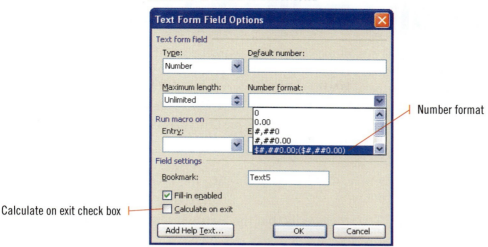

Number format

Calculate on exit check box

FIGURE M-9: Calculation options selected

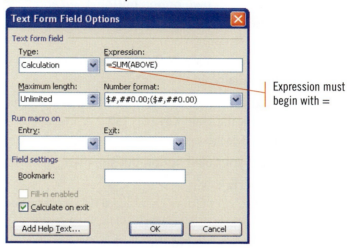

Expression must begin with =

FIGURE M-10: Calculation form field inserted

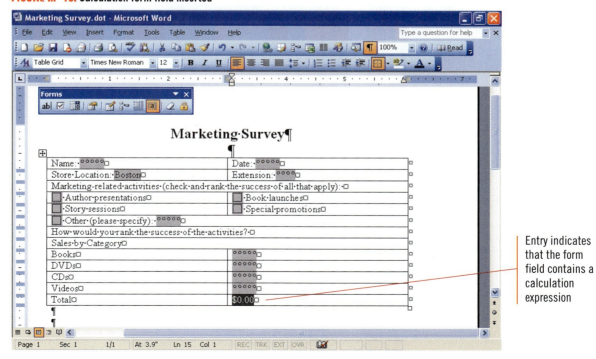

Entry indicates that the form field contains a calculation expression

Adding Help to a Form

You can help users fill in a form quickly and easily by attaching Help messages to selected form fields. For example, you can include a Help message in the Date form field that advises users how to enter a correctly formatted date. Help messages can be set to appear on the status bar or when the user presses the [F1] function key. ▰▰▰▰ You want to include instructions that advise store managers how to enter the date. You also want to add instructions about how to complete the Other (please specify): form field.

1. **Click the text form field to the right of Date:, then click the Form Field Options button 📰 on the Forms toolbar**

2. **Click Add Help Text, then verify that the Status Bar tab is selected**
   You can choose to include an AutoText entry such as a page number or the word "Confidential," or you can type your own Help message.

3. **Click the Type your own option button, then enter the Help text shown in Figure M-11**
   The text entered in the Status Bar text box will appear on the status bar when a user clicks the text form field next to Date.

4. **Click OK to exit the Form Field Help Text dialog box, then click OK to exit the Text Form Field Options dialog box**

5. **Click the text form field to the right of Other (please specify):, click 📰, click Add Help Text, then click the Help Key (F1) tab**
   You can enter a Help message containing up to 225 characters in the Help Key (F1) text box.

6. **Click the Type your own option button, then type the Help text shown in Figure M-12**

7. **Click OK, then click OK**
   The text form fields to which you have added Help messages do not appear to change. You will see the Help messages in the last lesson when you fill in the form as a user.

8. **With the text form field to the right of Other (please specify): still selected, click the Italic button 𝐼 on the Formatting toolbar, then click to the right of the text form field**
   The text form field does not appear to have changed. However, the Italic button on the Formatting toolbar is selected to indicate that any text entered in the text form field will appear in italic.

9. **Save the template**

FIGURE M-11: Status Bar Help

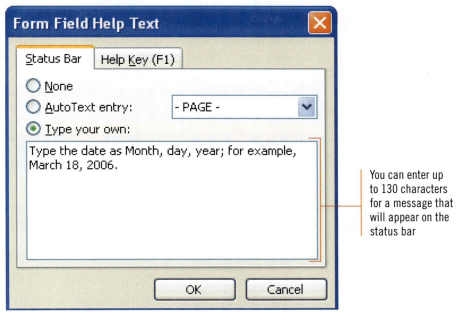

You can enter up to 130 characters for a message that will appear on the status bar

FIGURE M-12: Help Key (F1) text

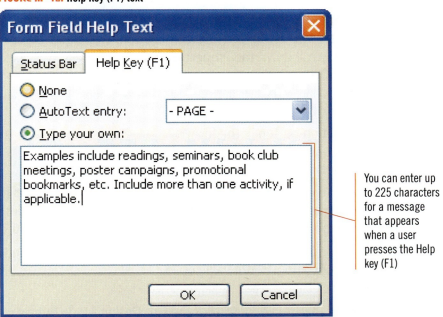

You can enter up to 225 characters for a message that appears when a user presses the Help key (F1)

UNIT M
Word 2003

Inserting Form Controls

The Forms toolbar contains the tools most commonly used to create a form that users complete in Word. You can further enhance a form by including some of the controls available on the Control Toolbox toolbar. These controls are referred to as ActiveX controls and are used to offer options to users or to run macros or scripts that automate specific tasks. One of the easiest controls to use in a form that users complete in Word is the Option button control. When you want users to select just one of several available options, you insert a series of Option button controls. You want the store managers to rank the effectiveness of the month's marketing activities. You decide to create a series of labeled Option buttons so that store managers can select one to indicate if the marketing activities yielded poor, good, or excellent results.

STEPS

QUICK TIP

Some controls in the Control Toolbox, such as the check box control, are also available on the Forms toolbar. To use most Control Toolbox controls, however, you need knowledge of Visual Basic.

1. **Click View on the menu bar, point to Toolbars, then click Control Toolbox**

   The Control Toolbox toolbar opens.

2. **Click the Design Mode button 🔲 on the Control Toolbox toolbar, click the blank area to the right of How would you rank the success of the activities?, then press the [Spacebar] one time**

   The Design Mode button becomes a floating toolbar, indicating that you are in Design Mode. You must be in Design Mode when you want to insert a control from the Control Toolbox toolbar to a selected cell.

3. **Click the Option Button button ◉ on the Control Toolbox toolbar to insert an option button control into the selected cell**

   Figure M-13 shows the option button with the button caption "OptionButton1" inserted in the selected cell. You need to change the properties of the control so that the label next to the option button shows the caption "Poor." A **property** is a named attribute of a control that you set to define one of the control's attributes such as its size, its color, and its behavior in response to user input.

QUICK TIP

You can move and resize the Properties window. To move the window, click the title bar and drag the window to its new location. To resize the window, move 🡔 over the lower-right corner of the Properties window, then click and drag 🡔 to resize the Properties window.

4. **Click the Properties button 🔲 on the Control Toolbox toolbar**

   The Properties window opens with the Alphabetic tab selected. The properties are listed in alphabetical order on the Alphabetic tab. In this window, you can identify properties such as the height and width of the option button and designate the label text to appear next to the option button.

5. **Select the text OptionButton1 next to Caption, type Poor, select 21.75 next to Height, type 17.25, scroll down the Properties window if necessary, select 108 next to Width, then type 50.25**

   The Properties window is shown in Figure M-14, and the caption "Poor" appears next to the option button in the Word form. The measurements are in pixels.

6. **Click the option button in the form**

   The size of the option button changes to match the Properties (Height = 17.25 and Width = 50.25) that you entered in the Properties window.

7. **With the option button box still selected, press [➡] once, press [Spacebar] two times, click ◉, replace OptionButton2 next to Caption in the Properties window with the word Good, change the Height to 17.25, then change the Width to 50.25**

8. **Repeat Steps 6 and 7 to enter an option button with the caption text Excellent, a Height value of 17.25, and a Width value of 75**

   The three option buttons appear, as shown in Figure M-15.

9. **Close the Properties window, click the Exit Design Mode button 🔲 on the Design Mode floating toolbar, close the Control Toolbox toolbar, then save the template**

   You must exit Design Mode after you insert a form control so that you can continue working with the form.

FIGURE M-13: OptionButton1 inserted

Control Toolbox toolbar

Design Mode button

Option Button button

Option Button control inserted

Design Mode button becomes a floating toolbar when Design Mode is active

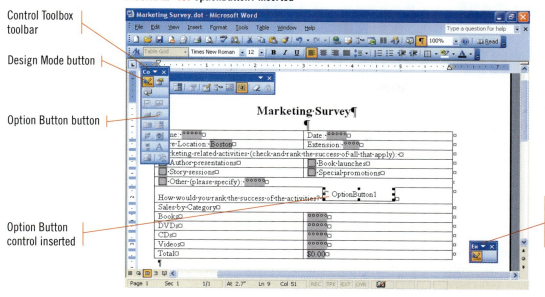

FIGURE M-14: Properties window

Alphabetic tab selected

"Poor" entered next to Caption

Height changed to 17.25 pixels

Width changed to 50.25 pixels

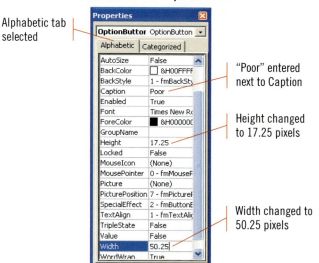

FIGURE M-15: Option buttons inserted

Drag toolbars and arrange as needed so you can see options while you work

Option buttons

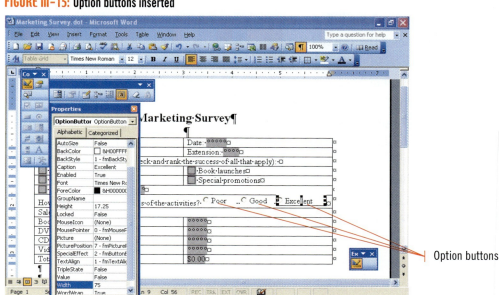

UNIT
M
Word 2003

Formatting and Protecting Forms

Forms should be easy to read onscreen so that users can fill them in quickly and accurately. You can enhance a table containing form fields and you can modify the magnification of a document containing a form so that users can easily see the form fields. You can then protect a form so that users can enter only the data required and *not* be able to change the structure of the form. When a form is protected, information can be entered only in form fields. You enhance the field labels, add shading to the form, and change the background color of the option button controls. Finally, you protect and then save the form template.

STEPS

1. Select **Name** in the first cell of the table, click the **Bold button** **B** on the Formatting toolbar, then enhance the following field labels with bold: **Date**, **Store Location**, **Extension**, and **Sales by Category**

> **TROUBLE**
> If the table move handle is not visible, click Table on the menu bar, point to Select, then click Table.

2. Click the **table move handle** ⊞ at the upper-left corner of the table to select the table, click **Table** on the menu bar, click **Table Properties**, click the **Row tab**, click the **Specify height check box**, enter **.3** in the text box, then click **OK**

3. Click **View** on the menu bar, point to **Toolbars**, then click **Tables and Borders**

    The Tables and Borders toolbar appears. You can use this toolbar to fill the entire table with shading.

4. With the entire table still selected, click the **Shading Color list arrow** 🔲▾ on the Tables and Borders toolbar, click **More Fill Colors**, click the **Custom tab**, enter settings in the Red, Green, and Blue text boxes as shown in Figure M-16, then click **OK**

5. With the entire table still selected, click the **Align Top Left list arrow** 🔲 on the Tables and Borders toolbar, click the **Align Center Left button** 🔲, click away from the table to deselect it, then close the Tables and Borders toolbar

    The option buttons still have white backgrounds. You can change the background color of an ActiveX form control in the Properties window.

6. Click **View** on the menu bar, point to **Toolbars**, click **Control Toolbox**, click the **Design Mode button** 🔲, click the **Poor option button** to select it, then click the **Properties button** 🔲 on the Control Toolbox toolbar to open the Properties window for the Poor option button

> **TROUBLE**
> After changing a control property, click the option button, then press [→] to deselect the option button.

7. Click the **cell** to the right of BackColor, click the **list arrow**, select the **Light Green color** in the top row as shown in Figure M-17

8. Repeat Step 7 to change the back color of the **Good** and **Excellent** option buttons to light green

9. Close the Properties window, click the **Exit Design Mode button** 🔲 on the Control Toolbox toolbar, then close the Control Toolbox toolbar

    After you modify an ActiveX control, you need to exit Design Mode so that you can protect the form. When the Design Mode button is selected, you cannot protect a form.

10. Click the **Protect Form button** 🔲 on the Forms toolbar, compare the completed form template to Figure M-18, close the Forms toolbar, then save and close the template

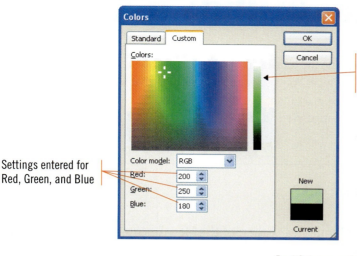

FIGURE M-16: Custom fill color

Black triangle shows custom color based on red, green, and blue settings

Settings entered for Red, Green, and Blue

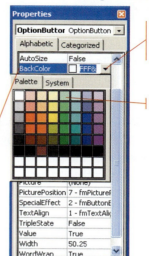

FIGURE M-17: Background color selected

BackColor list arrow appears after clicking in cell to the right of BackColor

Light Green

BackColor property

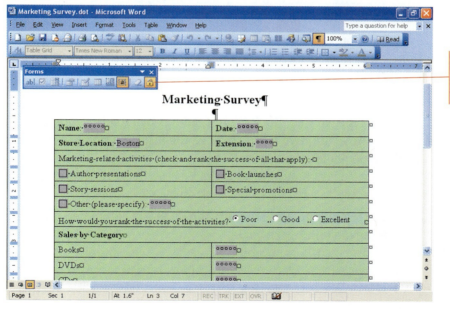

FIGURE M-18: Completed form template

Protect Form button selected indicating that the form is protected

Clues to Use

Locking form fields

When you protect a form using the Protect Form button on the Forms toolbar, the form information, such as field labels, is protected or locked. A user can input information only in form fields and the input information must match the type specified by the person who originated the form. Sometimes, however, instead of protecting an entire form, you might want to lock certain form fields. For example, if you are entering numbers in a form for a budget and you want to be sure that the numbers do not inadvertently get changed, you can lock the form field after you enter the numbers. To lock a form field, and prevent changes to the current field results, click the field, then press [Ctrl][F11]. If you need to unlock a field to update the field results, click the field, then press [Ctrl][Shift][F11].

Filling in a Form as a User

Before you distribute a form template to users, you need to test it to ensure that all the elements work correctly. For example, you want to make sure the total is calculated properly when numbers are entered in the form fields formatted with the Number type. You also want to make sure that selections appear in the list box, that the correct Help messages appear, and that you can easily select the check boxes and option buttons. ░░░░ You open a new document based on the template, then fill in the form as if you were the Houston store manager.

STEPS

1. **Click File on the menu bar, then click New**

   The New Document task pane opens.

2. **Click On my computer in the Templates section of the New Document task pane, click Marketing Survey.dot, verify that the Document option button in the Create New section of the Templates window is selected, then click OK**

   Notice that the Marketing Survey.dot file opens as a Word document, as indicated by the filename that appears on the title bar. The insertion point highlights the space following Name. The form is protected, so you can enter information only in spaces that contain text form fields, check boxes, drop-down lists, or option buttons.

3. **Type Your Name, then press [Tab]**

   The insertion point moves to the space following Date. Notice the Help message that appears in the status bar, telling you how to enter the date.

4. **Enter the current date in the required format, press [Tab], click the list arrow next to Boston, click Houston, then press [Tab]**

5. **Type 4455, press [Tab], then click the check box next to Author presentations, the check box next to Book launches, and the check box next to Other (please specify):**

6. **Press [Tab], then press [F1]**

   The Help message appears, as shown in Figure M-19.

7. **Click OK, type Mystery Book Night readings by Jonathon Grant, click the Good option button, press [Tab] two times to move the insertion point to the text form field next to Books, type 58000, then press [Tab]**

   The amount is automatically formatted with a dollar sign and the amount in the cell to the right of Total is updated automatically when you press [Tab] to move the insertion point out of the cell.

8. **Enter the remaining sales amounts shown in the completed form in Figure M-20; press [Tab] after you enter each value**

   The total—$112,000—is calculated automatically because this text field is a calculation type with the =SUM(ABOVE) formula. When you press [Tab] after entering the last value, the insertion point moves to the next text form field that accepts user input, which is the text form field after Name.

9. **Save the document with the name Houston Survey to the drive and folder where your Data Files are located, print a copy, then close the document**

   After you use the Monthly Marketing Survey template, it will be listed in the New from template section of the New Document task pane.

FIGURE M-19: F1 Help message

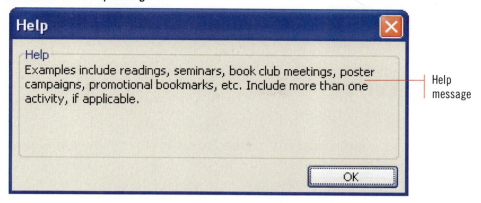

Help message

FIGURE M-20: Sales amounts entered

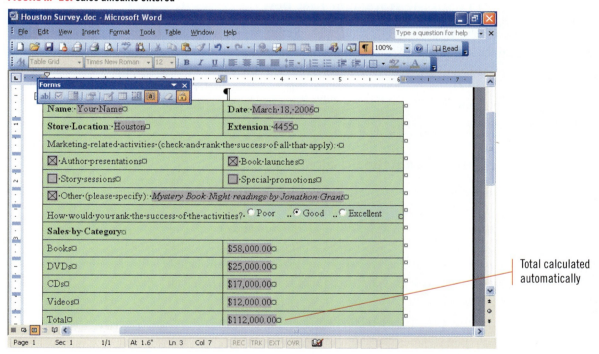

Total calculated automatically

Clues to Use

Editing a form template

To edit the structure of a form, you need to open the template, then click the Protect Form button on the Forms toolbar to deselect it. You can then make changes to the form by adding or removing form fields and modifying the appearance of the form. When you have finished modifying the form template, click the Protect Form button again, then save the template.

Practice

Identify each of the numbered buttons on the Forms toolbar shown in Figure M-21.

FIGURE M-21

Match each term with the statement that best describes it.

6. **Drop-down form field**	**a.** An area of a form into which users can enter information
7. **Control Toolbox**	**b.** A list of options in a form
8. **Text form field**	**c.** Contains a mathematical expression
9. **[F1]**	**d.** Contains a selection of ActiveX controls that can be inserted in a form
10. **Calculation form field**	**e.** One type of ActiveX control
11. **Option button**	**f.** Help key

Select the best answer from the list of choices

12. **What is a field label?**
    a. A space for users to enter variable information
    b. A placeholder for text such as a user's name or the current date
    c. A word or phrase, such as the user's current address, that is entered into a blank cell
    d. A word or phrase such as "Date" or "Location" that tells users the kind of information required for a given field

13. **What happens when you insert a text form field into a table cell?**
    a. A blank check box appears.
    b. A shaded rectangle with five dots appears.
    c. A blank bar outlined in black appears.
    d. A Help message appears to inform users what information to enter in the form field.

14. **How do you view the list of choices available in a drop-down form field?**
    a. Double-click the drop-down form field to insert a list arrow.
    b. Open the form as a user, click the drop-down form field, then click the list arrow.
    c. Right-click the drop-down form field, then click Activate.
    d. View the form in the Print Preview screen.

15. **How would you enter a Help message containing 200 characters?**
    a. Enter the Help message in the Type your own text box in the Status Bar tab of the Help Text dialog box.
    b. Enter the Help message in the form field.
    c. Edit the Help message so it contains only 130 characters, the accepted limit.
    d. Enter the Help message in the Type your own text box in the Help Key (F1) tab of the Help Text dialog box.

▼ SKILLS REVIEW

1. Construct a form template.

a. Start Word, open the New Document task pane if necessary, click the On my computer link, then create a new blank document as a template.

b. Check to ensure that Your Name Form Templates is designated as the folder to contain user templates. If necessary, refer to the lesson on Constructing a form template.

c. Type **Change of Grade Notification** as the title, then center the text and enhance it with Bold and a 20-point font size.

d. Two lines below the title, clear the formatting, then create a table consisting of four columns and 13 rows.

e. Refer to Figure M-22. Type the text as shown. Merge cells in rows 2, 10, 11, 12, and 13 as shown. Apply bold to field labels as shown. (*Note*: You will align text later in the exercise.)

f. Save the template as **Change of Grade Notification** to the Your Name Form Templates folder.

FIGURE M-22

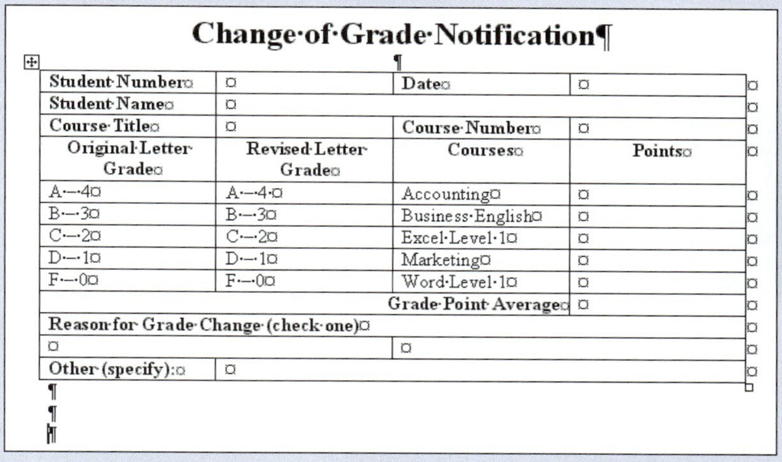
Change·of·Grade·Notification¶

Student·Number		**Date**	
Student·Name			
Course·Title		**Course·Number**	
Original·Letter·Grade	**Revised·Letter·Grade**	**Courses**	**Points**
A·—·4	A·—·4·	Accounting	
B·—·3	B·—·3	Business·English	
C·—·2	C·—·2	Excel·Level·1	
D·—·1	D·—·1	Marketing	
F·—·0	F·—·0	Word·Level·1	
		Grade·Point·Average	
Reason·for·Grade·Change·(check·one)			
Other·(specify):			

2. Add and modify text form fields.

a. Show the Forms toolbar, if necessary.

b. Insert text form fields in the blank cells to the right of the following field labels: Student Number, Date, Student Name, Course Number, and Other (specify).

c. Modify the text form field next to Student Number so that users can enter up to six numbers.

d. Modify the text form field next to Date so that users must enter a date formatted as M/d/yyyy.

e. Save your changes to the template.

3. Add drop-down and check box form fields.

a. Insert a drop-down form field after Course Title.

b. In the Drop-Down Form Field Options dialog box, enter the following list of items: **Accounting**, **Excel Level 1**, **Marketing**, **Business English**, and **Word Level 1**.

c. Move Business English up so that it appears immediately after Accounting.

d. Insert a check box form field and a space to the left of each letter grade in the Original Letter Grade and Revised Letter Grade columns.

e. Save the template.

4. Use calculations in a form.

a. Insert a text form field in the blank cell to the right of Accounting with the Number type, the Number format set to 0, and the Calculate on exit check box selected.

b. Copy the text form field with number formatting to the next four cells (Business English through Word Level 1).

c. Insert a text form field with the type set to Calculation in the blank cell to the right of Grade Point Average.

d. Type the expression **=SUM(ABOVE)/5**. This formula will add the numbers in the Points cells, then divide the total by 5 to determine the average.

e. Make sure the Number format is set to 0 and the Calculate on exit check box is selected before you exit the Text Form Field Options dialog box, then save the template.

5. Add Help to a form.

a. Add a status bar Help message in the Date form field that states: **Type the date in numerals as month, day, year; for example, 03/18/2006**.

b. Add a Help key (F1) Help message in the Other (specify): field that states: **Acceptable reasons include completion of work outstanding and acceptance of medical documentation.**

c. Save the template.

6. **Insert form controls.**
   a. Show the Control Toolbox toolbar. Make sure the Design Mode button is selected, then click the blank cell below the Reason for Grade Change field label.
   b. Insert an Option Button control with the following properties: Caption is **Calculation Error** and height is **18**.
   c. Insert an Option Button control in the next blank cell with the caption **Exam Retake** and a height of **18**.
   d. Close the Properties window, then exit Design Mode.
   e. Close the Control Toolbox toolbar, then save the template.

7. **Format and protect a form.**
   a. With the table selected, change the row height to **.35"**.
   b. Show the Tables and Borders toolbar, then change the text alignment for the entire table to Align Center Left.
   c. Align Top Center all four field labels in the row beginning with Original Letter Grade.
   d. Align Center all the form fields in the six cells under the cell with the Points label.
   e. Align Center Right the Grade Point Average field label.
   f. Select the table again, then change the colors in the Custom tab of the Colors dialog box to Red: **240**, Green: **220**, and Blue: **250**. (*Hint*: You should see a light lavender color.)
   g. View the Control Toolbox toolbar, then select Design Mode.
   h. With the Calculation Error option button selected, change the BackColor in the Properties window to light pink (last box in the top row of the color selections), which creates a two-tone effect—lavender for the form background and light pink for the option button.
   i. Repeat the preceding procedure to change the BackColor to light pink for the Exam Retake option button.
   j. Close the Properties window, then exit Design Mode. (*Note*: You must click the Design Mode button on the Control Toolbox toolbar to exit Design Mode.)
   k. Protect the form, then close the Forms toolbar, the Tables and Borders toolbar, and the Control Toolbox toolbar.
   l. Save and close the template.

8. **Fill in a form as a user.**
   a. Open a new document based on the Change of Grade Notification template. (*Hint*: Make sure the Document option button in the Create New section of the Templates dialog box is selected.)
   b. Type **337888** as the Student Number, press [Tab], type the **current date**, press [Tab], type your name, select Business English as the Course Title, enter **626** as the Course Number, select B as the Original Letter Grade, then select A as the Revised Letter Grade.
   c. Enter the points for each course as follows: Accounting: **3**, Business English: **4**; Excel Level 1: **4**; Marketing: **2**; and Word Level 1: **2**.
   d. Press [Tab] and verify that the value in the Grade Point Average cell is 3.
   e. Select the Exam Retake option button.
   f. Check the F1 Help Message in the Other (specify): field.
   g. Save the document with the filename **Business English Grade Change** to the drive and folder where your Data Files are located, print a copy, close the document, then exit Word.

▼ INDEPENDENT CHALLENGE 1

You work for the owner of Sun Sensations—a new company that sells tours to exotic sun spots around the world. The owner and some of the sales representatives have begun taking frequent business trips to tropical resorts in the South Pacific to set up tours. Your boss asks you to help expedite the bookkeeping by creating an expense report form that can be completed online in Word.

   a. Start Word and open the file WD M-1.doc from the drive and folder where your Data Files are located. Save it as a template called **Expense Report Form** to the Your Name Form Templates folder that you created to complete the lessons in this unit. (Refer to the first lesson in this unit, if necessary.)
   b. View the Forms toolbar.
   c. Insert text form fields for the Name, Report Date, Extension, and Purpose of Travel field labels.

▼ INDEPENDENT CHALLENGE 1 (CONTINUED)

d. Specify the date format of your choice for the Report Date form field.

e. Change the type of the text form field next to Extension to Number and specify a maximum of four numbers.

f. Add a status bar Help message to the Purpose of Travel form field that states: **Specify the location(s) you visited and the business goals accomplished**.

g. Insert a drop-down form field in the blank cell to the right of Department that includes the following entries: **Management**, **Marketing**, and **Sales**.

h. Insert a text form field in the first blank cell in the Date column, select Date as the type, specify the M/d/yy date format, then copy the text form field and paste it to all the blank cells in the Date column.

i. Insert a drop-down form field in the first blank cell in the Category column. Include the following entries in the drop-down list: **Meals**, **Hotel**, **Air Fare**, and **Other**. Put the entries in alphabetical order.

j. Copy the drop-down form field and paste it to all the blank cells in the Category column.

k. Insert a text form field in the first blank cell in the Details column, then copy the text form field and paste it to all the blank cells in the Details column.

l. Insert a text form field in the blank cell below Amount, then change the text form field options so the type is Number, the format is 0.00, and the Calculate on exit check box is selected. Copy the text form field with Number formatting and paste it to all the blank cells in the Amount column, except the cell next to Total.

m. Insert a text form field in the blank cell to the right of Total, then change the form field options so the type is Calculation, the format is 0.00, the Expression is =SUM(ABOVE), and the Calculate on exit check box is selected.

n. Right-align the form fields in the Amount column and Total cell.

o. Protect the form, then save and close the template.

p. Open a new document based on the template.

q. Type **your name** and the **current date**, select the Marketing Department, type **5555** for the extension, then describe the Purpose for Travel as **Evaluating the Paradise Palms Resort in Tahiti**.

r. Enter the following dates and expenses: **April 10: Return Air Fare from Seattle to Tahiti: $1800, April 11: Meals at Paradise Palms Resort: $200, April 12: Meals in various locations: $200, April 13: Meals including hosted dinner for Paradise Palms Resort Managers, $550, April 13: Hotel accommodation for three nights at the Paradise Palms Resort: $1200, and April 13: Other described as Taxis and Miscellaneous Expenses: $300**.

s. Verify the total expenses are 4250.00, then save the document as **Completed Expense Report** to the drive and folder where your Data Files are located.

Advanced Challenge Exercise

- Unprotect the form on the Expense Report Form.dot.
- Click below the form, press [Enter], then clear the formatting.
- Click the Insert Frame button on the Forms toolbar, draw a box approximately 4" wide and 1" tall, then enter text

FIGURE M-23

and the two check box controls as shown in Figure M-23. Note that you need to select True for the AutoSize property for both controls and change the font of the caption to Arial and 18 point. (Note: Adjust the boxes manually as needed.)

- Exit design mode, protect the form, then click the Agree check box.

t. Print a copy of the completed form, then close the document.

▼ INDEPENDENT CHALLENGE 2

You are the Office Manager at Atlantic Regional Securities, a company that has just instituted parking regulations for staff wanting to park in the new staff parking lot. Any staff member who wants to park in the lot must purchase a parking permit. You decide to create a Word form that staff members complete to purchase a parking permit. You will create the form as a Word template saved on the company's network. Staffers can open a new Word document based on the template, then complete the form in Word, or they can print the form and fill it in by hand.

a. Start Word, open the file WD M-2.doc from the drive and folder where your Data Files are located, and save it as a template called **Parking Permit Requisition** to the Your Name Form Templates folder that you created to complete the lessons in this unit. (Refer to the first lesson in this unit, if necessary.)

b. View the Forms toolbar.

c. Insert a text form field in the blank cell to the right of Date. Format the text form field to accept dates entered in the format you prefer. Include a Help message that appears on the status bar and tells users how to enter the date.

d. Enter a text form field in the blank cell to the right of Name.

e. Insert a drop-down form field in the blank cell to the right of Department that includes the following entries: **Accounting**, **Administration**, **Finance**, **Marketing**, **Sales**, and **Information Technology**.

f. Move entries so they appear in alphabetical order.

g. Insert a text form field in the blank cell to the right of Extension, then modify the text form field so that it accepts a maximum of four numbers. Include a status bar Help message that advises users to enter their four-digit telephone extension.

h. Insert check box form fields to the left of the selections in the fourth column (Full-time, Part-time, etc.). Leave a space between the check box and the first letter of each selection.

i. Insert an option button control in each of the blank cells in the last row of the form. The captions for the option buttons are as follows: **Check**, **Cash**, and **Pay Debit**.

j. Click the Exit Design Mode button on the Control Toolbox, then close the Control Toolbox.

k. Apply the Table Columns 5 Table AutoFormat to the table.

l. Show the Tables and Borders toolbar, then remove the shading from the cell that contains the Check option button.

Advanced Challenge Exercise

- Revise each of the three option buttons as follows:
- Change the foreground color (ForeColor) of each option button to Bright Blue. Note that the ForeColor is the text color.
- Change the Font to Impact and 16 point.
- Change the SpecialEffect to 0 – fmButtonEffectFlat.
- Change the TextAlign to 2 – fmTextAlignCenter.
- Set the width at 75 for the Check and Cash buttons and 100 for the Pay Debit button.
- Exit Design Mode.

m. Protect the form, then save and close the template.

n. Open a new document based on the template, then complete the form as a user. Type the **current date** and **your name**, select Executive status, select the Information Technology Department, enter any **four-digit extension**, then select Cash as the payment method.

o. Save the document as **Completed Parking Requisition** to the drive and folder where your Data Files are located, print a copy, close the document, then exit Word.

▼ INDEPENDENT CHALLENGE 3

You work for a company called Asian History Tours that specializes in taking small groups of people on educational tours to various areas in China, Southeast Asia, Korea, and Japan. One way you can measure the success of the tours is to ask customers to complete a feedback form after participating in a tour. You decide to create a Word form that you can e-mail to customers. Your customers can complete the form in Word, then send it back to you as an e-mail attachment.

a. Start Word, type **Asian History Tours** as the title and **Tour Feedback** as the subtitle, then enhance both titles attractively.

b. Save the document as a template named **Feedback Form** to the Your Name Form Templates folder you created to contain the form templates you created in this unit.

c. Plan a form that contains the following field labels: **Name**, **Tour Date**, **Tour Guide**, and **Tour Name** and a section for ranking tour components similar to Figure M-24.

FIGURE M-24

Asian History Tours Tour Feedback						
Name		Tour Date				
Tour Guide		Tour Name				
Please rank each of the following components on a scale from 1 (Poor) to 4 (Incredible)						
		1	2	3	4	
Meals						
Accommodations						
Tour Guide						
Educational Interest						
Overall						
Additional Comments						
May we contact you regarding new tours that may interest you?						

d. Enter text form fields in the cell to the right of Name, Tour Date, and Tour Guide, then enter a drop-down form field in the Tour Name cell that lists five tours. Type sample tour names such as Yangtze Odyssey, Great Wall Trek, and Temples of Japan. Be sure the names appear in alphabetical order in the drop-down list. Also be sure to assign the Date type to the Date form field, using a format of your choice.

e. Insert check box form fields in the ranking section of your form.

f. In the last row of the table, insert two Option Button controls: one labeled **YES!** and one labeled **No thanks**. Format the option buttons so that they fit the table cell.

g. Format the form attractively, using one of the Table AutoFormats if you wish. (*Hint*: You might need to increase the row height so that the option buttons fit.)

h. Protect the form, save it, then close the template.

i. Open a new document based on the form template, then save it as **Completed Feedback Form** to the drive and folder where your Data Files are located.

j. Fill in the form as if you had participated in one of your tours. Enter your name in the Name field.

k. Save the form, print a copy, close the form, then exit Word.

▼ INDEPENDENT CHALLENGE 4

Many companies and organizations that maintain Web sites include online forms that visitors can complete to participate in a survey, provide payment information, select products or services, and request information. You can learn a great deal about form design by studying some of the forms included on Web sites. You decide to search for Web sites that include forms, identify the form controls used in the forms, and then describe two unusual or creative ways in which form controls are used to request information.

a. Open your Web browser and conduct a search for companies that are likely to include forms that are used to gather information. Good choices include shopping Web sites such as an online bookstore that request payment information or travel site Web sites that request travel information.

b. Select two Web sites that include forms that users complete to provide information.

c. Open the file WD M-3.doc, then save it as **Form Evaluation** to the drive and folder where your Data Files are located.

d. Type **your name** and the **current date** in the spaces provided.

e. As directed in the Form Evaluation document, type the company name and copy the Web site address to the spaces provided, then follow the directions in the document to insert the required information.

f. Save the document, print a copy, then close it.

▼ VISUAL WORKSHOP

You are in charge of the audio-visual department at a local community college. Faculty members come to you to borrow projectors, DVD players, and computers to use in class presentations. You decide to make up a simple form that faculty members can complete online and then e-mail to you when they want to borrow audio-visual equipment. Create and enhance a form template, as shown in Figure M-25. Save the template as **Audio Visual Request Form** to the Your Name Form Templates folder containing all the form templates you've created for this unit. The items in the drop-down list for Department are **Arts**, **Business**, **Sciences**, **Education**, and **Technology**. The items in the drop-down list for Equipment are **DVD Player**, **Projector**, **Computer**, and **Television**. Protect the form, close the template, then open a new document based on the template. Complete the form with **your name**, the **current date**, the Business Department, Extension **4433**, a Projector, a **date** one week after the current date, a time of **2:00 p.m.**, one day checked, and special instructions of **Please deliver to Room 233**. Save the completed form as **My Audio Visual Form** to the drive and folder where your Data Files are located, print a copy, and close the document.

FIGURE M-25

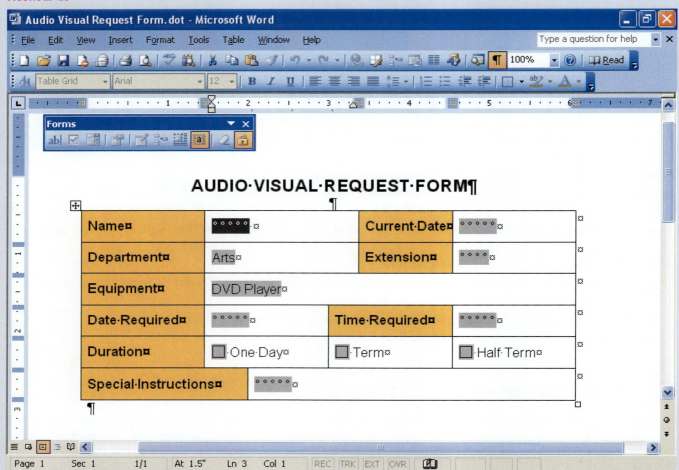

Working with Charts and Diagrams

OBJECTIVES

Define charts and diagrams

Create a column chart

Edit a chart

Create a pie chart

Import spreadsheet data into a chart

Create a diagram

Create an organization chart

Modify an organization chart

SAM

If you have a SAM user profile, you may have access to hands-on instruction, practice, and assessment of the skills covered in this unit. Log in to your SAM account and go to your assignments page to see what your instructor has assigned.

Word provides the tools you need to create and modify numerically based charts, such as bar charts, pie charts, and area charts. You can also create and modify diagrams such as Venn diagrams and cycle diagrams to show conceptual relationships that are not numerically based. Finally, you can create and modify an organization chart that shows hierarchical relationships, such as those among employees in a corporation. Graham Watson has just started working in the Marketing Department at MediaLoft. One of his first jobs is to prepare an analysis for MediaLoft management that highlights the success of online marketing efforts on MediaLoft's Web site at www.Media-Loft.com. Most of the data he needs is already entered in a Word document. You will help him present the information in chart and diagram form.

Defining Charts and Diagrams

A **chart** illustrates the trends, relationships, or patterns represented by a series of numbers in various combinations. Charts should clarify data for the reader. For example, when viewing a column chart about sales, a reader can see at a glance the relationship between the column representing the current year's sales and the column representing the previous year's sales, and then make decisions and draw conclusions accordingly. You can create different kinds of charts in Word, as shown in Figure N-1. You can also create six types of diagrams, as shown in Figure N-2. The Drawing toolbar includes the Insert Diagram or Organization Chart button, which you use to create diagrams and organization charts.  You are intrigued by the various charts and diagrams available in Word. You decide to investigate the purpose of each type of chart and diagram so that you can make appropriate choices when working with the data in the Marketing report.

DETAILS

You can create the following types of charts and diagrams:

- **Charts**

  Column charts compare values side by side, usually over time. For example, you can use a column chart to show total sales generated in each of four years, with each year represented by one column. Several variations on the column chart are available. You can select a **bar chart** to show values as horizontal bars; you can select **cylinder**, **cone**, and **pyramid charts** to show values in either horizontal or vertical format, similar to the rectangles used in column and bar charts.

  Circular charts show how values relate to each other as parts of a whole. For example, you can create a **pie chart** to show the breakdown of sales by product category for a store that specializes in sporting goods. Each product category, such as skis, boots, snowboards, and clothing, is represented by a slice of the pie chart. The most commonly used circular charts are pie charts and 3-D pie charts.

  Line style charts illustrate trends, where each value is connected to the next value by a line. An **area chart** shows data similarly to a line chart, except that the space between the lines and the bottom of the chart is filled, and a different band of color represents each value.

  Point-to-point charts are used to identify patterns or to show values as clusters. **XY charts** (also called **scatter charts**) are the most commonly used point-to-point charts.

- **Diagrams**

  An **organization chart** illustrates a hierarchy, most often in terms of how functional areas in a company or organization relate to each other. For example, you can use an organization chart to show relationships among executives, managers, supervisors, and employees in a company.

  A **Venn diagram** illustrates areas of overlap between two or more elements. You can use a Venn diagram to show how three departments in a company have individual responsibilities in addition to shared responsibilities.

  A **cycle diagram** illustrates a process that has a continuous cycle. You can use a cycle diagram to show the life cycle of a product from manufacturing to sales to consumer use to recycling into raw materials to manufacturing back into the same or a new product.

  A **pyramid diagram** illustrates a hierarchical relationship. Probably the most familiar pyramid diagram is the food diagram, which shows the food groups you should eat the most at the base of the pyramid and the food groups you should eat the least at the top.

  A **target diagram** illustrates steps toward a goal. You can use a target diagram to show the steps required to complete a specific project represented by the target area of the diagram.

  A **radial diagram** illustrates the relationships of several related elements to a core element. You can use a radial diagram to show how a group of individuals all report to the same supervisor.

FIGURE N-1: Sample chart types in Word

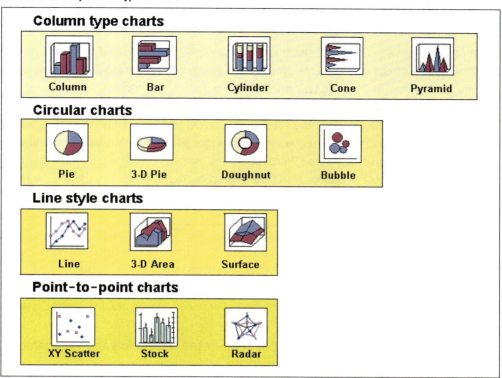

FIGURE N-2: Diagram Gallery

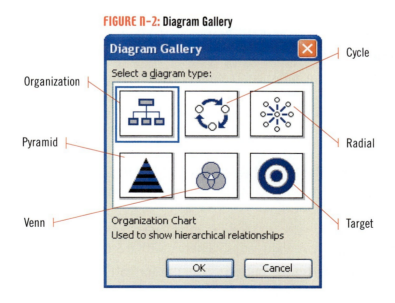

Creating a Column Chart

A column chart—or any of the charts available in Word—can be created from data you have entered into a Word table or from data you enter directly into a datasheet. A **datasheet** is a table grid that opens when you insert a chart in Word. The datasheet contains the values and labels that appear in the chart. A **value** is a number and a **label** is a word or two of text that describes the significance of the number. When you create a chart from data that you have entered into a Word table, the datasheet that appears contains the same information as the Word table. However, any changes you make to the labels or values in the datasheet are not reflected automatically in the Word table—and vice versa. You have created a Word table that shows the sales for each quarter of 2005 and each quarter of 2006. You use the data in this Word table to create a column chart.

STEPS

1. **Start Word, open the file WD N-1.doc from the drive and folder where your Data Files are located, save it as Online Marketing Analysis, then scroll through the document to get a sense of its contents**

   The data you want to chart is contained in a table under the Sales heading. You can create a chart from all the data in the table or just a portion of the data.

2. **Press [Ctrl][Home], move the pointer over the table below the Sales paragraph, then click the table move handle ⊞ to select the entire table**

   TROUBLE

   If the datasheet covers the chart, click the datasheet title bar and drag the datasheet to a new location.

3. **Click Insert on the menu bar, point to Picture, then click Chart**

   A column chart opens in the document, as shown in Figure N-3, because the default chart type is column. In addition, a datasheet opens that contains the same data shown in the Word table. The buttons required for working with charts appear on the Standard toolbar.

4. **Click Chart on the menu bar, click Chart Options, click the Titles tab if necessary, click in the Chart title text box, type Media-Loft.com Sales, then press [Tab]**

   The Chart title appears in the preview window in the Chart Options dialog box, as shown in Figure N-4.

5. **Click the Legend tab, click the Bottom option button, then click OK**

   The **legend** identifies the patterns or colors assigned to the data series in a chart.

6. **Click cell B1 in the datasheet (contains $70,000), type 50000, then click an empty cell in the datasheet**

   The value is formatted as currency and the column that illustrates the data in cell B1 changes to reflect the new data.

7. **Click outside the chart area to return to your Word document, click the cell below 2nd Quarter in the table, then change $70,000 to $50,000**

   You change the value in the Word table because the values in the table do not update automatically to reflect changes made to the datasheet.

   QUICK TIP

   If necessary, click View, then click Ruler to show the ruler bars.

8. **Click the chart to select it, then drag the lower-right corner down diagonally until the bottom of the chart aligns approximately with 6.5 on the vertical ruler**

9. **Click the Outside Border button ▦ on the Formatting toolbar, click away from the chart, then save the document**

   Figure N-5 shows the completed column chart.

FIGURE N-3: Inserted column chart

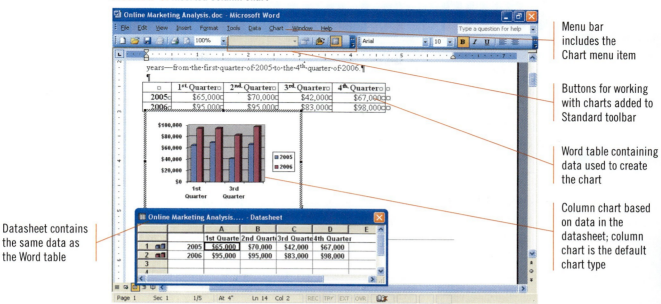

Datasheet contains the same data as the Word table

Menu bar includes the Chart menu item

Buttons for working with charts added to Standard toolbar

Word table containing data used to create the chart

Column chart based on data in the datasheet; column chart is the default chart type

FIGURE N-4: Chart Options dialog box

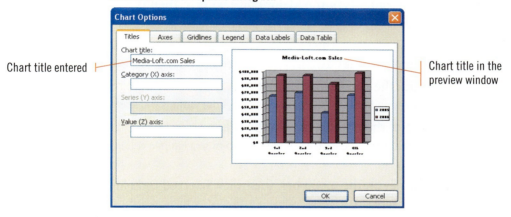

Chart title entered

Chart title in the preview window

FIGURE N-5: Completed column chart

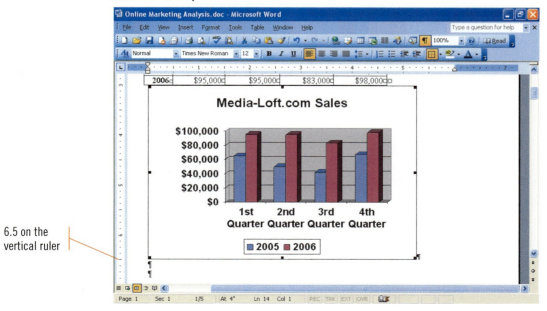

6.5 on the vertical ruler

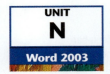

Editing a Chart

You can edit a chart in a variety of ways. For example, you can change the appearance of the columns representing each data series and you can change the font sizes of the various chart labels. You can also change the scale and appearance of each chart axis. In a two-dimensional chart, the **y-axis** is the vertical axis and the **x-axis** is the horizontal axis. You modify the y-axis and the x-axis of the chart and then change the font size of selected data labels. You also change the color of one of the data series and then change the column chart into a cone chart.

STEPS

1. **Right-click the column chart, point to Chart Object, then click Edit**
   The chart and datasheet open so that you can modify the chart. The y-axis of the chart is represented by the numbers to the left of the chart and the x-axis is represented by the text below the chart (1st Quarter, 2nd Quarter, and so forth).

2. **Right-click the y-axis, click Format Axis, then click the Scale tab**
   In the Scale tab of the Format Axis dialog box, you can change the values shown on the y-axis by changing the value of the major and minor units. For example, you can select the maximum value to appear on the y-axis and then you can set unit increments such as 5,000 or 50 between each value.

3. **Select the contents of the Major unit text box, then type 15000 as shown in Figure N-6**
   The check mark is removed from the Major unit check box when you set a specific unit.

4. **Click the Font tab in the Format Axis dialog box, change the font size to 10, then click OK**
   The information in the y-axis changes to reflect the settings you selected.

5. **Right-click the x-axis, click Format Axis, select the 10-point font size, then click OK**
   The information in the x-axis changes to reflect the settings you selected.

QUICK TIP
The maroon bars represent the year 2006.

6. **Click one of the maroon bars in the column chart**
   All the maroon bars are selected. When you point to a bar in a column chart a ScreenTip appears with information about what that bar represents.

7. **Click Format on the menu bar, then click Selected Data Series**
   You use the Format Data Series dialog box to modify the appearance of a data series. For example, you can select a new fill color or pattern.

8. **In the Format Data Series dialog box, select the Red color as shown in Figure N-7, then click OK**
   The bars representing the selected data series are now red.

QUICK TIP
You can also convert a column chart into a cylinder chart or a pyramid chart.

9. **Click Chart on the menu bar, click Chart Type, scroll down the Chart type list box, then click Cone**

10. **Click OK to exit the Chart Type dialog box, click outside the chart area to exit Edit mode, then save the document**
    The modified cone chart appears, as shown in Figure N-8. Notice that the columns representing each data series now appear as 3-D cones.

FIGURE N-6: Format Axis dialog box

Check mark removed to show value set manually

Major unit changed to 15000

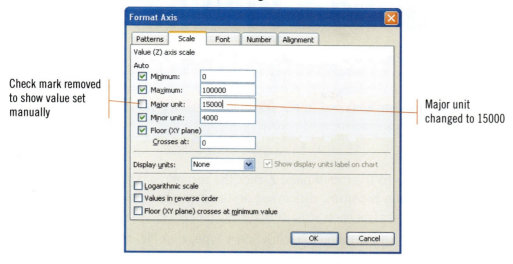

FIGURE N-7: Format Data Series dialog box

Red color selected

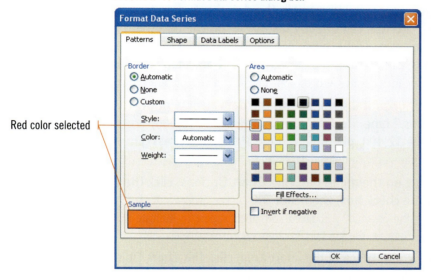

FIGURE N-8: Modified cone chart

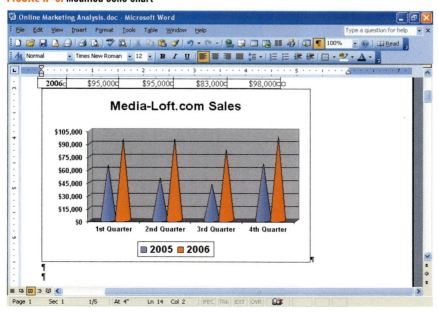

Creating a Pie Chart

Pie charts show data as parts of a whole. For example, you can create a pie chart to show the various expenses included in a budget. Each pie wedge represents a specific expense, such as Rent or Salaries. The size of the wedge depends on its numerical relationship to the overall budget. Taken together, all the wedges of a pie chart add up to 100%. 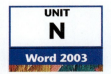 You create a pie chart to show the breakdown by category of the marketing expenses incurred in 2006.

STEPS

TROUBLE

If you don't see the paragraph marks, click the Show/Hide ¶ button to show formatting marks.

1. **Scroll down to the top of page 2, click the second paragraph mark below the paragraph on Marketing Expenses, click Insert on the menu bar, point to Picture, then click Chart**
   The default chart type opens and a datasheet with placeholder data and labels appears.

2. **Click Chart on the menu bar, click Chart Type, click Pie, then click OK**
   A pie chart based on the default data in the datasheet appears. In a pie chart, only the column labels and the values in the first row of the datasheet are used.

3. **Click the upper-left white cell in the datasheet, drag to select the default data, press [Delete], click the cell directly below "A" on the datasheet (contains "Slice 1"), type Brochures, press [Tab], type Magazine Ads, press [Tab], type Flyers, press [Tab], type Radio Ads, press [Tab], type E-Mail Marketing, then press [Enter]**
   The pie chart includes five wedges—one for each value represented by the labels.

4. **Drag the horizontal scroll bar on the datasheet window to the left, click the cell below "Brochures," type $15,000, press [Tab], type $10,000, press [Tab], type $5,000, press [Tab], type $2,400, press [Tab], type $900, then press [Enter]**
   Figure N-9 shows the completed datasheet.

5. **Click Chart on the menu bar, click Chart Options, click the Data Labels tab, click the Percentage check box, then click OK**
   The size of the pie chart is reduced and labels appear to indicate the percentage represented by each pie wedge. For example, the $15,000 Brochure expense is labeled 45%.

6. **Click any white space in the chart area, click the Chart Objects list arrow on the Standard toolbar, select Plot Area as shown in Figure N-10, then press [Delete]**
   You can select any component of a chart by clicking it or by selecting it from the Chart Objects list.

7. **Click Chart on the menu bar, click Chart Type, select the middle chart in the top row of the Chart sub-type section, then click OK**
   After changing a pie chart from a two-dimensional to a three-dimensional view, you can modify the appearance of the 3-D view.

8. **Click Chart on the menu bar, click 3-D View, type 45 in the Elevation text box, then click OK**

9. **Click outside the chart area, click the pie chart to select it, click Format on the menu bar, click Object, click the Size tab, change the Width to 4", click OK, click the Center button ≡ on the Formatting toolbar, click the Outside Border button ⊞, click away from the pie chart, then save the document**
   The completed pie chart is shown in Figure N-11.

FIGURE N-9: Data labels and values entered

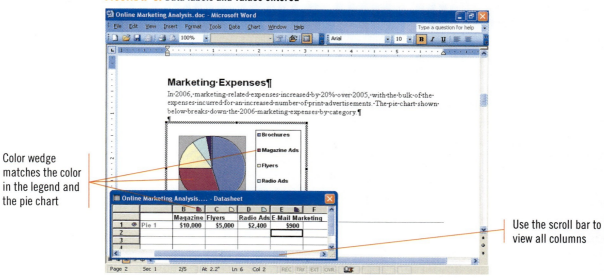

Color wedge matches the color in the legend and the pie chart

Use the scroll bar to view all columns

FIGURE N-10: Selecting the plot area

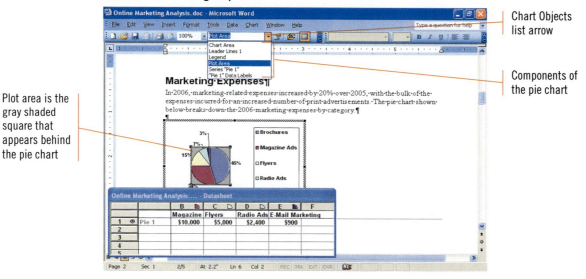

Plot area is the gray shaded square that appears behind the pie chart

Chart Objects list arrow

Components of the pie chart

FIGURE N-11: Completed pie chart

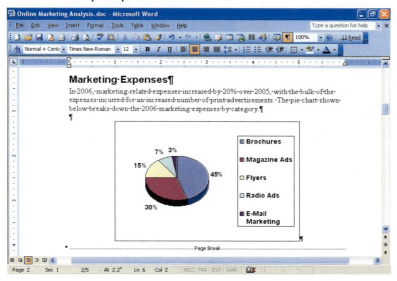

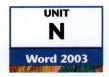

Importing Spreadsheet Data into a Chart

As you have learned, you can create a chart from data entered into a Word table or from data you enter in a datasheet. You can also create a chart from data you import from an Excel worksheet. You often choose this option when you have used Excel to enter data suitable for a chart and do not wish to re-create the data in Word. Importing the data in the Excel worksheet directly into the datasheet for a chart you create in Word can save you time. You have created an Excel worksheet containing data about the number of visitors Media-Loft.com has attracted over a two-year period. You import the Excel file into a datasheet for a chart you create in Word. You then change the chart type to a line chart.

STEPS

1. Scroll down to the top of page 3, click the **second paragraph mark** below the Web Site Visitors paragraph, click **Insert** on the menu bar, point to **Picture**, then click **Chart**

2. Click the **Import File button** on the Standard toolbar, navigate to the drive and folder where your Data Files are located, click **WD N-2.xls**, click **Open**, verify that **Web Site** in the Import Data Options dialog box is selected, then click **OK**

   The Web Site worksheet from the WD N-2.xls file is imported into the Word datasheet and the column chart changes to reflect the information in the datasheet. You can also choose to import specific cells from an Excel worksheet by selecting the Range Option button and identifying the cells to import.

3. Refer to Figure N-12: use ✛ to select the **framed cells** (three rows of five cells each) in the datasheet

4. Move the pointer over the left edge of the selected cells to show ⇖, use ⇖ to drag the **selected cells** left one column, click the **top border** of column E, then press **[Delete]**

   The placement of the columns shifts to reflect the change in the datasheet.

5. Click **Chart** on the menu bar, click **Chart Type**, click **Line**, then click **OK** to accept the default line chart style

   The column chart changes to a line chart with markers at each data value.

6. Right-click the **pink line** in the line chart, then click **Format Data Series**

   The Format Data Series dialog box opens with the Patterns tab selected.

7. Refer to Figure N-13: in the Line section select the **orange** color for the Line color, in the Marker section select the **triangle** style and the **orange** color for both the Foreground and the Background color of the marker, then click **OK**

   With the chart data completed, you can format the chart object so that it appears attractively in the Word document.

8. Click **outside the chart area**, right-click the **chart**, click **Format Object**, click the **Size tab**, change the Height to **3"** if necessary, then click **OK**

9. Center the chart and add an outside border, click away from the chart, then save the document

   The completed line chart is shown in Figure N-14.

FIGURE N-12: Moving imported data in the chart datasheet

Select framed cells

Column E heading

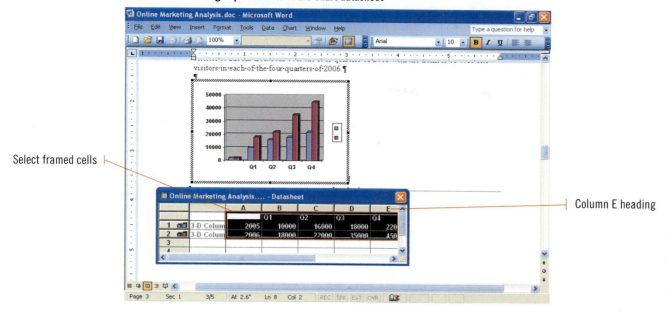

FIGURE N-13: Selecting options in the Format Data Series dialog box

Orange line color selected

Triangle marker style selected

Orange selected as Foreground and Background color

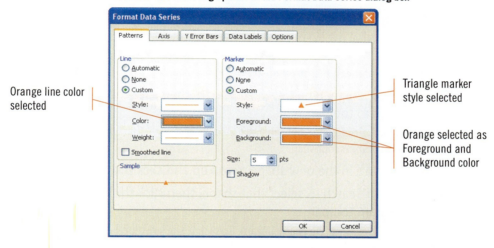

FIGURE N-14: Completed line chart

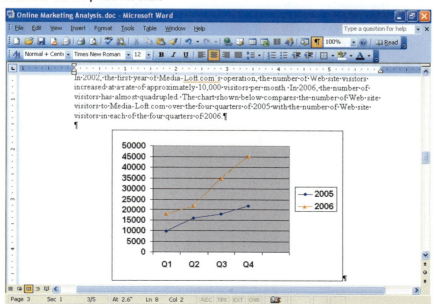

Creating a Diagram

You can create six kinds of diagrams with the Diagram tool. After you select a diagram type, you can enter text into the various sections of the diagram, then modify the size and fill color of the diagram. The diagram appears in a drawing canvas that you can size and position, just like you would any graphics object. You want to provide MediaLoft management a visual comparison of the four ways in which users access MediaLoft's Web site. You start by showing the Drawing toolbar and then creating and labeling a pyramid diagram.

STEPS

1. **Scroll down to the top of page 4, click the** second paragraph mark **below the Access Methods paragraph, show the Drawing toolbar, then click the** Insert Diagram or Organization Chart button 🔅 **on the Drawing toolbar**

   The Diagram Gallery dialog box opens.

2. **Click the** Pyramid Diagram, **then click** OK

   A pyramid diagram opens and the Diagram toolbar appears. Table N-1 describes the buttons on the Diagram toolbar for pyramid diagrams. The pyramid diagram consists of a series of shapes. The Insert Shape and Move Shape buttons change, depending on the diagram you create.

3. **Scroll down to see the bottom shape of the pyramid diagram, click the** bottom shape, **then type** MediaLoft Web Site Address **as shown in Figure N-15**

   Each shape in a diagram includes a text box. You can enter and then format text in each shape text box just as you would work with text in any text box.

4. **Click the next** shape, **type** Keyword Search, **then click the** Insert Shape button 🔺 Insert Shape **on the Diagram toolbar**

   The new shape is inserted to fit automatically under the shape that contains the insertion point. The pyramid diagram now contains four shapes.

5. **Type** Banner Ad **in the new shape, scroll up and click the** top shape, **then type** Links

6. **Click** Keyword Search **to select that shape, then click the** Move Shape Forward button 🔼 **on the Diagram toolbar**

   You use the Move Shape Forward button to switch the positions of the Keyword Search and Banner Ad shapes. The Banner Ad shape moves above the Keyword Search shape.

7. **Click the** AutoFormat button 🔅 **on the Diagram toolbar, then select** Primary Colors

   In the Diagram Style Gallery dialog box, you can select from a variety of interesting diagram formats. When you select a format, a preview of the selected format appears to the right of the Diagram Style list.

8. **Click** OK, **click the** Layout button Layout ▾ **on the Diagram toolbar, then click** Fit Diagram to Contents

   The Primary Colors scheme is applied to the diagram and the diagram is adjusted to fit the content.

9. **Click** outside the drawing canvas, **click the** Zoom list arrow, **click** 50% **and scroll to view the pyramid, then save the document**

   The completed pyramid diagram appears, as shown in Figure N-16.

FIGURE N-15: Text entered in the bottom shape of the pyramid diagram

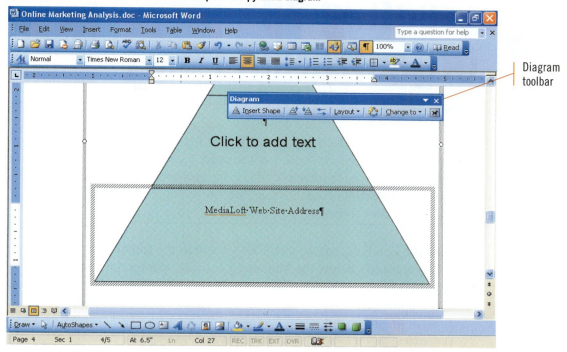

Diagram toolbar

FIGURE N-16: Completed pyramid diagram

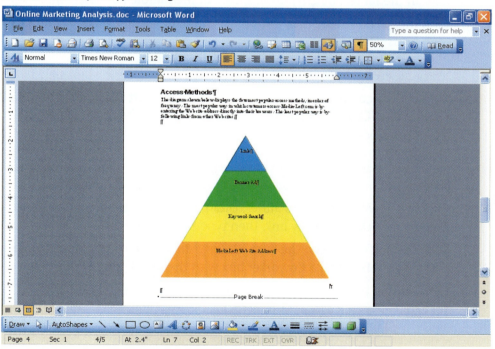

TABLE N-1: Buttons on the Diagram toolbar

button	use to	button	use to
Insert Shape	Insert a new shape in the diagram	Layout	Change the layout of the diagram
	Move a selected shape backward		Apply an AutoFormat
	Move a selected shape forward	Change to	Change the diagram to another diagram type
	Reverse the diagram		Adjust the text wrapping

Creating an Organization Chart

An organization chart shows information in the form of a hierarchy—the top box in the organization chart represents a top position, such as a president or supervisor, and the subordinate boxes represent secondary positions, such as vice presidents or clerks. You can also create an organization chart to show the relationships among related components, such as Web pages in a Web site.  You want to create a visual representation of the marketing activities related to the MediaLoft Web site. You create an organization chart to show two principal activities and their subactivities.

STEPS

1. **Click the Zoom list arrow, click 100%, scroll to the top of page 5, click the second paragraph mark below the Marketing Activities paragraph, click the Insert Diagram or Organization Chart button 🔄 on the Drawing toolbar, verify that the organization chart in the upper-left corner is selected, then click OK**

   An organization chart with two levels opens in a drawing canvas and the Organization Chart toolbar appears. The boxes in the organization chart contain placeholder text.

2. **Click in the top box, then type Marketing Activities**

3. **Click in the far left box, type Print, click in the middle box, then type Online**

4. **Click the far right box, click the border of the box to show the handles as in Figure N-17, then press [Delete]**

   When you delete a box in an organization chart, the remaining boxes increase in size, shift position, and are centered under the top box.

5. **Click the box containing the text "Print," click the Insert Shape list arrow 🔲 Insert Shape ▾ on the Organization Chart toolbar, then click Subordinate as shown in Figure N-18**

   A new box appears under the Print box. You select Subordinate when you want to show a component beneath another component in the organization chart. You select Coworker when you want to show a component on the same level as another component. You select Assistant when you want a component to appear off to the side, indicating a supportive role, rather than a subordinate or equal role.

   TROUBLE

   If you insert a Subordinate below the Brochures text box, click Edit, then click Undo.

6. **Click the new box, type Brochures, click the Insert Shape list arrow 🔲 Insert Shape ▾, select Coworker, click in the new box, then type Bookmarks**

7. **Click the box containing the text "Online," then add a Subordinate box with the text E-Mail Marketing and a Coworker box with the text Affiliate Programs**

8. **Click outside the drawing canvas, then save the document**

   The organization chart appears, as shown in Figure N-19.

FIGURE N-17: Organization chart box selected

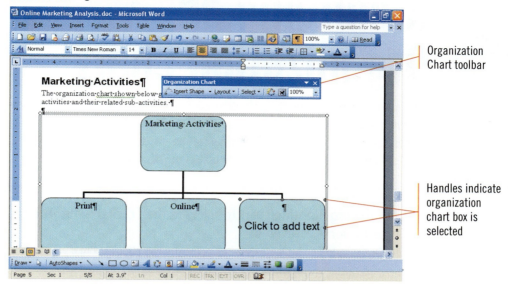

Organization Chart toolbar

Handles indicate organization chart box is selected

FIGURE N-18: Insert Shape menu options

Each diagram shows the placement of where a new box would be placed in relation to the selected box

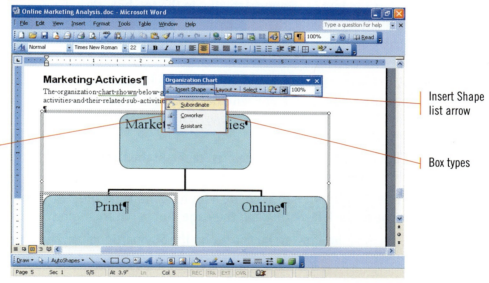

Insert Shape list arrow

Box types

FIGURE N-19: Completed organization chart

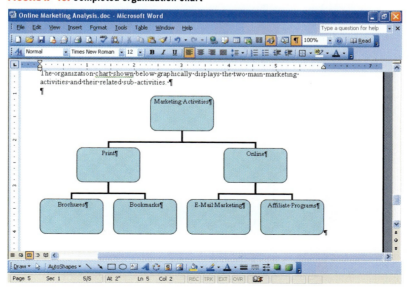

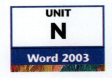
Modifying an Organization Chart

You can modify an organization chart by adding boxes to represent new coworkers or subordinates, or by removing boxes. You can also change the fill color of the boxes and modify the text. Finally, you can increase or decrease the size of the organization chart. You apply one of the AutoFormats to the organization chart and then modify the text in the various boxes.

STEPS

1. **Click the organization chart to select it, then click the AutoFormat button 🎨 on the Organization Chart toolbar**

   The Organization Chart Style Gallery opens. You can choose from a variety of interesting styles.

2. **Click Beveled Gradient as shown in Figure N-20, then click OK**

   The Beveled Gradient style is applied to the organization chart.

3. **Select the text Marketing Activities in the top box, click the Bold button B on the Formatting toolbar, then select the 12-point font size**

   You use the buttons on the Formatting toolbar to modify text in an organization chart box, just as you would modify any text in a Word document.

4. **With the text still selected, double-click the Format Painter button 🖌 on the Standard toolbar, then use the Format Painter to apply formatting to the text in all of the chart boxes**

   You can use the Format Painter to modify text in an organization chart, just as you would in a regular Word document.

5. **Click outside the drawing canvas, click 🖌, then compare the completed organization chart to Figure N-21**

6. **Press [Ctrl][Home], then create a footer containing the text Prepared by followed by your name at the left margin and the page number at the right margin**

7. **Click the Print Preview button 🔍 on the Standard toolbar, click the Multiple Pages button, then click 2 × 3 pages**

   The completed marketing analysis document appears on five pages, as shown in Figure N-22.

8. **Click Close on the Print Preview toolbar, save the document, print a copy, close the document, then exit Word**

> **TROUBLE**
> If the top border is missing on the first three charts in the printed document, change the text wrapping for each chart from inline to floating.

FIGURE N-20: Organization Chart Style Gallery

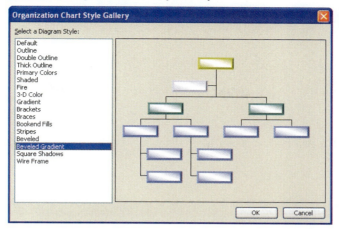

FIGURE N-21: Formatted organization chart

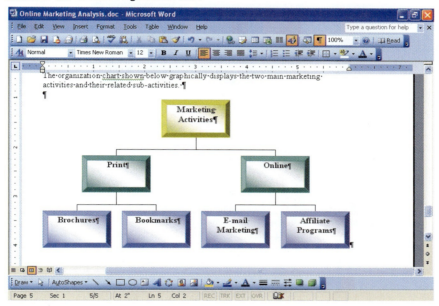

FIGURE N-22: Completed document in Print Preview

The top borders of some charts may not appear in Print Preview; however, they should appear in the printed document

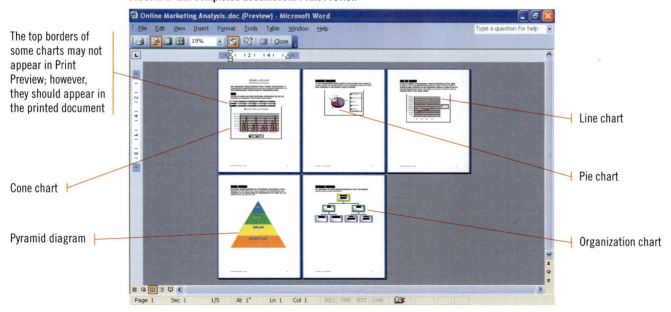

Cone chart

Pyramid diagram

Line chart

Pie chart

Organization chart

Practice

▼ CONCEPTS REVIEW

Label each of the elements in Figure N-23.

FIGURE N-23

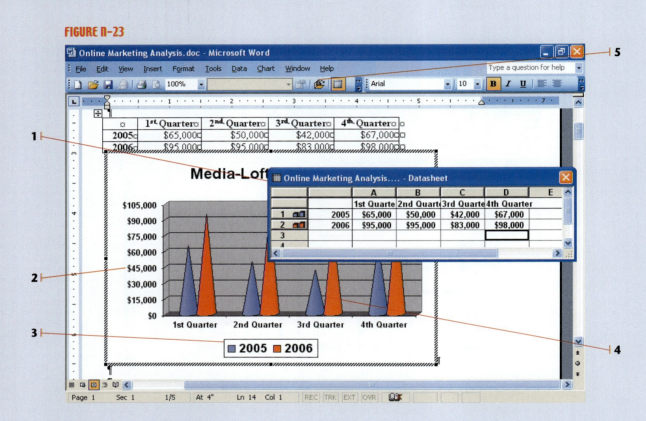

Match each term with the statement that best describes it.

6. Cone   a. Contains the data for a chart

7. Radial   b. Type of column chart

8. Legend   c. The key to the chart data

9. Label   d. A diagram that shows relationships to a core element

10. Datasheet   e. A kind of box included in an organization chart

11. Coworker   f. Describes the significance of a value

Select the best answer from the list of choices.

12. Which of the following chart types shows data as part of a whole?
   a. Column chart
   b. Pie chart
   c. Scatter XY chart
   d. Cylinder chart

13. Which term refers to a number represented by a data series in a chart?
   a. Label
   b. Legend
   c. Value
   d. Datasheet

14. Which tab in the Format Axis dialog box do you select to change the increments shown on an x-axis or y-axis?
   a. Scale
   b. Font
   c. Data series
   d. Legend

15. How many rows or columns of data can be represented in a pie chart?
   a. One
   b. Two
   c. Three
   d. Four

16. How do you import Excel spreadsheet data into a chart you create in Word?
   a. Click Insert on the menu bar, then select Chart Data.
   b. Click the Import File button on the Standard toolbar.
   c. Click the Insert File button on the Standard toolbar.
   d. Right-click a chart, then click Insert Data.

17. Which type of diagram do you use to show areas of overlap between elements?
   a. Venn diagram
   b. Target diagram
   c. Organization chart
   d. Pyramid diagram

18. Where does a Subordinate shape appear in an organization chart?
   a. Above the selected shape
   b. Below the selected shape
   c. To the right of the selected shape
   d. To the left of the selected shape

19. How do you enhance an organization chart with a preset format?
   a. Click the AutoFormat button on the Organization Chart toolbar.
   b. Click the Format Chart button on the Organization Chart toolbar.
   c. Double-click the top box in the organization chart, then click AutoFormat.
   d. Double-click the organization chart to enter Edit mode, then select a format from the AutoFormat gallery.

▼ SKILLS REVIEW

1. Create a column chart.

   a. Start Word, open the file WD N-3.doc from the drive and folder where your Data Files are located, then save it as **Pacific Rim Trading Report**.

   b. Select the table below the Sales paragraph near the top of the document, then insert a column chart.

   c. Open the Chart Options dialog box, then enter **Pacific Rim Trading Sales** as the chart title.

   d. Move the legend to the bottom of the chart.

   e. Change the 1st Quarter sales for 2004 to **$35,000** in the datasheet and in the table.

   f. Drag the lower-right corner sizing handle of the chart down to approximately the 7" mark on the vertical ruler bar and the 5" mark on the horizontal ruler.

   g. Enclose the chart with an outside border, center the chart, deselect the chart, then save the document

2. Edit a chart.

   a. Select the chart, double-click it, then change the Major unit of the y-axis from 20000 to **30000**.

   b. Change the font size of the y-axis to **10** point.

   c. Change the font size of the x-axis to **10** point.

   d. Change the font size of the legend to **10** point.

   e. Change the color of the data series representing 2005 to bright pink.

   f. Change the chart to a cylinder chart, then save the document.

3. Create a pie chart.

   a. Insert a chart below the Sales Expenses paragraph on the second page of the document.

   b. Convert the chart to a pie chart, then clear the placeholder data.

   c. Click Slice 1 in the datasheet, type **Web Site**, then enter **Print Ads**, **Radio Ads**, **Travel Expenses**, and **Special Events** as the labels for columns B through E.

   d. Click the cell below Web Site, type **$45,000**, then enter **$20,000**, **$15,000**, **$10,000**, and **$5,000** as the values for columns B through E.

   e. Open the Chart Options dialog box, then show the data labels as percentages.

   f. Click any white area in the chart, select Plot Area from the Chart Objects list, then delete the plot area.

   g. Convert the pie chart to a 3-D pie chart.

   h. Change the 3-D elevation of the chart to **35** degrees.

   i. Use the Format Object dialog box to change the width to **4"**, center the chart, add a border, then save the document.

4. Import spreadsheet data into a chart.

   a. Insert a chart at the second paragraph mark below the Retail Outlet Visitors paragraph on page 3 of the document.

   b. Import the file WD N-4.xls from the drive and folder where your Data Files are located, then click OK.

   c. Use the pointer to select cells with data under the columns labeled A–E in the datasheet (15 cells total), move the selected cells to the left, then delete column E.

   d. Convert the chart to a line chart. Accept the default chart subtype for a line chart.

   e. Format the data series that represents 2006 so that the line color and the foreground and background marker colors are light orange and the marker style is a circle.

   f. Use the Format Object dialog box to change the height of the chart to **3"**, center the chart, apply a border, then save the document.

5. Create a diagram.

   a. Scroll down to the top of page 4, click the second paragraph mark below the Supplier Countries paragraph, then show the Drawing toolbar, if necessary.

   b. Insert a radial diagram.

   c. Click the top circle, type **Japan**, then click the Insert Shape button twice so that the total number of circles is six, including the middle circle.

▼ SKILLS REVIEW (CONTINUED)

d. Enter text in the circles, as shown in Figure N-24.

e. Click the Thailand circle, then click the Move Shape Forward button so that Thailand and China change places.

f. Change the AutoFormat style to Fire.

g. Change the text Pacific Rim Trading to bold, 14 point, and white, then use the Format Painter to format the text in the remaining circles.

h. Save the document.

6. **Create an organization chart.**

a. Scroll to the top of page 5, click the second paragraph mark below the Store Management Structure paragraph, then insert an organization chart.

b. In the top box, type **Anita Chau**, press [Enter], then type **Store Manager**.

c. In the far left box, type **George West** followed by **Day Supervisor**; in the middle box, type **Yvonne Howe** followed by **Evening Supervisor**, then delete the far right box.

d. Insert a Subordinate below the George West box that contains the text **Marion Leung** followed by **Clerk**.

e. Insert a Coworker next to Marion Leung that contains the text **Sue Ng** followed by **Clerk**.

f. Insert a Subordinate below the Yvonne Howe box that contains the text **Sam Ramos** followed by **Clerk**.

g. Save the document.

7. **Modify an organization chart.**

a. Open the Organization Chart Style Gallery, then select the Stripes style.

b. Apply bold and 16 point to the name Anita Chau in the top box.

c. Use the Format Painter to apply the formatting to just the names in the remaining boxes.

d. Click outside the organization chart, create a footer that includes the text **Prepared by** followed by your name at the left margin and the page number at the right margin, then view all five pages in the Print Preview screen.

e. Close the Print Preview screen, print a copy of the document, save and close it, then exit Word.

FIGURE N-24

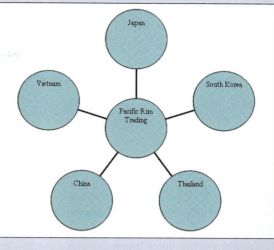

▼ INDEPENDENT CHALLENGE 1

As the assistant manager of a local art gallery, you are responsible for keeping track of how many people visit the gallery each month. At the end of six months, you compile the results into a column chart that you include in the gallery's semiannual report. The data for the column chart is already contained in an Excel worksheet.

a. Start Word, open a new blank document, then save it as **Gallery Attendance** to the drive and folder where your Data Files are located.

b. Type the text **Prairie View Art Gallery** as a heading formatted with bold, 16 point, and center alignment.

c. Press [Enter] twice after the heading, clear the formatting, then enter the following sentence: **The column chart shown below presents the gallery attendance figures for adults and children from July to December, 2006.**

d. Press [Enter] twice after the sentence, then create a column chart with the default settings.

e. Click the Import File button, then import the data from the Attendance worksheet in the file WD N-5.xls, which is stored in the drive and folder where your Data Files are located.

f. Edit the chart to change the color of the Adults data series.

g. Change the chart type to pyramid.

h. Enter **Gallery Attendance 2006** as the chart title, then move the legend to the bottom of the chart.

i. Use the Format Object dialog box to change the width to **6"** wide, then include a border line.

j. Edit the chart, change the font size of the y-axis, x-axis, and the legend text to **10** point.

▼ INDEPENDENT CHALLENGE 1 (CONTINUED)

Advanced Challenge Exercise

- Remove the gray walls from the chart. (*Hint*: Right-click an area of the gray wall, click Format Walls, then change the color to None.)
- Change the 3-D view to an elevation of **20** and a rotation of **30**. (*Hint*: Right-click the chart, then click 3-D View).
- Add the value to each data point. (*Hint*: Click the Data Labels tab in the Chart Options dialog box).
- Reduce the font size of both sets of value labels to **10** point.

k. Double-click two lines below the chart, type **Prepared by** followed by your name left-aligned, save the document, print a copy, close the document, then exit Word.

▼ INDEPENDENT CHALLENGE 2

Six months ago, you started a new online business called Linen Barn that sells designer towels and linens. As part of a report for your investors, you want to include a pie chart that shows online sales of your products by category.

a. Start Word, open a new document, then save it as **Linen Barn Sales** to the drive and folder where your Data Files are located.

b. Create a 3-D pie chart based on the data that follows.

Category	Sales
Bath Towels	**$87,000**
Bed Linens	**$71,000**
Bedspreads	**$46,000**
Hand Towels	**$18,000**
Bath Accessories	**$12,000**

c. Add the title **Online Sales by Category**, position the legend at the top of the chart, below the title, then add data labels to show the percentage represented by each slice of the pie.

d. Remove the shaded plot area, then change the color of the Bath Towels data point to bright green. (*Hint*: You need to click the pie chart, then click just the pie slice that represents Bath Towels.)

e. Increase the 3-D tilt to 45 degrees.

f. Use the Format Object dialog box to increase the width of the chart to **5"**, enclose the chart in an outside border, then center the chart.

g. Edit the chart by changing Bath Accessories to **$18,000**, then change the font size of the legend text to **10** point and the data labels to **9** point.

h. Double-click below the chart, type **Prepared by** followed by your name left-aligned, save the document, print a copy, close the document, then exit Word.

▼ INDEPENDENT CHALLENGE 3

You have just started working for Masterworks Tours, an English-language tour company based in Vienna, Austria, that specializes in tours to sites frequented by classical composers such as Beethoven and Mozart. One of your jobs is to help prepare the company's annual report. Included in the report will be a page that describes the company personnel. You suggest creating an organization chart to show the hierarchy of positions.

a. Start Word, open a new document, then save it as **Masterworks Tours** to the drive and folder where your Data Files are located.

b. Type **Masterworks Tours Organization Chart** as a title enhanced with 18 point, bold, and center alignment.

c. Two blank lines below the title, insert an organization chart.

d. Refer to Figure N-25 to enter the text and add the boxes required for your organization chart.

e. Apply the Stripes AutoFormat, then apply bold to the names.

▼ INDEPENDENT CHALLENGE 3 (CONTINUED)

Advanced Challenge Exercise

- Add an Assistant box to the top box.
- Type **Jason Kane** as the name and **Executive Assistant** as the title.
- Remove the Stripes AutoFormat and restore the Default AutoFormat.
- Click just the border of the top box, click the Fill Color list arrow on the Drawing toolbar, then select the Gold fill color.

FIGURE N-25

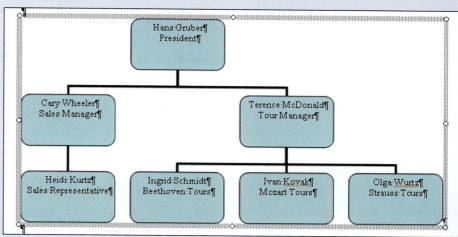

- Fill the assistant's box with Light Turquoise, then fill the two boxes related to Sales positions with Light Orange and the four boxes related to Tour positions with Sky Blue.
- Open the Clip Art task pane, search for **Beethoven** (you must be connected to the Internet to find suitable clip art), then insert one of the Beethoven pictures that appears.
- Change the layout of the picture to Square, then move the picture into the blank area of the organization chart to the right of the top box. Resize the picture if necessary, then position it so that the bottom-left corner is slightly overlapped by Terence McDonald's box. Note that you will need to change the stacking order of the picture to Send to Back.

f. Double-click below the organization chart, type **Prepared by** followed by your name left-aligned, print a copy of the document, save and close the document, then exit Word.

▼ INDEPENDENT CHALLENGE 4

You use radial diagrams to illustrate relationships of several related elements to a core element. As a Web designer in the process of designing a new Web site for a company of your choice, you have been checking out your competitors' Web sites. To help you determine the features you want your new Web site to have, you create a radial diagram that shows six features included on a competitor's Web site that sell similar products or services.

a. Open your Web browser and conduct a search for a company that sells a product or service that interests you. You can enter keywords related to the product, such as **lawn furniture**, **garden tools**, and **hiking tours**, and you can enter generic domain names such as **www.garden.com** or **www.hiking.com** in the Address box of your Web browser.

b. Explore the Web site you have selected and identify six features. Features include a search tool, shopping cart, free gift offer, product-related content, and a Frequently Asked Questions page.

c. Start Word. In a new Word document, enter a title such as **Radial Diagram of an Online Garden Store**. In place of the word **Garden** use a word that describes the type of stores you researched.

d. Insert a radial diagram that contains the name of the Web site in the center circle and one feature in each of the six surrounding circles. (*Note:* You need to add three new circles.)

e. Format the diagram with the AutoFormat of your choice.

f. Format the text so that it appears attractive and easy to read. (*Note:* You might need to scale the diagram and then drag the sizing handles so that the text doesn't wrap inappropriately.)

g. Type **Prepared by** and your name below the diagram.

h. Save the document as **Web Site Radial Diagram** to the drive and folder where your Data Files are located, print a copy, close the document, then exit Word.

▼ VISUAL WORKSHOP

You are working with the Web Development Group at ZooPlace.com to plan and launch a new Web site that sells a wide assortment of exotic stuffed animals—from manatees to moose. To help your investors understand the development process, you've created a target diagram that illustrates the steps toward the goal of launching the Web site. The largest circle of the target diagram represents the first step in the process and the target area of the diagram represents the final goal. In a new Word document, enter the title and create the target diagram shown in Figure N-26. Note that you will need to fill each of the five circles and enhance the corresponding text with the colors shown in Figure N-26 or of your own choosing. Save the document with the name **Web Launch Target Diagram**, print a copy, then close the document.

FIGURE N-26

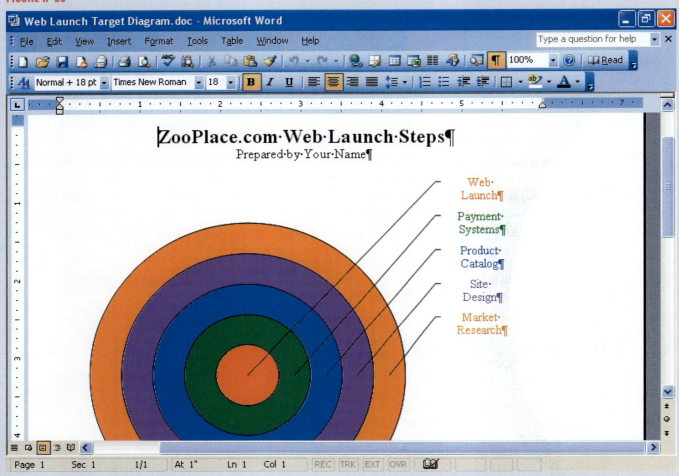

UNIT O

Collaborating with Workgroups

OBJECTIVES

| Explore collaboration options |
| Include comments in a document |
| Track changes |
| Accept and reject changes |
| Create document versions |
| Compare documents and merge changes |
| Use Find and Replace options |
| Protect documents |

If you have a SAM user profile, you may have access to hands-on instruction, practice, and assessment of the skills covered in this unit. Log in to your SAM account and go to your assignments page to see what your instructor has assigned.

Word includes a variety of functions designed to let you work on a document as part of a team. You can include comments in a document, highlight the changes you've made to the document text, create different versions of a document, compare these versions, and then merge changes to create a finished document that all members of the team can approve. You can also use Find and Replace options to find special characters and formatting. Finally, you can protect documents against unauthorized changes and set permission options. Nazila Sharif in the Marketing Department at MediaLoft has written several questions for an online survey that visitors to MediaLoft's Web site can complete. You collaborate with Nazila to develop a version of the survey that you can submit to Alice Wegman, the department manager, for final approval.

O

Word 2003

Exploring Collaboration Options

You can collaborate with colleagues in different ways. For example, you can distribute printed documents that show all the changes made by one or more colleagues, along with the comments they've made, or you can share the electronic file of the document, which also shows the changes and comments. ▧▧▧▧ Before you start working with colleagues to develop questions for an online survey, you investigate collaborative features available in Word.

The collaborative features in Word include the following:

- **Reviewing toolbar**

  You use the buttons on the Reviewing toolbar to access commands that allow you to share a document between two or more people. Table O-1 describes the buttons on the Reviewing toolbar.

- **Insert comments**

  You insert comments into a document when you want to ask questions or provide additional information. When several people work on the same document, their comments appear in different colored balloons along the right side of the document in Print Layout view. Figure O-1 shows a document containing comments made by two people.

- **Track changes**

  When you share documents with colleagues, you need to be able to show them where you have inserted and deleted text. In Word, inserted text appears in the document as underlined text in the color assigned to the person who made the insertion. This same color identifies that person's deletions and comment text. For example, if Nazila's comment balloons are green, then the text she inserts or deletes in a document will also be green. Text that is deleted appears in a balloon along the right side of the document in Print Layout view, along with the comment balloons. Figure O-1 includes new text inserted in the document and two balloons containing deleted text.

- **Create versions**

  Sometimes you might want to maintain two or three versions of the same document so you can keep an ongoing record of changes. To save disk space, you can save several versions of one document within the same document file. You can then view each version of the document at any time.

- **Compare and merge documents**

  You use the Compare and Merge Documents feature to compare any two documents to show the differences between the two. Compare and Merge is often used to show the differences between an original document and an edited copy of the original. It is also used to merge the changes and comments of multiple reviewers into a single document when each reviewer edits the document using a separate copy of the original. When you compare and merge two documents, you have the option of merging the changes into one of the documents or of merging the changes into a new third document. Figure O-2 shows the three locations possible for displaying the compare and merge results. The differences between the two documents are shown in the merged document as tracked changes. You can then examine the merged document, edit it, and save it with a new filename.

TABLE O-1: Buttons on the Reviewing toolbar

button	use to	button	use to
🔁	Show the previous change in a document	🔤	Highlight selected text
🔁	Show the next change in a document	📄	Insert voice comment
📝	Accept the highlighted change	📝	Turn Track Changes on/off
📝	Reject the highlighted change or delete the currently selected comment	📑	Open the Reviewing Pane
📁	Insert a new comment		

FIGURE O-1: Document showing tracked changes and comments

Reviewing toolbar

Inserted text

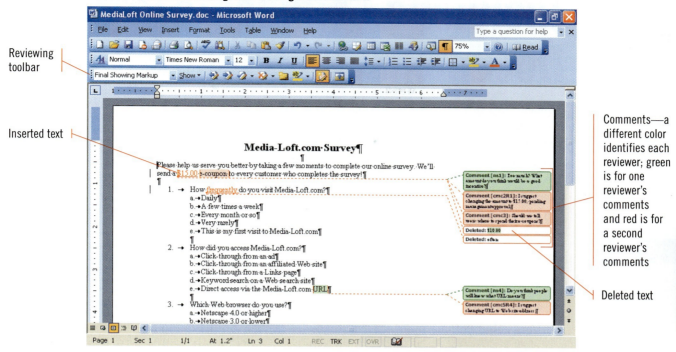

Comments—a different color identifies each reviewer; green is for one reviewer's comments and red is for a second reviewer's comments

Deleted text

FIGURE O-2: Options for merging document changes

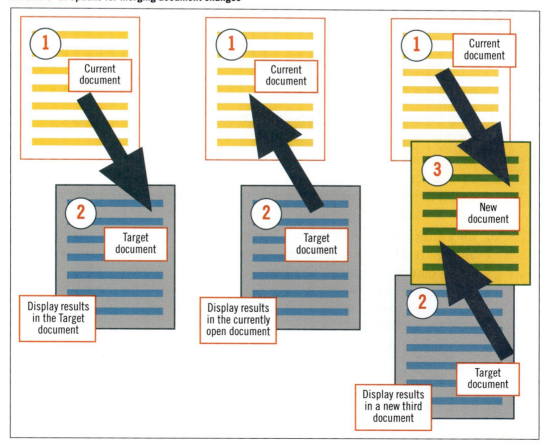

Including Comments in a Document

Sometimes when you review a document that someone else has written, you want to insert a comment relating to the document text, the document formatting, or any number of related issues. A **comment** is text you insert in a comment balloon that appears, by default, along the right side of your document in Print Layout view. A comment mark appears in the document at the point where you inserted the comment. A line leads from the comment mark to the comment balloon.  Your colleague Nazila has already inserted some comments in the document containing the list of survey questions. You open the document, add a new comment and then edit one of the comments that Nazila inserted. You work in Page Layout view so you can see the comments in comment balloons in the right margin.

STEPS

1. **Start Word, open the file WD O-1.doc from the drive and folder where your Data Files are located, then verify that the Show/Hide ¶ button ¶ is selected**

2. **Verify that you are in Print Layout view, click View on the menu bar, point to Toolbars, click Reviewing, click the Zoom list arrow on the Standard toolbar, click Page Width, scroll the document to view its contents, then save it as MediaLoft Online Survey**

   The Reviewing toolbar opens above the document window and the two comments that Nazila inserted appear in colored balloons in the right margin of the document. Comment markers appear in the document itself.

3. **Select the word e-coupon in the first paragraph, then click the Insert Comment button on the Reviewing toolbar**

   Comment markers appear around the word "e-coupon" and a comment balloon appears in the right margin in a color that is different from Nazila's comment. When inserting a comment, you select a word or two of the text so that the comment markers enclose the selected words and the words are shaded with the same color as the corresponding comment balloon.

4. **Click the Zoom list arrow, click 100%, then if necessary scroll right to view the comment balloon**

5. **Type Should we tell users where to spend their e-coupons?, then click anywhere outside the balloon**

   You increase the zoom percentage so you can read text in a balloon. Your comment appears in a new balloon, as shown in Figure O-3.

6. **Click after incentive in the first comment balloon, click , type I suggest changing the amount to $15.00, pending management approval. in the new balloon, then click anywhere outside the comment balloon**

   A comment balloon with your response appears between the two existing comments. You click in a comment balloon and then click the Insert Comment button on the Reviewing toolbar to keep the original comment and the response together.

7. **Scroll down, click in Nazila's second comment balloon, click , then in the new balloon type I suggest changing URL to Web site address.**

   You can also choose to view comments in the Reviewing Pane.

8. **Click the Reviewing Pane button on the Reviewing toolbar, then scroll down the Reviewing Pane to view the comments**

   Figure O-4 shows comments in the Reviewing Pane.

9. **Click to close the Reviewing Pane, then save the document**

FIGURE O-3: Comment balloons

Insert Comment button

Comment marker in text

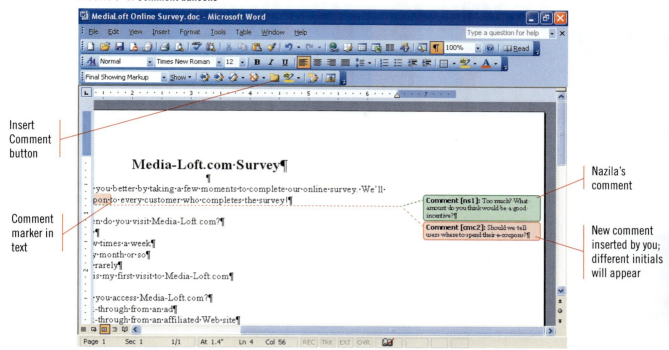

Nazila's comment

New comment inserted by you; different initials will appear

FIGURE O-4: Comments in the Reviewing Pane

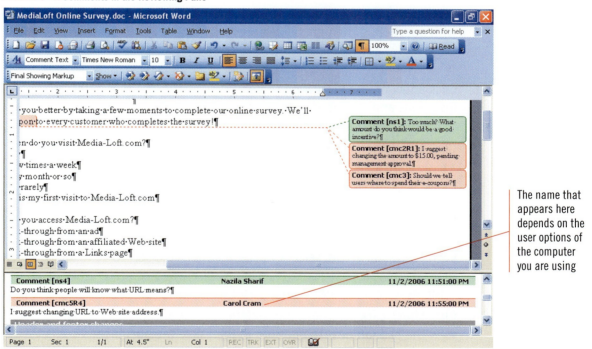

The name that appears here depends on the user options of the computer you are using

Tracking Changes

When you work on a document with two or more people, you want to be able to see where changes have been made. You use the Track Changes command to show inserted text and deleted text. In Page Layout view, the deleted text appears in a balloon, similar to a comment balloon, and the inserted text appears in the color assigned to the reviewer and underlined in the document. You go through the survey that Nazila prepared and make some editing changes. You then review changes by type and reviewer.

STEPS

1. **Press [Ctrl][Home] to move to the top of the document, then click the Track Changes button on the Reviewing toolbar**

   Now that Track Changes is turned on, every change you make to the document will appear in colored text.

2. **Select $10.00 in the first paragraph (but not the space following it), then press [Delete]**

   The deleted text appears in a balloon in the right margin. The ballon outline is the same color as your comment balloon; the text in the balloon matches Nazila's color because her comment is associated with the deleted text.

3. **Type $15.00**

   As shown in Figure O-5, the inserted text appears underlined and in the same color as the color of the comment you inserted in the previous lesson.

4. **Select often in question 1, then type frequently**

   The deleted text appears in a new balloon and the text "frequently" appears in colored underlined text.

5. **Scroll down the document to question 6, select all the text (Have you...No ¶) included with question 6, then press [Delete] twice**

   The deleted text appears in a balloon in the right margin along with a balloon that shows the formatting associated with the deleted text.

6. **Click Show on the Reviewing toolbar, click Comments to deselect it, click Show, click Insertions and Deletions to deselect it, click Show, then click Formatting to deselect it**

   You deselect all tracked changes and comment balloons so that you can review changes by type and reviewer.

7. **Click Show, then point to Reviewers**

   A menu opens listing the reviewers and showing the color assigned to each, as shown in Figure O-6. You can choose to view comments either for all reviewers or for individual reviewers. A check mark next to a reviewer's name means that the comments and tracked changes for that reviewer appear in the document window. If you do not want to view a reviewer's comments and tracked changes, click the check box next to that reviewer's name to deselect that reviewer and remove the check mark. You leave All Reviewers selected.

8. **With Show still active, select Comments, then scroll up to view the comment balloons**

   Since you left All Reviewers selected, comment balloons for all reviewers appear in the right margin. The different colors match the colors assigned to the reviewers in the reviewers list.

9. **Click Show, click Insertions and Deletions, click Show, click Formatting, scroll down to view the balloon next to question 6, then save the document**

   The insertions appear as underlined text in the document and the deletions appear in balloons in the right margin. Formatting changes appear in their own balloons.

FIGURE O-5: Text inserted with Track Changes feature active

New inserted text

Track Changes button (also available on the Tools menu)

Deleted text appears in a new balloon

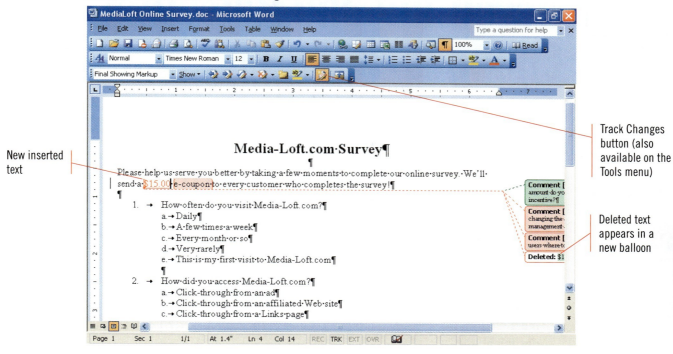

FIGURE O-6: List of Reviewers

Additional names may appear, depending on reviewing actions performed by others using your computer

Your name may appear here

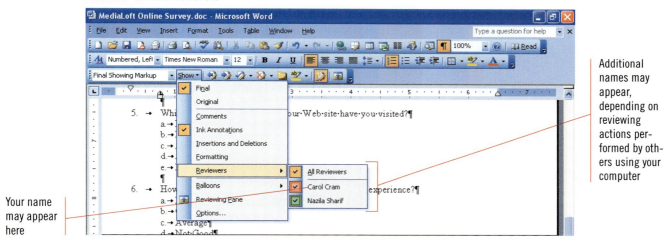

Clues to Use

Modifying Track Changes options

You modify the appearance of tracked changes using the Track Changes dialog box, which is shown in Figure O-7. To open this dialog box, click Show on the Reviewing toolbar, then click Options. In the Track Changes dialog box, you can change the formatting of insertions and select a specific color for them, and you can modify the appearance of the comment balloons. For example, you can increase or reduce the width of the balloons and you can choose to display the balloons in either the left or the right margin of the document.

FIGURE O-7: Track Changes dialog box

Accepting and Rejecting Changes

When you receive a document containing tracked changes, you will want to accept or reject the changes before you print the document as a final copy. When you accept a change, inserted text becomes part of the document and deleted text is permanently removed. You use the Reviewing toolbar to accept and reject changes in a document and to find and remove comments. Now that you've added your own changes to the document, you use the Reviewing toolbar to accept or reject the tracked changes and to remove the comments.

STEPS

1. **Press [Ctrl][Home], click the Zoom list arrow on the Standard toolbar, click Page Width, click the Display for Review list arrow on the Reviewing toolbar, then click Original Showing Markup**
   In this view, the inserted text appears in a balloon, as shown in Figure O-8.

2. **Click the Display for Review list arrow, click Final Showing Markup, then click the Next button on the Reviewing toolbar to move to the first tracked change ($10.00) in the document**
   The insertion point moves to the balloon containing the deleted text $10.00.

3. **Click the Accept Change button on the Reviewing toolbar**
   The balloon containing the deleted text and the comments associated with that deletion are removed from the right margin. The insertion point appears in the document before the next tracked change, which is $15.00.

4. **Click to select the next tracked change ($15.00), click , then click e-coupon to deselect the text**
   The amount $15.00 appears in black text in the document, which indicates that it has been accepted as the new amount.

5. **Click to move to the next tracked change which is the comment you inserted in a previous lesson, then click the Reject Change/Delete Comment button on the Reviewing toolbar to remove the comment and balloon from the right margin**

6. **Click to move to the next change (often), click to restore the word "often", click , then click to reject the insertion of the text "frequently"**
   Question 1 is restored to its original wording. You can continue to review and accept or reject changes individually, or you can choose to accept the remaining changes in the document.

7. **Click , then click Accept All Changes in Document**
   All the tracked changes in the document are accepted.

8. **Click the Reject Change/Delete Comment list arrow , then click Delete All Comments in Document**
   Scroll through the document. Notice that all tracked changes and comments are removed from the document. See Figure O-9.

9. **Click the Track Changes button on the Reviewing toolbar to turn off Track Changes, then save the document**

FIGURE O-8: Original Showing Markup view

Original Showing Markup selected

Display for Review list arrow

Deleted text appears in strikethrough formatting

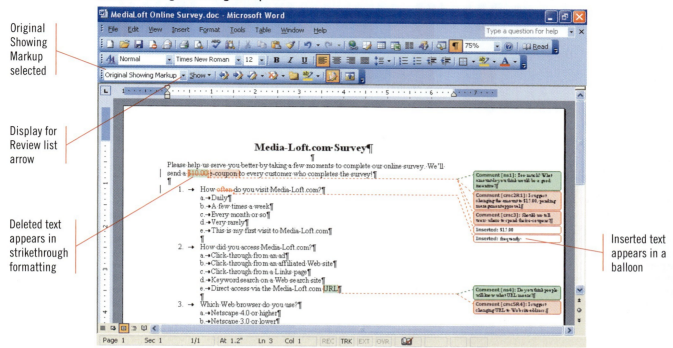

Inserted text appears in a balloon

FIGURE O-9: Tracked changes and comments accepted or rejected

Accept Change button

Reject Change/Delete Comment button

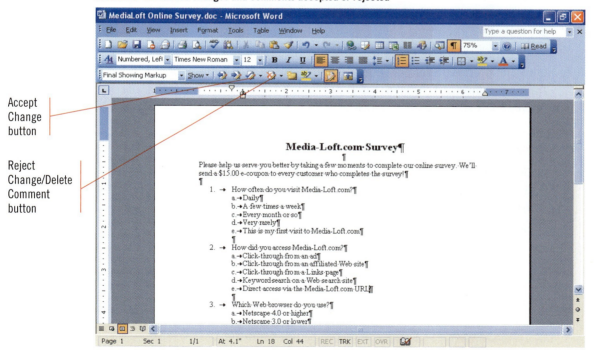

Distributing documents for revision

When you work with several people on a document, you can e-mail each person a copy of the document and ask for their input. To save time, you can use the Send To command that automatically asks a recipient to review the attached document. To send the active document, click File on the menu bar, point to Send To, then click Mail Recipient (for Review). In a few moments, the default e-mail client window opens. If you are already connected to the Internet, you just enter the e-mail address of the recipient in the To: text box, and then click Send.

Creating Document Versions

You can use the Versions command to create two or more versions of a document. Each version can contain text that differs from every other version. You create versions of a document when you want to keep a record of the changes you've made to a document and store all versions of the document within the same filename.  Although you are pleased with the revised questions, you decide to create two versions of the survey document. One version will contain the changes you have just accepted and the other version will contain a new question.

STEPS

1. **Click File on the menu bar, then click Versions**

   The Versions in MediaLoft Online Survey.doc dialog box opens. Depending on your computer settings, you may see a version with the comment "Auto version for sharing."

2. **Click Save Now**

   The Save Version dialog box opens. In this dialog box, you can type a short description of the version.

3. **Type Survey with 6 questions as shown in Figure O-10, then click OK**

   The Versions dialog box closes and the version of the document containing six survey questions is saved to the drive and folder where the original document is located.

4. **Switch to 100% view**

5. **Click at the end of item e. in Question 2, press [Enter] twice, type 3., press [Tab], type Have you ever visited a MediaLoft real world store?, press [Enter], press [Tab], type Yes, press [Enter], then type No**

   The new question appears in the document, as shown in Figure O-11.

6. **Click File on the menu bar, then click Versions**

   The Versions in MediaLoft Online Survey.doc dialog box opens and information about the document version you've already saved appears in the Existing versions area.

7. **Click Save Now, type Survey with 7 questions, then click OK**

   A second version of the MediaLoft Online Survey document is saved.

8. **Click File on the menu bar, then click Versions**

   Both versions of the document appear in the Versions in MediaLoft Online Survey.doc dialog box, as shown in Figure O-12.

9. **Click Close, then save and close the document**

Clues to Use

Using versions

To work on a version of a document, be sure that document is the active document, click File on the menu bar, then click Versions to open the Versions dialog box. In the Versions dialog box, all versions of the document that you've saved are listed. The versions are listed with the most recently saved version first. You select the version you want to work on, and then click Open. When you open a version, two Word windows are open at the same time. The document you are working on appears in the top part of the window and the version you just opened appears in the bottom of the window. The title bar of the window containing the version includes the date and time the version was created.

FIGURE O-10: Save Version dialog box

Shows the current date and time

Type description and notes about version here

The name assigned to User Information in the Options dialog box appears here

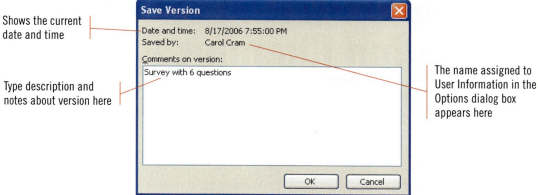

FIGURE O-11: New question inserted

New question

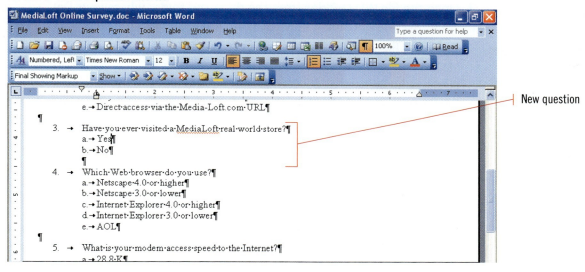

FIGURE O-12: Versions in MediaLoft Online Survey.doc dialog box

Most recent version appears first

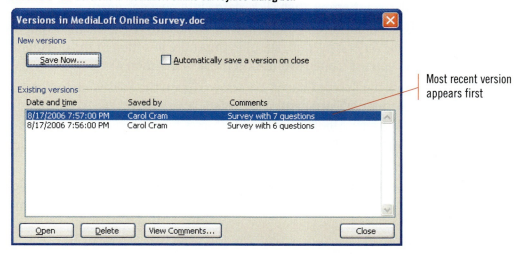

UNIT

O

Word 2003

Comparing Documents and Merging Changes

The Compare and Merge Documents feature in Word allows you to merge two documents at a time so you can compare the documents and determine where changes have been made. Word shows the differences between the documents as tracked changes. To use the Compare and Merge Documents feature, the files you want to compare must be the same document saved using different filenames. You cannot use the feature to compare versions of the document saved within the same filename. Refer back to Figure O-2 to review options for merging documents.  Alice has reviewed the document and sent you her revision of the survey questions. In addition, Chris Williams in Customer Service has sent his revision of the survey questions. After opening and saving these documents, you use the Compare and Merge Documents features to check the changes Alice and Chris have made.

STEPS

1. **Open the file WD O-2.doc from the drive and folder where your Data Files are located, then save the document as MediaLoft Online Survey_Alice**

> **QUICK TIP**
> In order to merge these documents, these files must be saved to the drive and folder that contains the MediaLoft Online Survey document.

2. **Open the file WD O-3.doc, then save it as MediaLoft Online Survey_Chris**

   MediaLoft Online Survey_Chris is the active document. In the Compare and Merge process, the active document is called the **current document**.

3. **Click Tools on the menu bar, then click Compare and Merge Documents**

   The three survey documents appear in the Compare and Merge Documents dialog box. First, you want to merge the document from Alice into the MediaLoft Online Survey document created by Chris. After reviewing that merge, you will merge the original document with the merged document you just created into a new document.

4. **Click MediaLoft Online Survey_Alice, then click the Merge list arrow to view the list of Merge options as shown in Figure O-13**

   You use the Merge command to display results in the target document, which is the document created by Alice. You use the Merge into current document command to display the results in the currently open document, which is the document created by Chris. You use the Merge into new document command to display results in a new document.

> **QUICK TIP**
> Scroll through the document to get a feel for its contents.

5. **Click Merge into current document**

   The document appears, as shown in Figure O-14.

6. **Click Tools, click Compare and Merge Documents, click MediaLoft Online Survey, click the Merge list arrow, then click Merge into new document**

> **QUICK TIP**
> To reject specific changes, click the Next button until the text to delete is highlighted, then click the Reject Change/Delete Comment button.

7. **Use the buttons on the Reviewing toolbar to reject the following tracked changes: A few, two, Very rarely, find, an, URL, the entire insertion of the question Which Web browser do you use?, and Favorites (in the new question 4)**

8. **Click the Accept Change list arrow 🖉▾ on the Reviewing toolbar, click Accept All Changes in Document**

   After accepting the combined tracked changes, the new document contains five questions.

9. **Scroll to the bottom of the document, type your name where indicated, then save the document as MediaLoft Online Survey_Final**

10. **Click Window on the menu bar, click MediaLoft Online Survey_Alice, close the document, click Window on the menu bar, click MediaLoft Online Survey_Chris, then save and close it**

   MediaLoft Online Survey_Final is the only active Word document.

FIGURE O-13: Compare and Merge Documents dialog box

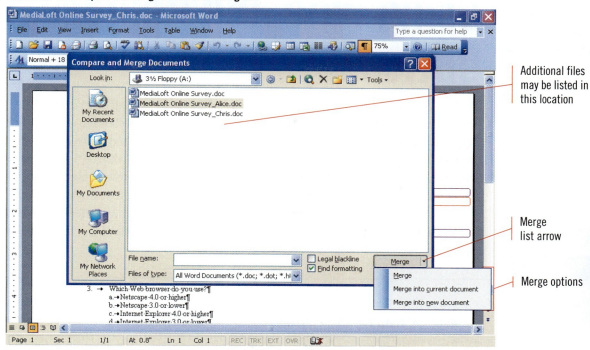

Additional files may be listed in this location

Merge list arrow

Merge options

FIGURE O-14: Document showing merged changes

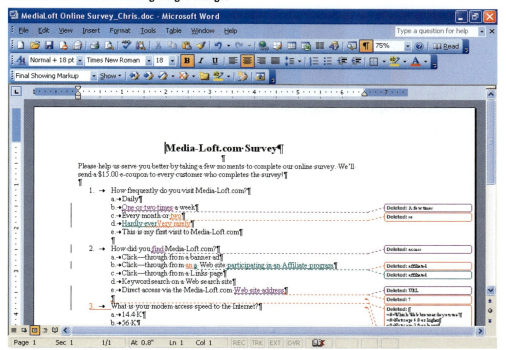

Using Find and Replace Options

Word offers advanced find and replace options that allow you to search for and replace formats, special characters, and even nonprinting elements such as paragraph marks (¶) and section breaks. For example, you can direct Word to find every occurrence of a word or phrase of unformatted text and then replace it with the same text formatted in a different font style and font size.  You are pleased with the final version of the survey questions. Now you need to consider how best to format the questions for delivery over the Internet. You decide that every instance of the Web site name Media-Loft.com should appear in bold and italic. You use the Find and Replace feature to find every instance of Media-Loft.com and replace it with ***Media-Loft.com***. You then notice that an em dash (—) appears between the words "Click" and "through" in three entries in question 2. You decide to replace the em dash with the smaller en dash (–).

STEPS

1. Press [Ctrl][Home] to move to the top of the document, click Edit on the menu bar, click Replace, then type Media-Loft.com in the Find what text box

2. Press [Tab], type Media-Loft.com in the Replace with text box, then click More
   The Find and Replace dialog box expands.

3. Click in the Replace with text box

QUICK TIP
You can also click Format on the menu bar and then click Font to open the Font dialog box.

4. Click Format at the bottom of the Find and Replace dialog box, click Font to open the Replace Font dialog box, select Bold Italic in the Font style list, then click OK
   The format settings for the replacement text Media-Loft.com appear in the Find and Replace dialog box, as shown in Figure O-15.

5. Click Find Next, move the dialog box as needed to see the selected text, click Replace All, click OK, click Close, then click the first paragraph to deselect the text
   All instances of Media-Loft.com are replaced with ***Media-Loft.com***.

6. Press [Ctrl][F] to open the Find and Replace dialog box, click the Replace tab, then press [Delete] to remove Media-Loft.com from the Find what text box

7. Click Special, click Em Dash, press [Tab], click Special, then click En Dash
   Codes representing the em dash and en dash are entered in the Replace tab in the Find and Replace dialog box.

8. Click the No Formatting button at the bottom of the Find and Replace dialog box to remove the formatting assigned to the text in the Replace with text box so the Find and Replace dialog box appears as shown in Figure O-16

9. Click Find Next, click Replace All, click OK, click Close, then save the document

FIGURE O-15: Expanded Find and Replace dialog box

Click Less to return the dialog box to its original size

Format button

Formatting selected for the Replace with text

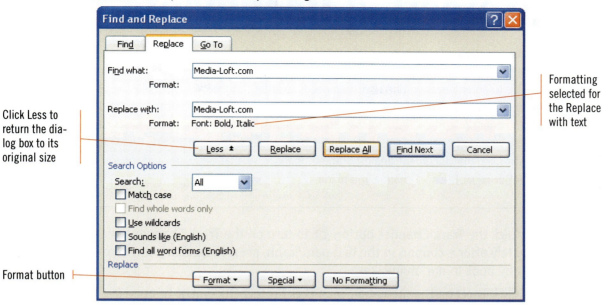

FIGURE O-16: Special characters inserted in the Find and Replace dialog box

Em dash code

En dash code

No Formatting button

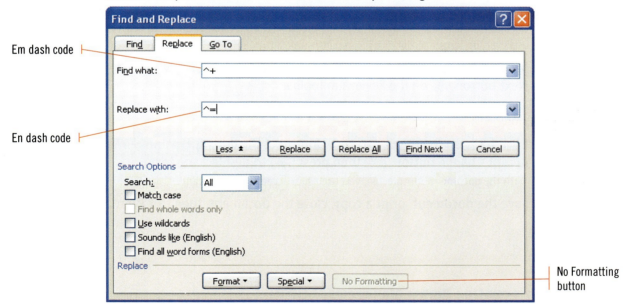

Protecting Documents

You can protect a document so that no one else can make changes or insert comments. When you protect a document, you choose the level of protection you want to impose on the document and then you can choose to enter a password. A user then needs to enter this password to make the permitted editing or formatting changes to the document. For a higher level of security, you can use the new Information Rights Management feature to restrict access to documents and ensure that documents cannot be distributed to people who do not have rights to view the content. You make one more change to the document and protect the document against tracked changes so that any user who opens the document cannot accept or reject the new change you made.

STEPS

1. **Click the Track Changes button** to turn on the Track Changes feature, click immediately after **e-coupon** in the first paragraph, press **[Spacebar]**, then type **redeemable for any book in our online store**

2. **Click Tools on the menu bar, then click Protect Document to open the Protect Document task pane**

   In the Protect Document task pane, you can select the formatting and editing restrictions you want to place on the document.

3. **Click the check box in the Editing restrictions section of the Protect Document task pane, then click the No changes (Read only) list arrow to view the editing restrictions you can choose as shown in Figure O-17**

   QUICK TIP
   Passwords generally consist of letters and numbers in a combination that is almost impossible to decipher.

4. **Select Tracked changes, click Yes, Start Enforcing Protection, enter mrk2$7# as the password, press [Tab], type mrk2$7# again, then click OK**

   For security reasons, the password you entered appears as a series of bullets. Now that you have protected the document, the Track Changes button on the Reviewing toolbar is dimmed. With the document protected, users can no longer accept or reject changes unless they enter the password.

5. **Save and close the document, open MediaLoft Online Survey_Final.doc, then click the Next button on the Reviewing toolbar**

   The tracked change is highlighted, but you cannot accept or reject the change because the document is protected.

6. **Click Tools on the menu bar, click Unprotect Document, type mrk2$7#, click OK, click the Accept Change button, then press [→] to deselect the text**

   With the document unprotected, you can again accept or reject changes.

7. **Save the document, print a copy, close the document, then exit Word**

Clues to Use

Understanding Information Rights Management (IRM)

You use the IRM feature when you want to specify exactly who can access a document and what activities they are authorized to perform. You can specify three access levels. Users with Read access can read the document, but they cannot edit, print, or copy the document. Users with **Change** access can read, edit, and save changes to a document, but they cannot print the document. Users with **Full Control** access can do anything with the document that the document author can do. By default, you have Full Control access to a document that you create. To specify an access level for a document, you click Restrict permission at the bottom of the Protect Document task pane or you click the Permission (Unrestricted Access) button on the Standard toolbar. You will then be asked to install the Windows Rights Management client, which you use to set access levels. You can install the IRM client only if you have administrative rights to your computer.

FIGURE O-17: Protect Document task pane

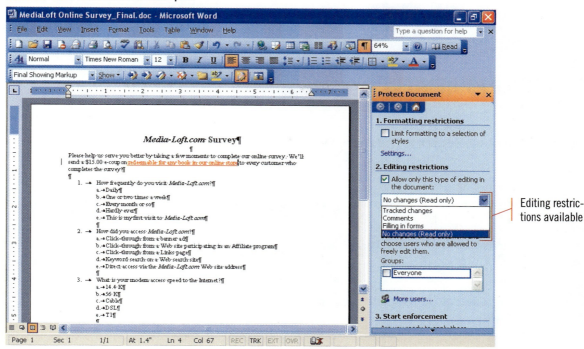

Editing restrictions available

Clues to Use

Obtaining and attaching a digital signature

You can authenticate yourself as the author of a document by inserting a digital signature. A **digital signature** is an electronic stamp that you attach to a document to authenticate the document. The highest-level digital signature is encryption-based and secure, which assures the recipient that the document originated from the signer and has not been altered. To obtain a secure digital signature, you need to first obtain a digital certificate from a certificate authority such as VeriSign, Inc. A digital certificate is an attachment for a file that vouches for the authenticity of the file, provides secure encryption, or supplies a verifiable signature. You or your organization must submit an application to obtain a digital certificate from a commercial certification authority. You must obtain a digital certificate in order to generate an authenticated digital signature.

To attach a digital signature, click Tools on the menu bar, click Options, click the Security tab, click Digital Signatures, and then click Add in the Digital Signatures dialog box. Read the message boxes that open, clicking "Yes" or "OK" as needed to accept the default certificate. Click View Certificate to see the default digital certificate attached to your document. See Figure O-18.

FIGURE O-18: Digital Signature information

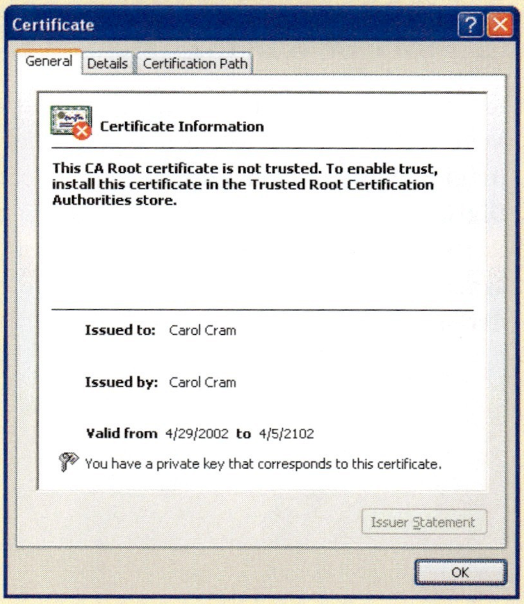

Certificate

General | Details | Certification Path

Certificate Information

This CA Root certificate is not trusted. To enable trust, install this certificate in the Trusted Root Certification Authorities store.

Issued to: Carol Cram

Issued by: Carol Cram

Valid from 4/29/2002 **to** 4/5/2102

You have a private key that corresponds to this certificate.

Issuer Statement

OK

Practice

▼ CONCEPTS REVIEW

Label each of the elements in Figure O-19.

FIGURE O-19

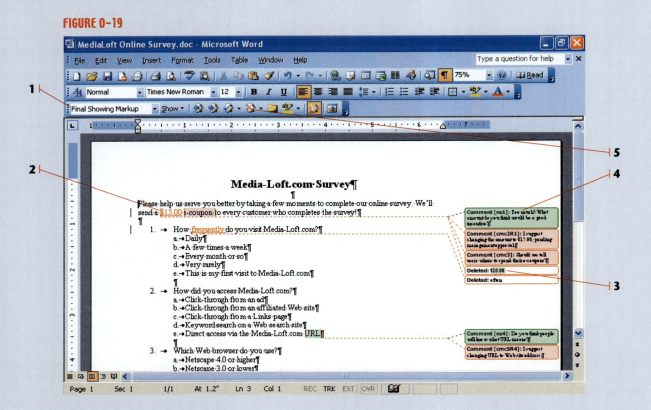

Match each term with the statement that best describes it.

6. **Balloon**

7. **Next button**

8. **Original Showing Markup**

9. **Digital signature**

10. **Reviewing Pane**

11. **Tracked Changes dialog box**

a. Use to move to another change

b. View that shows deleted text in strikethrough form

c. Contains a comment and appears in the right margin

d. Use to verify the identity of the person who created the document

e. Use to view comments at the bottom of the document window

f. Use to change the appearance of tracked changes.

Select the best answer from the list of choices.

12. How are comments inserted by two or more individuals differentiated in a document?

    a. The initials of the individual are inserted in the document next to the comment.

    b. The comment balloon is a different color for each individual.

    c. The comment balloon appears in a different location for each individual.

    d. The full name of the individual appears at the end of the comment text.

13. Which view do you choose when you want the text of the document and the comment balloons to be visible on the screen at the same time?

    a. Original Showing Markup view

    b. Final Showing Markup view

    c. Page Width view

    d. 100% view

14. Where can you see the name of an individual associated with a specific comment?

    a. In the Reviewing Pane

    b. In the comment balloon

    c. At the location where the comment was inserted

    d. In the Track Changes pane

15. In Print Layout view, how is deleted text shown in the Final Showing Markup view?

    a. As strikethrough text that ~~looks like this~~

    b. As bold and colored text in the document

    c. As double-underlined text in the document

    d. In a balloon along the right side of the document

16. Which of the following merge options do you select when you want to display results in the target document?

    a. Merge

    b. Merge into current document

    c. Merge into target document

    d. Merge into new document

17. How do you e-mail document revisions to a colleague?

    a. Select Mail Recipient from the Send To menu.

    b. Select Mail Recipient (for Review) from the Send To menu.

    c. Select Reviewers from the Show menu.

    d. Select Mail Reviewers from the File menu.

18. How do you protect a document against tracked changes?

    a. Select Document Protection from the File menu.

    b. Select Protect Document from the Edit menu.

    c. Select Protect Document from the Tools menu.

    d. Select Protect Document on the Safety tab in the Options dialog box.

19. Which of the following statements best describes a digital signature?

    a. It confirms that the document originated from the signer and has not been altered.

    b. It confirms that the document originated from a certification authority.

    c. It confirms that the document is password protected.

    d. It confirms that the document has been approved by VeriSign.

20. Using the Information Rights Management (IRM) feature, which of the following permissions is *not* an option?

    a. Read access

    b. Write access

    c. Full Control access

    d. Change access

▼ SKILLS REVIEW

1. Include comments in a document.

    a. Start Word, open the file WD O-4.doc from the drive and folder where your Data Files are located.

    b. Change the zoom to 90% or whatever value allows you to see the document and the comments without having to scroll horizontally, and then scroll vertically to view the two comments.

    c. Select **service** at the end of the second line in the Company Overview section, return to 100% view, then insert this comment: **We need to change this sentence to mention Demarco Designs.**

    d. Scroll to the end of the paragraph in the Company Background section, click in the comment, then insert a new comment with the text **Good idea.**

    e. Open the Reviewing Pane to view the names of the two reviewers.

    f. Close the Reviewing Pane.

    g. Save the file as **Design Signs Company Description**.

2. Track changes.

    a. Press [Ctrl][Home], then turn on Track Changes.

    b. Delete **no other design consultation services operates** in the first paragraph, then type **the only local competition comes from Demarco Designs, a small consulting firm that opened just three months ago**.

    c. Replace **objects d'art** at the end of the first paragraph with **collectibles**.

    d. Scroll down to the Expansion Plans section of the document, then replace **$50,000** with **$75,000**.

    e. Save the document.

3. Accept and reject changes.

    a. Change the Display for Review view to Original Showing Markup view, note the deletions made to the document, then return to Final Showing Markup view.

    b. Use the Reviewing toolbar to accept the changes in the first paragraph and to delete the comment associated with the first paragraph.

    c. Delete the comments associated with the Company Background paragraph. (*Hint*: Right-click a comment, then click Delete Comment on the shortcut menu.)

    d. Reject deleting the original amount of $50,000 and reject inserting $75,000 in the third paragraph.

    e. Save the document.

4. Create document versions.

    a. Save the active document as a version with the comment **Three new employees**. (*Note:* You will be able to save document versions only if you are saving to a hard drive.)

    b. Scroll to the Expansion Plans sections, then select the text **two apprentice designers and an administrative assistant** and type **three designers and an office manager**.

    c. Save the document as a version with the comment **Four new employees.**

    d. Accept all tracked changes, save the document, then close the document.

5. Compare documents and merge changes.

    a. Open the file WD O-5.doc from the drive and folder where your Data Files are located and save the document as **Design Signs_Donald**, open WD O-6.doc, then save it as **Design Signs_Julia**.

    b. Be sure Design Signs_Julia is the active document, then select Compare and Merge Documents from the Tools menu.

    c. Select the document Design Signs Company Description, click the Merge list arrow, then select Merge into a new document.

    d. With the new document the active document, select Compare and Merge Documents from the Tools menu, select Design Signs_Donald, then select Merge into current document. (Note: If a warning box appears, be sure Your Document is selected, then click Continue with Merge.)

    e. Show all the reviewers who have worked on the document. In addition to yourself, you'll see Donald Vogt and Julia Pirelli.

    f. Show changes by type: comments only, insertions and deletions only, formatting only, and then all three types again.

    g. Use the Reviewing toolbar to remove the following text: **a** before **an**, **consulting**, **three**, **antiques** and **ten**, and then delete all comments.

    h. Scroll to the bottom of the document, insert your name where indicated, then accept all the changes to the document.

    i. Reduce the top and bottom margins to **.5** so that all the text fits on one page.

    j. Save the document as **Design Signs_Final**, close the other Word documents so only Design Signs_Final is open.

6. Use Find and Replace options.

    a. Open the Find and Replace dialog box, select any text in the Find what text box and type **Design Signs**, expand the Find and Replace dialog box if necessary, then assign Italic formatting to the text in the Find what text box.

▼ SKILLS REVIEW (CONTINUED)

b. Select any text in the Replace with text box and type **Design Signs**, then assign Bold Italic formatting to the text in the Replace with text box.

c. Find and replace all instances of Design Signs formatted in Italic with Design Signs formatted in Bold and Italic.

d. Click in the Find what text box, delete Design Signs, show the list of Special characters, select Manual Line Break, then clear the formatting assigned to text in the Find what text box. (*Hint:* Click the No Formatting button at the bottom of the Find and Replace dialog box.)

e. Click in the Replace with text box, delete **Design Signs**, show the list of Special characters, select Paragraph Mark, then clear the formatting assigned to text in the Replace with text box.

f. Find and replace all instances of a Manual Line Break with a Paragraph Mark. (*Note:* If a message box appears, click Yes to continue the search.)

g. Close the Find and Replace dialog box, then save the document.

7. Protect documents.

a. Turn on Track Changes, then delete **freelance** in the Company Background section.

b. Protect the document for Tracked changes with the password **R2D3%12**.

c. Save the document.

d. Press [Ctrl][Home], then move to the tracked change and try to accept it.

e. Unprotect the document with the **R2D3%12** password, then accept the change.

f. Save the document, print a copy, close the document, then exit Word.

▼ INDEPENDENT CHALLENGE 1

You work for Adelphi Solutions, a large application service provider based in Durham, England. The company is sponsoring a conference called E-Business Solutions for local businesses interested in developing or enhancing their online presence. Two of your coworkers have been working on a preliminary schedule for the conference. They ask for your input.

a. Start Word, open the file WD O-7.doc from the drive and folder where your Data Files are located, then save it as **E-Business Solutions Conference**.

b. Save a version of the document with the comment **Changes by Mark and Winnifred**. (*Note:* You will be able to save document versions only if you are saving to a hard drive.)

c. Scroll through the document to read the comments and view the changes made by Mark Smythe and Winnifred Reese.

d. In the 9:00 to 10:00 entry, select E-Payment Systems, then insert a comment with the text **I suggest we change the name of this session to E-Cash in the New Millennium.**

e. Be sure the Track Changes feature is active. In the 3:00 to 4:00 entry, delete the text Nirvana, and then type **Heaven**.

f. Type your name where indicated at the bottom of the document, then accept all the changes, but do not delete the comments.

g. Save a new version of the document with the comment **Changes by** followed by your name.

Advanced Challenge Exercise

- Open the Versions dialog box, then delete the version with the comment Changes by Mark and Winnifred.
- Open the version you created, then maximize the window containing the version. (*Note:* A new window opens containing the version.)
- With Track Changes turned on, select the text **Library Building University of Durham**, then apply highlighting to the text.
- Accept the formatting change you just made.
- Save the document as **E-Business Solutions Conference ACE**. (*Hint:* Click the Save button to open the Save as dialog box.)

h. Print a copy of the document, close all open Word files, and then exit Word.

▼ INDEPENDENT CHALLENGE 2

You work as an editor for Rex Harding, a freelance author currently writing a series of articles related to e-commerce. Rex sent you the first draft of his article titled **Web Security Issues**. You edited the article, then sent it back to Rex, who reviewed your changes, accepted or rejected them, inserted some new changes of his own, responded to some of your comments, and then added some new comments. You've just received this latest revision of the article. Now you need to review Rex's new changes and then prepare the final document. Rex has also asked you to use the Find and Replace feature to apply formatting to selected text included throughout the article.

a. Start Word, open the file WD O-8.doc from the drive and folder where your Data Files are located, then save it as **Web Security Issues Article**.

b. Turn on Track Changes, then scroll through the document to get a feeling for its contents.

c. Open the Reviewing Pane. Notice there were two reviewers—Rex and you, as indicated by Your Name in the Reviewing Pane. Close the Reviewing Pane.

d. Find and accept the first change (the formatting of Rex's name as the author of the article at the top of the document).

FIGURE O-20

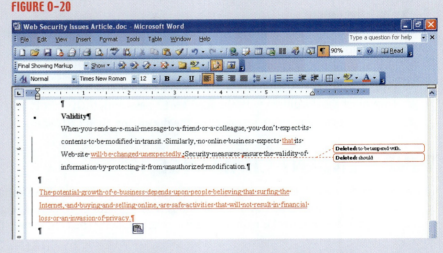

e. Move to the first comment, read it, delete it, then move to the next comment and delete it. As requested in the comments, move the last sentence in paragraph 1 to the end of the article (following the paragraph on Validity), as shown in Figure O-20. (*Note*: As you cut and paste text, the text is tracked as a change. You will accept the change later.)

f. Move to the comment that states Could you switch the Protection and Access Control sections?, then perform the action requested. (*Hint*: Select the Protection section (including the heading), press [Ctrl][X], click to the left of the Access Control section, then press [Ctrl][V].)

g. Accept all the remaining changes in the document, delete all the comments from the document, then turn off the Track Changes feature.

h. Scroll to the top of the document, then use the Find and Replace feature to find all instances of **Web** and replace it with **Web** formatted in Italic. You should make nine replacements.

i. Clear formatting assigned to the text in the Replace with text box, and then close the Find and Replace dialog box.

Advanced Challenge Exercise

- Click Show on the Reviewing toolbar, then click Options.
- Change Markup options as follows: Double-underline for insertions and Italic for deletions.
- Change the width of the comment balloons to 1".
- Show balloons in the Left margin, then close the Track Changes dialog box.
- Turn on track changes, select harm in the second sentence and add the comment **Should we also mention financial harm?**
- Select the word harm in the last sentence of the introduction (in the phrase from potential harm or failure), and change it to **danger**.
- Switch to the Original Showing Markup view to verify that harm appears in italic, then switch back to Final Showing Markup view.
- Print a copy of the document, then reject the change you just made and delete the comment.
- Open the Track Changes dialog box again and return the settings to their defaults: Underline for insertions, Strikethrough for Deletions, and 2.5" balloon width appearing in the right margin.

j. Create a header that includes your name and the date, proofread the document making formatting changes as needed, save the document, print a copy, close the document, then exit Word.

▼ INDEPENDENT CHALLENGE 3

The Southern Alps Institute in Wanaka, New Zealand, offers teens and young adults courses in various winter and summer mountain sports. As the course programmer, you are responsible for approving all the course descriptions included on the school's Web site. Three of your colleagues, Malcolm Pascal, Teresa Lopez, and Gregg Luecke have each revised descriptions of the three summer courses offered at the school. You use the Compare and Merge Documents feature to merge the documents so that you can see the changes made by the reviewers. You review the changes and add some additional changes. Finally, you protect the document so that only you or your colleagues with access to your password may accept or reject your changes.

a. Start Word, open these files from the drive and folder where your Data Files are located, then save them as indicated: WD O-9.doc as **Summer Courses_Malcolm**, WD O-10.doc as **Summer Courses_Teresa**, and WD O-11.doc as **Summer Courses_Gregg**.

b. Use the Compare Documents and Merge feature to merge the Summer Courses_Malcolm (target file) and the Summer Courses_Gregg (active) documents into the current document (accept the default setting to keep formatting changes from your document), then merge Summer Courses_Teresa into a new document (again, accept the default to keep the formatting changes from your document).

c. Review the changes in the merged version of the document.

d. Accept all the changes and delete any comments, then save the document as **Summer Courses_Final**.

e. If you have e-mail capability, e-mail this revision to yourself and then continue revising the e-mailed document; otherwise, continue revising the current document.

f. Be sure the Track Changes feature is active, then change the name of the Mountaineering Course to **Wilderness Survival**.

g. Password protect the document for Tracked Changes with a password of your choice, then try to accept the tracked change to verify that the file is protected.

h. Unprotect the document, then accept the changes.

i. Add a digital signature, if available.

j. Create a header containing your name and the date, save the document, print a copy, close all documents without saving changes, then exit Word.

▼ INDEPENDENT CHALLENGE 4

You are thinking about launching a small business that sells a product or service of your choice. As part of your start-up, you decide to find out more about digital signatures and digital certificates.

a. Open your Web browser and conduct a search for information on digital signatures and digital certificates. You can try entering the keywords **digital signature definition** and **digital certificate definition**.

b. Start Word, open the file WD O-12.doc from the drive and folder where your Data Files are located, then save it as **Digital Signatures**.

c. Use information from the Web sites you accessed as well as the Word Help system to answer the questions.

d. Type your name and the current date in the header section.

e. Close your browser when you have completed your research.

f. Print a copy of the Word document, close the document, then exit Word.

▼ VISUAL WORKSHOP

You work for a company called Paradise Found that sells gardening supplies and plants. Your coworker has prepared a mission statement for the company and she asks you to edit it. Open the file WD O-13.doc, then save it as **Paradise Found Mission Statement**. Turn on the Track Changes feature, then insert comments and add changes so that the edited mission statement appears as shown in Figure O-21. Ensure that your name and the current date appear in the footer, save the document, print a copy, then close the document.

FIGURE O-21

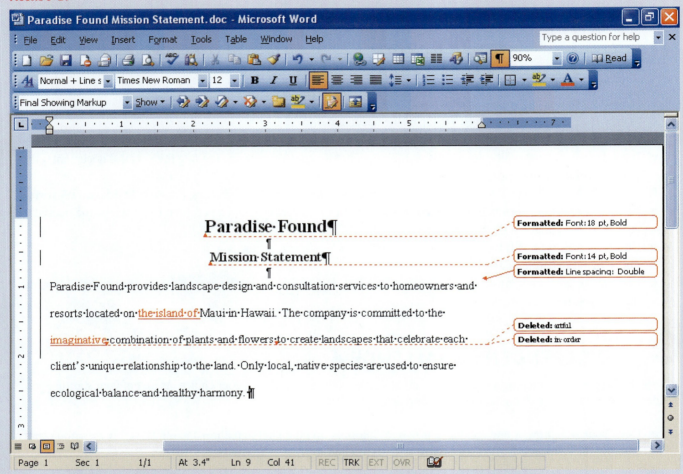

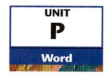

UNIT
P
Word

Customizing Word

OBJECTIVES

Plan a macro

Create a macro

Run a macro

Edit a macro in Visual Basic

Rename, delete, and copy macros

Create a custom toolbar

Customize menus

Modify options

Summarize content using automated tools

If you have a SAM user profile, you may have access to hands-on instruction, practice, and assessment of the skills covered in this unit. Log in to your SAM account and go to your assignments page to see what your instructor has assigned.

You can customize Word to suit your working style by creating macros to automate a series of tasks and procedures that you perform frequently, selecting only the options you use frequently on customized toolbars and menus, and even changing default options such as measurement units and custom dictionaries. Finally, you can use the AutoSummarize feature to examine a document, highlight the main points, and even create a summary. Graham Watson in the Marketing Department at MediaLoft has asked you to produce a booklet containing excerpts from novels featured at book signing events. You have already received excerpts from several authors, but each excerpt is formatted differently. You decide to create a macro to automate the formatting and saving tasks. Then you modify menus and default settings to help you work more efficiently. Finally, you use the AutoSummarize feature to quickly summarize the contents of a guidelines document.

Planning a Macro

If you perform a task repeatedly in Microsoft Word, you can automate the task by using a macro. A **macro** is a series of Word commands and instructions that you group together as a single command to accomplish a task automatically. You create a macro when you want to quickly perform multiple tasks usually by clicking a button or using a shortcut key. For example, you can create a macro that inserts a table with a specific number of rows and columns and with a particular border style, or you can create a macro to perform a series of complex tasks that involve multiple keystrokes. 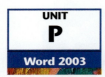 You want to create a macro to format each book excerpt document consistently, enter a title at the top of each document, and then save and close each document. You carefully plan the steps you will perform to create the macro.

DETAILS

- ### Macro tasks

    When planning a macro, the first step is to determine the tasks you want the macro to accomplish. For example, the macro could apply consistent formatting such as size, text wrapping, and borders to a series of graphics in a document, insert a fill-in text field so you can enter a caption for each graphic, and then perform commands such as saving, printing, and closing the document. Table P-1 lists all the tasks that you want your macro to perform when you open a document containing a book excerpt.

- ### Macro steps

    Table P-1 also lists all the steps required to accomplish each task. You plan and practice these steps before you create a macro so that you can perform the steps without error when you create the macro. If you make an error while recording the steps in the macro, you usually need to stop recording and start over because the recorded macro will include not only the correct steps but also the errors. By rehearsing the steps required before recording the macro, you ensure accuracy. While recording a macro, you can only use keystrokes or mouse clicks to complete all the macro steps, except selecting text. To select all the text in a document, you use the [Ctrl][A] or Edit, Select All commands. To select just a portion of text, first you use arrow keys to move the insertion point to the text, then you press the [F8] key to turn on select mode, and finally you use arrow keys to select the required text.

- ### Macro information

    Once you have practiced the steps required for the macro, you are ready to determine the information related to the macro. Figure P-1 shows the Record Macro dialog box. You use this dialog box to name the macro, assign the macro to a button to be placed on a toolbar or to a keyboard shortcut, and enter a short description of the macro. This description is usually a summary of the tasks the macro will perform. You also use this dialog box to assign the location where the macro should be stored. The default location is in the Normal template so that the macro is accessible in all documents that use the Normal template. The date and name of the person who created the macro appear in the description section. The name of the person is based on the user information listed on the User Information tab in the Options dialog box.

- ### Record macro procedure

    When you click OK after completing the Record Macro dialog box, the Stop Recording toolbar opens, as shown in Figure P-2. The buttons on the Stop Recording toolbar are toggle buttons. You click the Pause button if you want to pause recording temporarily to fix an error; you click the Stop button when you have completed all the steps required for the macro. You must click the Stop button before you close the Stop Recording toolbar because simply closing the toolbar does not stop the macro recording function.

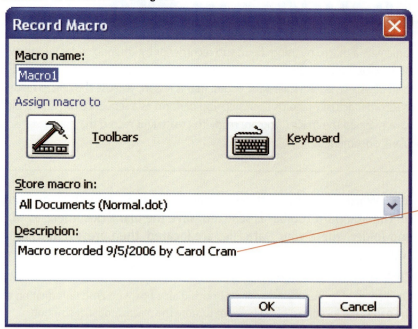

Your name or the name listed on the User Information tab in the Options dialog box appears here; you can also choose to enter a more detailed description of the macro in the Description box

FIGURE P-2: Stop Recording toolbar

Toolbar options list arrow

Pause Recording button

Stop Recording button

TABLE P-1: Macro tasks and steps to complete the tasks

tasks	steps
Select all the text	Press [Ctrl][A]
Change the line spacing to 1.5 lines	Click Format on the menu bar, click Paragraph, click the Line spacing list arrow, click 1.5 lines, click OK
Select the Comic Sans MS font and 14 pt	Click Format on the menu bar, click Font, select the Comic Sans MS font, select 14 pt, click OK
Insert a fill-in field text box into which a page title can be typed	Press [↑] once to deselect the text and move to the top of the document, click Insert on the menu bar, click Field, scroll down the list of Field names, click Fill-in, click OK, click OK
Save and close the document	Click the Save button, click File on the menu bar, click Close

UNIT
P
Word 2003

Creating a Macro

You can create a macro by using the macro recorder or by entering codes into the Visual Basic Editor. For most routine macros, you use the macro recorder. For complex macros, you use the Visual Basic Editor and enter macro steps as a series of Visual Basic codes. In this lesson, you use the macro recorder to create a macro. The macro recorder actually records each step you perform as a sequence of Visual Basic codes. Now that you have planned the macro, you are ready to create and record the macro steps. You create the macro in a new blank document.

STEPS

QUICK TIP

You create the macro in its own blank document so that if you make errors, you do not affect the formatting of a completed document.

1. **Start Word, close the Getting Started task pane, verify that the Show/Hide ¶ button ¶ on the Standard toolbar is selected, save the blank document as Macro Setup to the drive and folder where your Data Files are located, then press [Enter] four times**
   With the paragraph marks visible, you can see the formatting changes you make as part of your macro steps.

2. **Click Tools on the menu bar, point to Macro, then click Record New Macro**
   The Record Macro dialog box opens. In this dialog box, you enter information about the macro, including the name, the location where you want to store the macro, and a description.

3. **Type FormatExcerpts, then press [Tab] three times to move to the Store macro in list box**
   You can store the macro in the Normal.dot template so that it is available to all new documents or you can store the macro in the current document. Since you want the new macro to format several different documents, you accept the default storage location, which is the Normal.dot template.

4. **Press [Tab] to move to the Description box, then type the description shown in Figure P-3**
   By default, the Description box contains the name of the person who is recording the macro and the date the macro is recorded. You can keep this information, you can add to it, or you can overwrite it as you did in Step 4.

5. **Click OK**
   The Stop Recording toolbar opens, the pointer changes to 🖱, which indicates that you are in record macro mode.

6. **Press [Ctrl][A], click Format on the menu bar, click Paragraph, click the Line spacing list arrow, click 1.5 lines, then click OK**
   The line spacing between the paragraph marks changes to 1.5 spacing.

7. **Click Format on the menu bar, click Font, select the Comic Sans MS font, select 14 pt, then click OK**
   The size of the paragraph marks changes to show 14 pt Comic Sans MS.

8. **Press [↑] once to move to the top of the document, click Insert on the menu bar, click Field, select Fill-in from the list of Field names, then click OK**
   A fill-in field text box appears, as shown in Figure P-4. If necessary, you can move the Fill-in Text box so that the Stop Recording toolbar is still visible. When you run the macro, you will enter text in the fill-in field text box.

QUICK TIP

You should no longer see 🖱.

9. **Click OK, click the Save button 🖫 on the Standard toolbar, click File on the menu bar, click Close, then click the Stop Recording button ▪ on the Stop Recording toolbar**
   The Macro Setup file is saved and closed. The macro steps are completed and the Stop Recording toolbar closes. When you run the macro on a document that you open, the Save command saves the document with the filename already assigned to it. When you run the macro on a document that has not been saved, the Save command opens the Save As dialog box so that you can enter a filename in the File name text box, click Save, and then continue running the macro.

FIGURE P-3: Description entered in the Record Macro dialog box

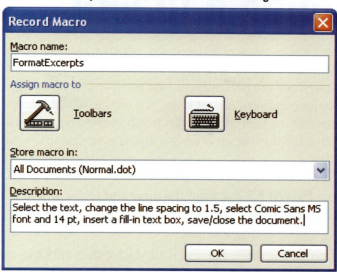

FIGURE P-4: Fill-in field text box

Stop Recording toolbar

Fill-in field text box; text typed in the fill-in field text box while the macro is running will appear at the top of the document

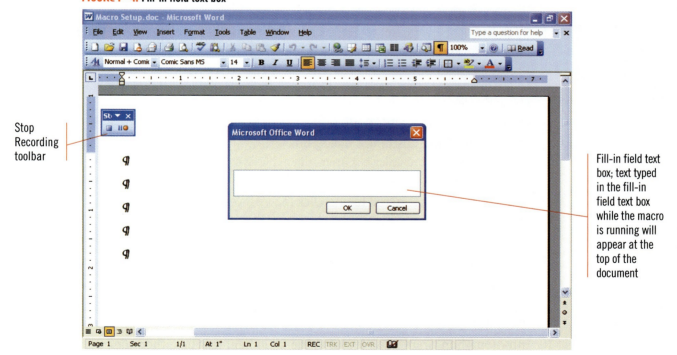

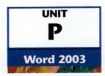

Running a Macro

When you run a macro, the steps you recorded are performed. You can choose to run a macro in three different ways. You can select the macro name in the Macro dialog box and click the Run button, you can click a button on a toolbar if you have assigned a toolbar button to the macro, or you can press a keystroke combination if you have assigned shortcut keys to the macro. You open one of the novel excerpts you want to format and run the FormatExcerpts macro by selecting the macro name in the Macro dialog box and clicking Run. You then decide to assign a keyboard shortcut to the macro.

STEPS

> **TROUBLE**
> The document contains spelling errors that you will correct later.

1. **Open the file WD P-1.doc from the drive and folder where your Data Files are located, then save it as Novel Excerpt_Emily Chow**

   The file contains an excerpt from Emily Chow's new novel *Dragon Swindle*.

2. **Click Tools on the menu bar, point to Macro, then click Macros**

   The Macros dialog box opens. In this dialog box, you select a macro and then the action you want to perform such as running, editing, or deleting the macro. The FormatExcerpts macro is listed, as well as any other macros that other users created in the Normal template. The name of the macro selected in the list box appears in the Macro name text box.

3. **Be sure FormatExcerpts is selected, then click Run**

   The macro selects all the text, changes the line spacing to 1.5, selects the Comic Sans MS font and 14 pt, then opens a fill-in field text box.

4. **Type Emily Chow's Dragon Swindle in the fill-in field text box, then click OK,**

   The macro saves and then closes the document.

> **TROUBLE**
> If the title is not shaded, your computer is not set to display field shading. You display field shading by selecting options on the View tab of the Options dialog box.

5. **Open the file Novel Excerpt_Emily Chow.doc from the drive and folder where your Data Files are located, then compare it to Figure P-5**

   The text you entered in the fill-in field text box appears at the top of the page. The document text uses 1.5 line spacing and 14-pt Comic Sans MS. The title text you typed appears shaded because you entered it in a fill-in field text box. The shading will not appear in the printed document.

6. **Close the document, click Tools on the menu bar, click Customize, then click Keyboard at the bottom of the Customize dialog box**

   The Customize Keyboard dialog box opens. In this dialog box, you can assign a keystroke combination to a macro or you can create a button for the macro and identify on which toolbar to place the button.

7. **In the Categories list, scroll to and click Macros, verify that FormatExcerpts is selected, click in the Press new shortcut key text box, then press [Alt][E]**

   Figure P-6 shows the settings assigned to the FormatExcerpts macro to create a keyboard shortcut.

8. **Click Assign, click Close, then click Close**

9. **Open the file WD P-2.doc from the drive and folder where your Data Files are located, save it as Novel Excerpt_Jonathon Grant, then press [Alt][E]**

   The macro runs to the point where the fill-in field text box appears.

10. **Enter Jonathon Grant's Sea Swept in the fill-in field text box, then click OK**

    The macro saves and closes the document.

FIGURE P-5: Document formatted with the FormatExcerpts macro

Comic Sans MS font and 14 pt formatting applied to text

Title created by entering text in the Fill-in field text box

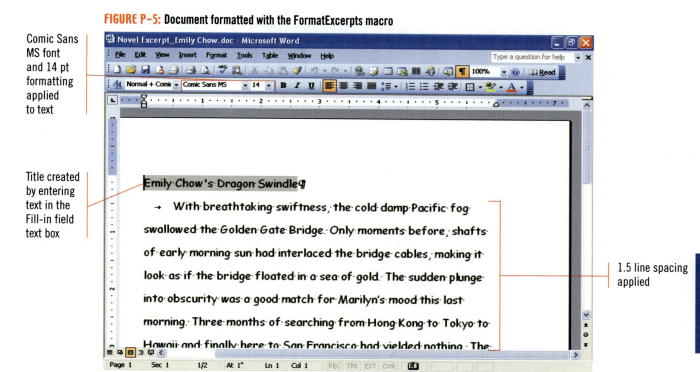

1.5 line spacing applied

FIGURE P-6: Customize Keyboard dialog box

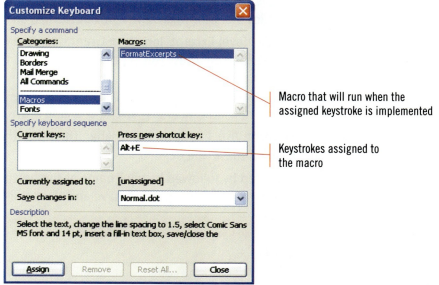

Macro that will run when the assigned keystroke is implemented

Keystrokes assigned to the macro

Editing a Macro in Visual Basic

You can make changes to a macro in two ways. First, you can delete the macro and record the steps again, or second, you can edit the macro in the Microsoft Visual Basic window. You use the second method when the change you want to make to the macro is relatively minor—such as changing the font style or font size, or removing one of the commands. You decide to increase the font size that the macro applies to text from 14 pt to 16 pt and then remove the close document command.

1. **Click Tools on the menu bar, point to Macro, then click Macros**
   The FormatExcerpts macro appears in the list of available macros in the Macros dialog box.

2. **Verify that FormatExcerpts is selected, then click Edit**
   The Microsoft Visual Basic window opens. The green text in the right pane is the description of the macro you entered when you created the macro. A list of codes appears in the right pane below the description. These codes were created as you recorded the steps for the FormatExcerpts macro. The text that appears to the left of the equal sign represents the code for a specific attribute such as SpaceBefore or KeepWithNext. The text to the right of the equal sign represents the attribute setting.

3. **Close the left pane, maximize the Microsoft Visual Basic window if necessary, scroll down the page to the With Selection.Font section, then find Size = 14 as shown in Figure P-7**

4. **Select 14, then type 16**

5. **Scroll down to the last End With section, then find ActiveDocument.Close shown in Figure P-8**

6. **Select the ActiveDocument.Close command, then press [Delete]**
   With the Close document code removed from the Visual Basic window, the macro will no longer close the document after saving it.

7. **Click the Save Normal button 🔲 on the Standard toolbar in the Microsoft Visual Basic window, then click the View Microsoft Word button 🔳 on the Standard toolbar**

8. **Open the file Novel Excerpt_Jonathon Grant.doc from the drive and folder where your Data Files are located, press [Alt][E] to run the macro, then click Cancel to close the fill-in field text box**
   The second time you run the macro you don't need to enter a title in the fill-in field text box. The font size of the document is now increased to 16 pt and the document is saved, but not closed.

9. **Click Microsoft Visual Basic on the taskbar, then click the Close button on the Microsoft Visual Basic window title bar**

10. **Type Formatted by followed by your name at the bottom of the Novel Excerpt_Jonathon Grant document, print a copy, then save and close the document**

Clues to Use

Locating Visual Basic codes

Sometimes you might want to insert a Visual Basic code into a macro. You find the correct code by searching Microsoft Visual Basic Help. To access Help, click Tools on the menu bar, point to Macro, click Visual Basic Editor, then click the Microsoft Visual Basic Help button on the Standard toolbar in the Microsoft Visual Basic window. You may then be prompted to install the required Help files. The Visual Basic Help task pane opens, which includes a Table of Contents and a Search feature. You use the Table of Contents to select links to various topics and you use the Search feature to generate a list of links to information about a specific action you want to perform. To use the Search feature, you type a brief description of the action you want to perform and then search for the required codes. Once you have found the code you want to use, you must paste the code above the "End Sub" code and either above or below any of the codes related to other tasks. All codes related to a specific task, such as format paragraph spacing, must stay together in their own sections.

FIGURE P-7: Font size code in Visual Basic

With
Selection.Font
section

Code to
change the
font size

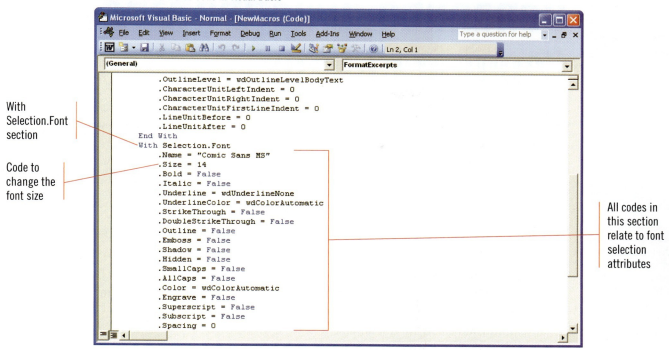

All codes in
this section
relate to font
selection
attributes

FIGURE P-8: ActiveDocument.Close code in Visual Basic

Save Normal
button

View Microsoft
Word button

Code to save
the active
document

Code to close
the active
document

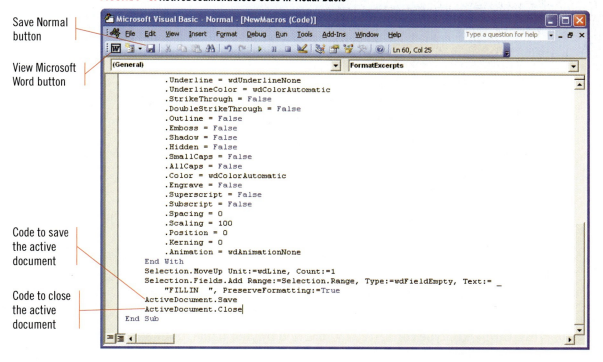

Renaming, Deleting, and Copying Macros

If you save a macro in the current document, you can choose to copy the macro to other documents in which you wish to run the macro. You can also choose to copy the macro to the Normal.dot template so that the macro is available to all documents. You use the Organizer dialog box to copy macros from one document to another document.  Graham Watson, your supervisor, asks you to use a different macro to format the novel excerpts. He sends you a document containing a new macro, which you copy to an unformatted novel excerpt

STEPS

1. Click Tools, point to Macro, click Security, then click the Medium option button

   With the security level set to Medium, you can choose whether or not to open documents containing macros.

2. Click OK, open the file WD P-3.doc from the drive and folder where your Data Files are located, click Enable Macros when the Security Warning appears, save the document as Novel Excerpt Macro, open the file WD P-4.doc, save it as Novel Excerpt_Charles Sheldon, then close the document

   The Novel Excerpt Macro document is the active document. You will copy the macro from the Novel Excerpt Macro document to the Novel Excerpt_Charles Sheldon document.

3. Click Tools on the menu bar, point to Macro, click Macros, then click Organizer

   In the Organizer dialog box, shown in Figure P-9, you copy macros from a source file to a target file.

4. Click Close File under the right-hand list in the Organizer dialog box, click Open File, navigate to the drive and folder where your Data Files are located, click the Files of type list arrow, click All Word Documents, click Novel Excerpt_Charles Sheldon.doc, then click Open

5. Be sure NewMacros is selected in the list box on the left (see Figure P-9), click Copy, click Close in the lower right corner of the Organizer dialog box, then click Yes to save the document

6. Close the Novel Excerpt Macro document, open Novel Excerpt_Charles Sheldon.doc, click Enable Macros, click Tools on the menu bar, point to Macro, click Macros, select NovelExcerptMacro, then click Run

   The macro formats the text with 1.5 line spacing and 14-pt Arial Narrow, and then saves the document.

7. Press [Alt][E], type Charles Sheldon's Spade Murders, then click OK

   The original FormatExcerpts macro reformats the document.

8. Click Tools on the menu bar, point to Macro, click Macros, click NovelExcerptMacro, click Delete, then click Yes

9. Click FormatExcerpts, click Edit, replace FormatExcerpts in two places with Book (see Figure P-10), then click the Close button on the Microsoft Visual Basic title bar to close Microsoft Visual Basic and return to Word

   The FormatExcerpts macro is renamed Book.

10. Press [Ctrl][End], type Formatted by followed by your name, print a copy, then save and close the document

FIGURE P-9: Organizer dialog box

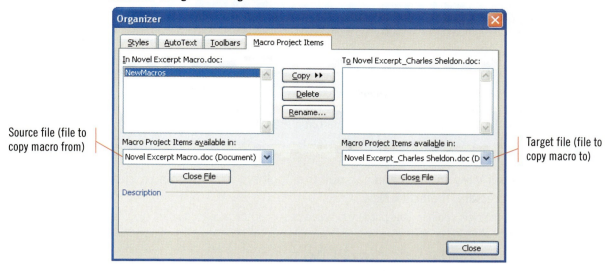

Source file (file to copy macro from)

Target file (file to copy macro to)

FIGURE P-10: Renaming the macro in Visual Basic

Book entered here

Book entered here

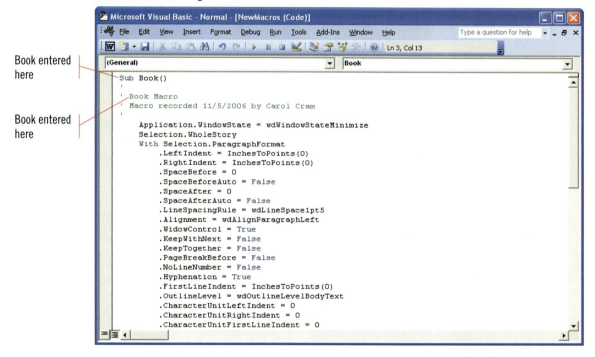

Clues to Use

Setting security levels

If you frequently receive documents containing macros, you might need to change the security level, depending on the source of the macros. A macro can introduce a virus into your system. As a result, you want to ensure that any macro included with documents you open in Word are created by sources you trust. You can select three security levels. A High security level (the default setting) allows you to open only digitally signed macros from trusted sources. Any macro that is not digitally signed will be automatically disabled. A Medium security level provides you with a prompt when you open a document containing a macro. You can then choose to enable or disable the macros. A Low security level accepts any document containing any number of macros, and you are not protected from unsafe macros.

Creating a Custom Toolbar

You can create a custom toolbar that contains only the buttons you want to use to perform a specific number of tasks. The custom toolbar can include a button that you click to run a macro, along with buttons for other functions such as checking spelling or drawing an AutoShape. You decide to create a toolbar that includes a button to count the words in the document, a button to add an outside border at the position of the insertion point, and a button to run the Book macro.

STEPS

1. **Click View on the menu bar, point to Toolbars, click Customize, click the Toolbars tab if necessary, then click New**

   In the New Toolbar dialog box, you type a name for the new toolbar and you assign a location in which to store the toolbar.

2. **Type Novel Excerpts, then click OK**

   The new toolbar appears next to the Customize dialog box and contains no buttons.

3. **Click the Commands tab in the Customize dialog box, select Tools in the Categories list, scroll down the list of commands, click Word Count, then drag Word Count to the Novel Excerpts toolbar as shown in Figure P-11**

   The I-beam shows where the command you are dragging to the toolbar will be placed.

4. **Scroll down the Categories list, click Borders, scroll down the Commands list, click Outside Borders, then drag the Outside Borders button to the Novel Excerpts toolbar**

5. **Scroll down the Categories list, click Macros, click Normal.NewMacros.Book in the Commands list, then drag Normal.NewMacros.Book to the Novel Excerpts toolbar**

6. **Click Modify Selection in the Customize dialog box, point to Change Button Image, click the red diamond shape, click Modify Selection, click Text Only (in Menus), click Close to close the Customize dialog box, then click the New Blank Document button 🗋 on the Standard toolbar**

   The selections on the Novel Excerpts toolbar are activated as shown in Figure P-12.

7. **Close the new document without saving it, open the file Novel Excerpt_Emily Chow.doc from the drive and folder where your Data Files are located, then click Word Count on the Novel Excerpts toolbar**

   The Word Count dialog box opens, as shown in Figure P-13.

8. **Click Close to close the Word Count dialog box, click the red diamond on the Novel Excerpts toolbar to run the macro, click Cancel to close the fill-in field text box, select Emily Chow's Dragon Swindle including the paragraph mark, click the Outside Border button 🔲 on the Novel Excerpts toolbar, click anywhere in the first paragraph, save the document, then compare it to Figure P-14**

9. **Click View on the menu bar, point to Toolbars, click Customize, click the Toolbars tab, scroll to the bottom of the list to view Novel Excerpts, click the check box to deselect it, click Delete, click OK, then click Close**

   The customized toolbar is deleted. Next, you delete the macros you created.

10. **Click Tools, point to Macro, click Macros, select Book if necessary, click Delete, click Yes, then close the dialog box**

FIGURE P-11: Word Count dragged to the Novel Excerpts toolbar

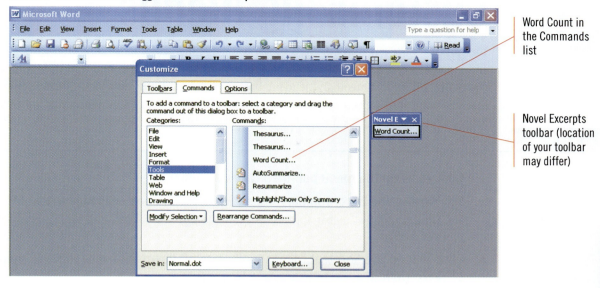

Word Count in the Commands list

Novel Excerpts toolbar (location of your toolbar may differ)

FIGURE P-12: Novel Excerpts custom toolbar

Your toolbar buttons may appear in a different order

FIGURE P-13: Word Count dialog box

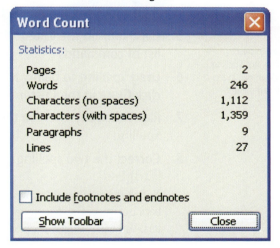

FIGURE P-14: Title enhanced with an outside border

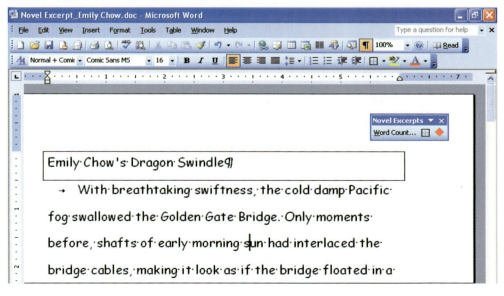

Customizing Menus

You can customize any menu in Word by removing commands, by renaming commands, and by displaying an icon and text for a command. You can also copy a command from one menu to another menu. You can choose to customize a menu on the menu bar, or you can customize a shortcut menu. You decide that you want the Spelling command to appear on the shortcut menu when you right-click the mouse. Then you can quickly check the spelling in each novel excerpt you format.

1. **Click Tools on the menu bar, then click Customize**

2. **Scroll down the list of toolbars, then click the check box next to Shortcut Menus**
   The Shortcut Menus toolbar appears, as shown in Figure P-15. You can modify Text, Table, and Draw shortcut menus.

3. **Click Text on the Shortcut Menus toolbar, scroll down the list of shortcut menus that appears, then click Text as shown in Figure P-16**
   The Text shortcut menu appears when you right-click a line of text.

4. **Drag the Customize dialog box title bar as needed so you can see the Commands tab, then click the Commands tab in the Customize dialog box**

5. **Click Tools in the Categories list, scroll down the Commands list, then click Spelling in the list of commands**

6. **Drag Spelling to below Hyperlink in the shortcut menu as shown in Figure P-17, then click Close in the Customize dialog box**

7. **Right-click anywhere in the document to show the modified shortcut menu, then click Spelling**

8. **Correct the two spelling errors ("sholders" and "radioe"), save the document, then press [Ctrl][End]**
   Notice that the word "copyright" at the bottom of the document is misspelled as COPYWRIGHT. That is because one of the default options in Word is to not check the spelling of a word if it is in all uppercase letters. You will change the option setting and correct this spelling error in the next lesson.

FIGURE P-15: Shortcut Menus toolbar

Shortcut Menus toolbar

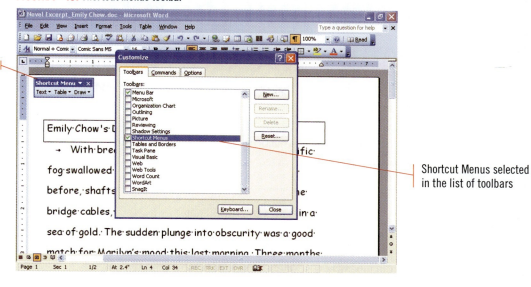

Shortcut Menus selected in the list of toolbars

FIGURE P-16: Text shortcut menu selected

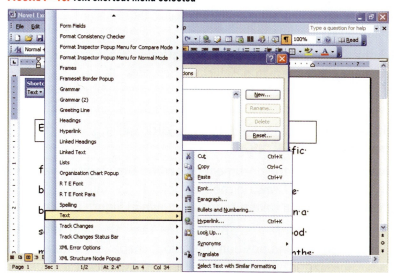

FIGURE P-17: Spelling added to the Text shortcut menu

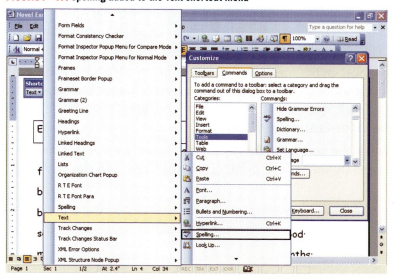

Modifying Options

Word includes many default settings designed to meet the needs of most users. For example, the default setting for entering text is black text on a white background. You can change this default to enter text another way, such as white text on a blue background. You modify default settings by selecting or deselecting options in the Options dialog box from the Tools menu. After working with Word for several months, you have identified some default options that do not suit your working style. You decide to change these options in the Options dialog box. First, you modify one of the Spelling options and then you deselect the option that automatically creates a drawing canvas each time you insert an AutoShape.

STEPS

1. **Click Tools on the menu bar, then click Options**

   In the Options dialog box, you can change settings in eleven categories. For example, you can enter new information via the User Information tab, you can change the location where files are stored via the File Locations tab, and you can modify how a document is printed via the Print tab.

2. **Click the Spelling & Grammar tab, then click the Ignore words in UPPERCASE check box to deselect it**

   Now when you use the Spelling command to check the spelling of a document, Word will check the spelling of words entered in uppercase.

3. **Click the General tab, click the Automatically create drawing canvas when inserting AutoShapes check box to deselect it, then click OK**

   Now you can draw an AutoShape independent of the drawing canvas—something you often need to do when you want to draw just one AutoShape such as a horizontal line or a small geometric shape.

4. **Right-click anywhere in the document, click Spelling, then change COPYWRIGHT to the correct spelling—COPYRIGHT**

5. **Move to the top of the document, show the Drawing toolbar if necessary, click AutoShapes on the Drawing toolbar, point to Callouts, click the Rounded Rectangular Callout, then draw a callout shape as shown in Figure P-18**

6. **Type Nominated for Mystery Book of the Year!, then enhance the text with Bold, center the text, then size and position the callout shape (see Figure P-19)**

   If you are working on a computer that other users access, you should restore the default options and remove the Spelling command from the shortcut menu.

7. **Click outside the callout shape, click Tools on the menu bar, click Options, click the Automatically create drawing canvas when inserting AutoShapes check box to select it, click the Spelling & Grammar tab, click the Ignore words in UPPERCASE check box to select it, then click OK**

8. **Click Tools on the menu bar, click Customize, click the Toolbars tab, click the Shortcut Menus check box, click Text on the Shortcut Menus toolbar, select the Text shortcut menu, click Spelling in the shortcut menu, drag it to a blank area of the screen, then click Close in the Customize dialog box**

9. **Move to the bottom of the document, press [Enter] after the last line, type Formatted by followed by your name, print a copy, then save and close the document**

FIGURE P-18: Callout shape drawn

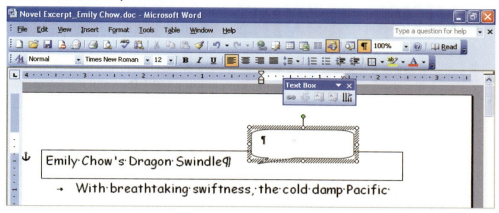

FIGURE P-19: Completed callout shape

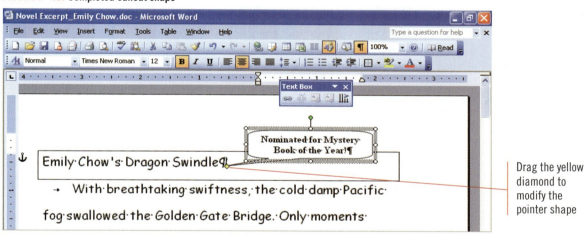

Drag the yellow diamond to modify the pointer shape

Clues to Use

Creating and using custom dictionaries

You can use a custom dictionary to prevent Microsoft Word from flagging words that are spelled correctly, but that do not appear in Word's main dictionary. For example, you can create a custom dictionary to contain terms you use frequently, such as medical terms, technical terms, or surnames. You use this dialog box to change the default dictionary, add a dictionary, and edit a dictionary. To create a new custom dictionary, you open the Spelling & Grammar tab in the Options dialog box, click Custom Dictionaries, click New, type a name for the custom dictionary, save it, then click Modify to add words to it. Each custom dictionary, including the default dictionary, appears in the list of dictionaries shown in the Custom Dictionaries dialog box. If you do not want a custom dictionary to be activated for a particular document, you can remove the green check box that appears next to it in the Custom Dictionaries dialog box. Figure P-20

shows the Custom Dictionaries dialog box containing the default dictionary and a new custom dictionary called Names.

FIGURE P-20: Custom Dictionaries dialog box

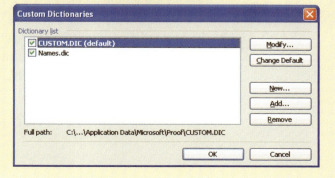

Summarizing Content with Automated Tools

You can use AutoSummarize to identify the key points in a document and then present them in the form of an easy-to-read summary. AutoSummarize produces the summary by analyzing a document and assigning a score to each sentence. High scores are assigned to sentences that contain words used frequently in the document. You can choose how you want AutoSummarize to display the summary. For best results, you use AutoSummarize to analyze documents such as reports, proposals and scientific or academic papers that already have a definite structure. 🎨 You realize that AutoSummarize is designed to analyze business and academic documents, rather than fiction. As a result, you decide to use AutoSummarize to produce an executive summary of the Meet the Author Guidelines you created in a previous unit.

STEPS

1. **Open the file WD P-5.doc from the drive and folder where your Data Files are located, save it as Author Guidelines, then scroll through the document to get a sense of the content**

2. **Return to the top of the document, click Tools on the menu bar, then click AutoSummarize**

   The AutoSummarize dialog box appears as shown in Figure P-21. In this dialog box, you can choose to highlight key points or insert an executive summary or abstract at the top of the document, in a new document, or in the same document but with the principal text hidden.

3. **Click OK to accept the Highlight key points option**

   The key sentences that AutoSummarize has identified are highlighted and the AutoSummarize tool bar appears as shown in Figure P-22. By default, 25% of the sentences are highlighted.

4. **Scroll through the document to view the highlighted sentences, then click Close on the AutoSummarize toolbar to remove the highlighting**

5. **Click Tools on the menu bar, click AutoSummarize, select the Insert an executive summary or abstract at the top of the document option, then click OK**

6. **Read the summary**

7. **Click File on the menu bar, click Properties, click the Summary tab if necessary, then read the text inserted in the Comments section**

   By default, AutoSummarize updates the document properties to include keywords and comments related to the document contents as shown in Figure P-23. You can edit these keywords and comments in the Properties dialog box, just as you would any text.

8. **Click OK, click the Undo button 🔄 on the Standard toolbar to remove the summary, click Tools on the menu bar, click AutoSummarize, select the option next to Create a new document and put the summary there, click the Percent of original list arrow, click 20 sentences, then click OK**

9. **Press [Ctrl][End], type Summarized by followed by your name, save the document as Author Guidelines Summary, print a copy, save and close the document, save and close the Author Guidelines document, then exit Word**

FIGURE P-21: AutoSummarize dialog box

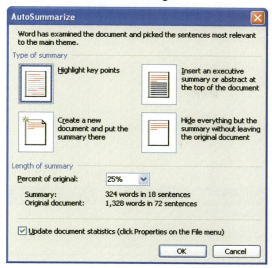

FIGURE P-22: AutoSummarize applied to a document

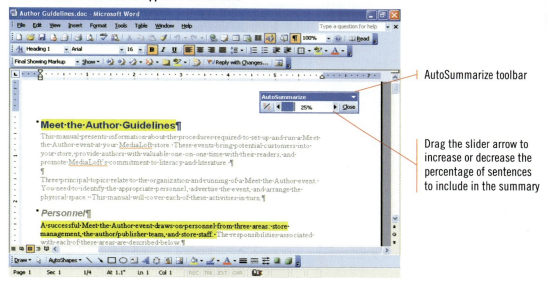

AutoSummarize toolbar

Drag the slider arrow to increase or decrease the percentage of sentences to include in the summary

FIGURE P-23: Document Properties

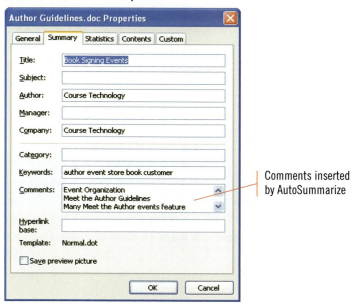

Comments inserted by AutoSummarize

Practice

▼ CONCEPTS REVIEW

Label each of the elements in Figure P-24.

FIGURE P-24

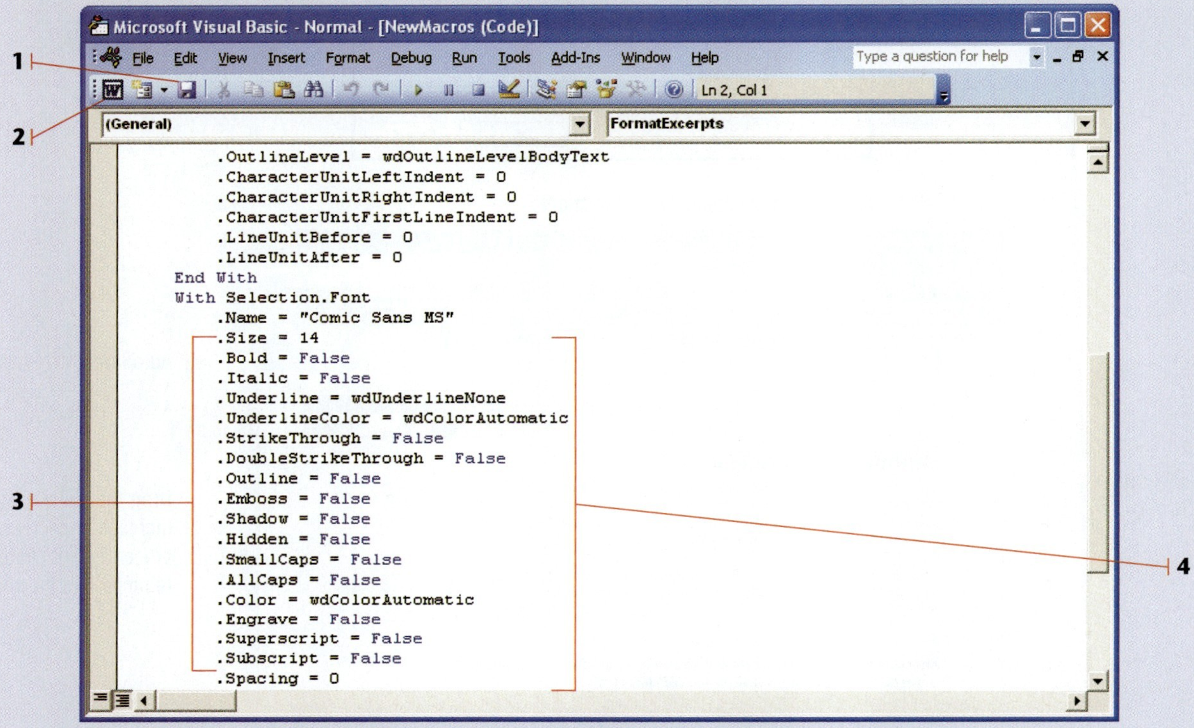

Match each term with the statement that best describes it.

5. **Stop Recording toolbar**	a. Contains the buttons of your choice
6. **AutoSummarize**	b. Analyze the document and assign a score to each sentence
7. **Custom toolbar**	c. Contains the buttons used to stop and pause a macro
8. **Customize**	d. Command selected to modify a shortcut menu
9. **Options**	e. Used to run macros
10. **Macros dialog box**	f. Selection on the Tools menu used to modify default settings

Select the best answer from the list of choices.

11. **What is a macro?**
    a. A series of procedures
    b. A series of Word commands and instructions that you group together as a single command
    c. Tasks that you cannot perform manually
    d. A series of tasks that Word performs when you select Run Macro from the Tools menu

12. **Which dialog box do you open when you want to copy a macro from one document to another document?**
    a. Organizer dialog box
    b. Organizing Macros dialog box
    c. Record Macro dialog box
    d. Copy Macro dialog box

▼ SKILLS REVIEW

1. **Create a macro.**
   a. Start Word, open the file WD P-6.doc from the drive and folder where your Data Files are located, then save it as **Press Release_Lake Towers Hotel**.
   b. Open the Record Macro dialog box, then type **PressReleaseFormat** as the macro name.
   c. Enter the following description after the identification information: **Select all the text, change the Before and After spacing to 3 pt, enhance the title with Arial Black, 24 pt, Bold, then apply the Table List 8 AutoFormat to the table.**
   d. Click OK, press [Ctrl][A] to select all the text, open the Paragraph dialog box, then change the Before spacing to **3 pt** and the After spacing to **3 pt**.
   e. Exit the Paragraph dialog box, press [➡] once, press [Ctrl][Home], press [F8] to turn on text select mode, then press [End] to select the document title (Lake Towers Hotel).
   f. Open the Font dialog box, then select the Arial Black font, Bold, and 24 pt.
   g. Exit the Font dialog box, press [Ctrl][End], press [↑] to move into the table, click Table on the menu bar, click Table AutoFormat, then apply the Table List 8 AutoFormat.
   h. Click [↓] once, then click the Stop Recording button on the Stop Recording toolbar.
   i. Scroll up to view the formatted document, then save and close the document.

2. **Run a macro.**
   a. Open the file WD P-7.doc from the drive and folder where your Data Files are located, then save it as **Press Release_Saskatoon Classic Hotel**.
   b. Open the Macros dialog box, select the PressReleaseFormat macro, then click Run.
   c. Type **Formatted by** followed by your name at the bottom of the document, scroll up and view the formatted document, print a copy, then save and close it.
   d. Open the Customize dialog box from the Tools menu, click Keyboard, select Macros from the Categories list, select the PressReleaseFormat macro, assign the [Alt][H] keystrokes to the FormatPressRelease macro, then close the dialog boxes.
   e. Open the file WD P-8.doc from the drive and folder where your Data Files are located, save it as **Press Release_Atlantica Hotel**, press [Alt][H] to run the macro, scroll up to view the formatted document, then save the document.

3. **Edit a macro in Visual Basic.**
   a. Open the Macros dialog box, verify the PressReleaseFormat macro is selected, then click Edit.
   b. Find the .SpaceAfter = 3 in the paragraph format section, then change the spacing to **6**.
   c. Scroll down as needed to find the .Size = 24 code in the Font section, then change the size to **36**.
   d. Save the macro, close the Visual Basic window, verify Press Release_Atlantica Hotel is the active document, then use the [Alt][H] keystrokes to run the revised macro.
   e. Verify that the security level for macros is set to Medium. (*Note:* If the security setting was *not* Medium, return to the original security setting when you have completed this Skills Review.)
   f. Save the document, then close it.

4. **Rename, delete, and copy macros.**
   a. Open the file WD P-9.doc from the drive and folder where your Data Files are located, click Enable Macros, then save the document as **Hotel Macro Sample**.
   b. Open the Macros dialog box, then open the Organizer dialog box.
   c. Close the file in the list on the right side, then open the Press Release_Atlantica Hotel.doc file. (*Note*: You must change the Files of type to All Word Documents.)
   d. Copy the macro from the Hotel Macro Sample file to the Press Release_Atlantica Hotel file, then close the Organizer dialog box and click Yes to save the Press Release_Atlantica Hotel file.
   e. Close the Hotel Macro Sample file, open the Press Release_Atlantica Hotel.doc file, click Enable Macros, then run the HotelMacro using the Macros dialog box.
   f. Scroll through the document to view the results of the HotelMacro, then run the [Alt][H] macro.
   g. Delete the HotelMacro macro from the Macros dialog box.

h. Click PressReleaseFormat in the Macro name list if necessary, click Edit, change the name of the macro PressReleaseFormat to **Hotel** in two places, save, then close Visual Basic to return to Word.

i. Type **Formatted by** followed by your name at the bottom of the Press Release_Atlantica Hotel document, print a copy, then save and close the document.

5. Create a custom toolbar.

a. Click View on the menu bar, point to Toolbars, click Customize, click the Toolbars tab if necessary, then click New.

b. Enter **Hotels** as the name of the new custom toolbar.

c. From the Commands tab, select Drawing in the Categories list, scroll down the list of commands, then drag the Shadow Style button to the Hotels toolbar. (*Note*: When you drag a button that includes a black list arrow at the right side of the Commands list, the options associated with the list arrow move with the button.)

d. Select Macros in the Categories list, then select Normal.NewMacros.Hotel in the Commands list and drag it to the toolbar.

e. Modify the Macro button so that it shows the key shape and appears as text only in menus, then close the Customize dialog box.

f. Open the file Press Release_Lake Towers Hotel.doc from the drive and folder where your Data Files are located, click the picture of the waiter, click the Shadow Style button on the Hotel toolbar, select Shadow Style 2, then deselect the image.

g. Click the Hotel macro button on the Hotel toolbar to run the revised macro.

h. Delete the Hotel toolbar from the Customize Toolbars dialog box, then save the document.

6. Customize menus.

a. Open the Customize dialog box, then click the check box next to Shortcut Menus in the Toolbars tab to select it.

b. Click Table on the Shortcut Menus toolbar, then select the Table Text shortcut menu.

c. Click the Commands tab in the Customize dialog box, click Table in the Categories list, select the Sort Ascending button from the list of commands, drag it to the Table Text shortcut menu so that it appears above Borders and Shading, then close the Customize dialog box.

d. Scroll to the bottom of the document, click anywhere in the Price column (contains the room rates) of the table, right-click to show the modified Table Text shortcut menu, click Sort Ascending, then save the document.

7. Modify options.

a. Open the Options dialog box from the Tools menu, click the General tab, click the Measurement units list arrow, then select Centimeters.

b. Close the Options dialog box, right-click the picture at the top of the document, click Format Picture, click the Size tab, change the Height of the picture to **8** centimeters, then exit the Format Picture dialog box.

c. Open the Options dialog box, then change the Measurement unit in the General tab back to inches.

d. Open the Customize dialog box, then remove the Sort Ascending button from the Table Text shortcut menu. (*Hint*: Repeat steps 6a–6b. When the Table Text shortcut menu appears, drag Sort Ascending to a blank area of the screen.)

e. Scroll to the bottom of the document, type **Formatted by** followed by your name, print a copy of the document, then save and close it.

f. Open the Macros dialog box, delete the Hotel macro, close the Macros dialog box, then exit Word.

8. Summarize Content Using Automated Tools

a. Open the file WD P-10.doc from the drive and folder where your Data Files are located, then save the document as **Back Country Tours**.

b. Read through the document, then use AutoSummarize to highlight key points.

c. Use AutoSummarize to insert an executive summary at the top of the document, then read the summary.

d. Remove the three bulleted points: Sea Kayaking, Wildlife Photography, and Mountain Biking.

e. Add a page break below the summary, then type **Summarized by** followed by your name at the bottom of the summary page.

f. Center "Summary" at the top of the page and increase its font size to 24 pt.

g. Save and close the document, then exit Word.

▼ INDEPENDENT CHALLENGE 1

You've just started working for Organics Forever, a company that delivers fresh, organic fruits and vegetables to its customers throughout Wellington, New Zealand. Your supervisor wants you to automate some tasks related to the company documentation. First, he asks you to use AutoSummarize to create a summary of the company description for use on the company's Web site. He then asks you to create a macro that will speed up the tasks required to prepare each week's price lists.

a. Start Word, open the file WD P-11.doc from the drive and folder where your Data Files are located, then read through the document to get a sense of the contents.

b. Use AutoSummarize to insert an executive summary in a new document.

c. Save the new document as **Organics Forever_About Us**, type **Summarized by** followed by your name at the end of the document, print a copy, then save and close it.

d. Close WD P-11.doc without saving it.

e. In a new Word document, type **Starting Date**, press [Enter], type **Date**, press [Enter] two times, type **Special of the Week**, press [Enter], type **Weekly Special**, then press [Enter]. This text is sample text that you can use as you create the macro.

f. Press [Ctrl][Home], open the Record Macro dialog box, then enter **PriceList** as the macro name.

g. Click the Store macro in list arrow and select Document1 (document).

h. Enter the following description for the macro: **Macro created by [your name] on [the current date]. Select Date, insert the current date, select Weekly Special, then insert a fill-in text box.**

i. Click Keyboard in the Record Macro dialog box and assign the [Alt][P] shortcut key combination.

j. Click Assign and Close, then perform the steps required for the macro as follows:
   • Press [↓], press [F8], then press [End] to select Date.
   • Press [Delete], click Insert on the menu bar, click Date and Time, click the format corresponding to March 29, 2006, verify that the Update automatically check box is selected, then click OK.
   • Press [Enter], press the [↓] twice, press [F8], press [End] to select Weekly Special, click Insert on the menu bar, click Field, click Fill-in, click OK, then click OK.
   • Click the Stop Recording button on the Stop Recording toolbar.

k. Save the document as **Price List Macro**.

l. Open the file WD P-12.doc from the drive and folder where your Data Files are located, save it as **Organics Forever Price List_[Current Date]**, then close the document.

m. Copy the macro in the Price List Macro document to the Organics Forever Price List_[Current Date] document.

n. Set the Security setting to Medium if necessary, close the Price List Macro document, open the file Organics Forever Price List_[Current Date].doc, click Enable Macros, then run the [Alt][P] macro. In the fill-in box, type **Papayas on sale: $2.00 each**, then click OK.

o. Change the name of the PriceList macro in the Visual Basic window to SalePrice, then close Visual Basic and return to the document.

Advanced Challenge Exercise

■ Open a new blank document, then create a table consisting of 4 rows and 4 columns.

■ Position the insertion point in the table, then create a new macro called FormatTable stored in all documents that selects the entire table, changes the table fill to light yellow, changes the vertical alignment of each cell to Center, and changes the row height to .3. Be sure to save the document after you stop recording. (*Hint*: Practice the steps before you create the macro. Remember that you need to use menus to perform all the steps, including selecting the table.)

■ Create a new table, place the insertion point in the table, and then run the macro to test it.

■ Close the document without saving it, then run the macro in the tables in the Organics Forever Price List.

p. Type **Formatted by** followed by your name at the bottom of the document, print a copy of the document, save it, close it, then exit Word.

▼ INDEPENDENT CHALLENGE 2

As the office manager of the Black Belt Academy, you prepare a gift certificate that you can give to new members. Since you will need to create several of these certificates each week, you decide to create a custom toolbar that contains the buttons you'll use most often to personalize each certificate.

a. Start Word, then open the Customize dialog box.

b. Click the Toolbars tab, then create a new toolbar named **Gift Certificate** and save in the Normal.dot template.

c. Click the Commands tab in the Customize dialog box. From the Drawing category, add the Change AutoShape button and the Fill Color button; from the AutoShapes category, add the Line button. (*Note*: Make sure you select the "Line" button, *not* the Lines button.)

d. Compare the completed Gift Certificate toolbar to Figure P-25, then close the Customize dialog box.

FIGURE P-25

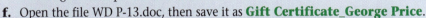

e. Open the Options dialog box from the Tools menu, click the General tab if necessary, then click the Automatically create drawing canvas when inserting AutoShapes check box to deselect it.

f. Open the file WD P-13.doc, then save it as **Gift Certificate_George Price**.

g. Click the hexagon shape, click the Change AutoShape button on the Gift Certificate toolbar, point to Stars and Banners, then select the Change Shape to Explosion 2 shape.

h. Right-click the explosion shape, click Add Text, type **George Price** on two lines, then enhance the text with Bold, 14 pt, and center alignment.

i. Click the Fill Color list arrow on the Gift Certificate toolbar, then select the Light Turquoise fill color.

j. Click next to To:, click the Line button, click the straight line, press and hold the [Shift] key, draw a line approximately six inches from To: to the right margin, then draw a line next to Date:.

k. Click next to To:, type **George Price, 202 West 4th Street, Milwaukee, WI**, then remove Bold.

l. Click next to Date:, then type the current date. If necessary, adjust the line so that it appears under the date.

Advanced Challenge Exercise

- Open the Customize dialog box, then click Commands.
- Select Built-in Menus, then drag Font to the Gift Certificate toolbar.
- Click Rearrange Commands in the Customize dialog box, then click the Toolbar option button and select the Gift Certificate toolbar.
- Move the Change AutoShape button on the Gift Certificate toolbar to the bottom of the list of four buttons.
- Click Line, click Modify Selection, then change the name of the Line button to Info Line.
- Select Edit Button Image from the list of selections, then click squares below the current line to make a thicker line. See Figure P-26.
- Exit all dialog boxes.
- Select the text **George Price** in the explosion shape, click the Font button on the Gift Certificate toolbar, then select the BrushScript MT font (or a similar script-like font).
- Click the new Line button, then draw a line under Gift Certificate. Use Shift to keep the line straight.

FIGURE P-26

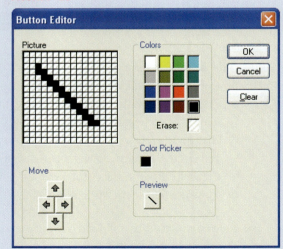

m. Type **Prepared by** followed by your name at the bottom of the document, print a copy, then save and close the document.

n. Delete the Gift Certificate toolbar from the toolbars list in the Customize dialog box, close the document, then exit Word.

▼ INDEPENDENT CHALLENGE 3

You work for Blossom Inc., a florist shop in Nashville, Tennessee. The company has moved recently. As a result, several letters include an incorrect address in the letterhead. You decide to create a macro that replaces the address, phone number, and fax number of the old location with the correct contact information.

a. Start Word, open the file WD P-14.doc from the drive and folder where your Data Files are located, then save it as **Catalog Request_Farrell.**

b. Open the Record Macro dialog box, name the new macro **BlossomLetterhead**, then enter the following text in the Description text box: **Select the address, type a new address, change the zip code, change the phone and fax numbers, apply italic.** Close the dialog box.

c. Press [▼] once, then press [◄] once to position the insertion point at the beginning of the address line.

d. Press [F8] to turn on select mode, then press [►] repeatedly to select just 1801 Bower Avenue.

e. Press [Delete], then type **150 Mainline Avenue**.

f. Press [►] to move just before the 0 in the zip code, type **22**, then press [Delete] two times to delete 01.

g. Press [▼] two times, then press [Home] to move to the beginning of the Phone number line.

h. Press[►] to move to the last four digits of the phone number (7766), type **4455**, press [Delete] four times to delete 7766, press [►] to move to the last four digits of the fax number (7768), type **6641**, then press [Delete] four times to delete 7768.

i. Press [Home] to move to the beginning of the line, press [F8], then press [End].

j. Press [Ctrl][I] to turn on italic, press [▼] once, then click the Stop Recording button on the Stop Recording toolbar.

k. Enter your name in the closing where indicated, print a copy of the letter, then save and close it.

l. Open the Macros dialog box, click BlossomLetterhead in the list of macros, click Edit to enter the Visual Basic window, then change the name of the macro to **Letterhead** (in two places).

m. Scroll down toward the end of the Letterhead code to find the code Selection.Font.Italic = wdToggle, then delete the line of code. (*Note*: If you make a mistake, click Edit Undo.)

n. Save the revised macro, then close the Visual Basic window.

o. Open the file WD P-15.doc from the drive and folder where your Data Files are located, save it as **Catalog Request_Deville**, run the Letterhead macro, press [▼] to remove highlighting if necessary, enter your name in the complimentary closing, print a copy of the letter, save, then close the document.

p. Delete the Letterhead macro, then exit Word.

▼ INDEPENDENT CHALLENGE 4

You can obtain custom dictionaries from many Web sites on the World Wide Web and then add them to Microsoft Word so that you can check documents that contain specialized terms such as medical or scientific terms. You decide to check out some of the resources available on the Web with respect to custom dictionaries that you can use with Spell Checker.

a. Conduct a search for keywords such as "spelling dictionaries" and "spell checking dictionaries."

b. Find two Web sites that provide spelling dictionaries you can download and add as custom dictionaries to Microsoft Word. Some of the Web sites will offer spelling dictionaries for free and some will sell them.

c. Open WD P-16.doc from the drive and folder containing your Data Files, then save it as **Spelling Dictionaries**.

d. Complete the document with the required information about the spelling dictionaries available from the Web sites you've selected.

e. Add a summary paragraph explaining the steps you would follow to make one of these custom dictionaries the default dictionary.

f. Enter your name where indicated in the document, print a copy, then save and close the document and exit Word.

▼ VISUAL WORKSHOP

Open the file WD P-17.doc from the drive and folder where your Data Files are located, click Enable Macros, then save the file as **Birthday Card_Sara**. The file contains text and a macro called BirthdayCard. Open the Visual Basic window for the BirthdayCard macro (see Figure P-27), then edit the code as follows: Change the font attribute from Arial to **Georgia**, scroll down, then change the line spacing attribute from wdLineSpaceDouble to wdLineSpaceSingle. (*Note*: You only need to replace Double with Single in the attribute code.) Save the revised macro, close the Visual Basic window, then run the revised macro and enter **Sara** in the fill-in box. Switch to Whole Page view, then compare the completed birthday card to Figure P-28, adjust formatting as needed. Type **Formatted by** followed by your name at the bottom of the document, print a copy, then save and close the document.

FIGURE P-27

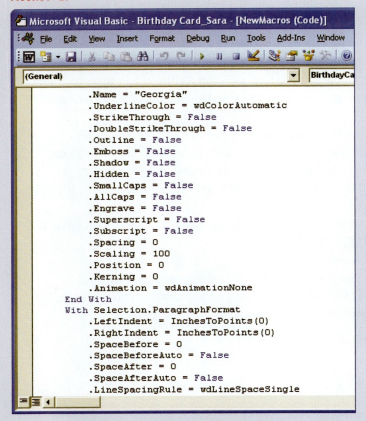

FIGURE P-28

Working with XML

OBJECTIVES

Work with XML Schema

Manage XML Documents and Options

If you have a SAM user profile, you may have access to hands-on instruction, practice, and assessment of the skills covered in this unit. Log in to your SAM account and go to your assignments page to see what your instructor has assigned.

Word 2003 includes the features needed to create and work with XML documents. **XML** stands for eXtensible Markup Language and is used to structure, store, and send information. You can attach an XML schema to a document, select XML options, and save a document in XML format. Information about customers, suppliers, and products currently contained in documents can, through the use of XML, be coded, extracted, and stored, and then distributed across the Internet to facilitate a variety of business operations from marketing to strategic planning. In the past, information, such as customer names and addresses, could be accessed easily only if it was stored in a database. Now XML can be used to extract and use information that can be contained in a wide variety of documents. Graham Watson in the Marketing Department at MediaLoft asks you to learn more about how XML can be used to code documents in Word.

Working with XML Schema

Before you can convert a Word document into an XML document, you need to attach an XML schema. An **XML schema** is a formal specification that is written in XML code. When attached to a document, an XML schema defines the structure of an XML document. The schema includes the names of **elements** that can be defined in the document and defines which **attributes** are available for each element. XML is based on user-defined tags and XML schemas are usually created within a company for use with the company's documents. Companies develop their own custom schemas that they then apply to documents containing information required for a wide variety of business operations. Graham Watson has received an XML schema from MediaLoft's XML experts and asks you to attach it to a Word document containing a list of authors and their books. The file containing the schema is called BookList_Schema. Figure XML-1 shows the Book List schema in Notepad. You attach this schema to a Word document in Word and then you attach XML tags to relevant content.

STEPS

TROUBLE

Make sure that the Show/Hide ¶ button ¶ is selected so that paragraph marks are visible.

1. **Start Word, open the file WD XML-1.doc from the drive and folder where your Data Files are located, then save it as Book List**

   The document contains the names of three authors and the titles of their books.

2. **Click View on the menu bar, click Task Pane, click the Other Task Panes list arrow in the task pane, then click XML Structure**

   The XML Structure task pane opens and advises you that you need to select a schema before you can apply XML elements to a Word document.

3. **Click Templates and Add-Ins, then click the XML Schema tab if it is not already selected**

   Using options available on the XML Schema tab, you can add a schema, access the schema library where you can modify schema settings and delete schemas you no longer need, and modify XML options.

4. **Click Add Schema, navigate to the drive and folder where your Data Files are located, click BookList_Schema.xsd, then click Open**

   The .xsd extension identifies the file as an XML schema.

TROUBLE

If Book List already appears in the dialog box, type Book List1 or another number to give the schema a unique name.

5. **In the Schema Settings dialog box, type Book List, press [Tab], type Book List, then click OK**

6. **Click OK to attach the Book List schema to the document**

   The XML Structure task pane appears as shown in Figure XML-2. Next you add XML tags to selected text in your document.

TROUBLE

If you do not see {Book List}, click Book and continue.

7. **Click Books {Book List} in the Choose an element to apply to your current selection list box, then click Apply to Entire Document in the Apply to entire document message box**

   The Books tag defines the content of the entire document.

8. **Click [↓] once to deselect the text, then save the document**

   In the next lesson you will finish adding the required tags from the XML schema to the Book List document.

FIGURE XML-1: Book List schema viewed in Notepad

Code to create an element

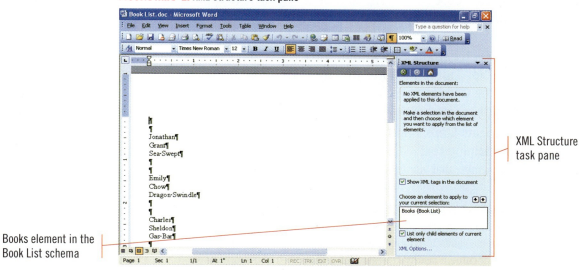

FIGURE XML-2: XML Structure task pane

XML Structure task pane

Books element in the Book List schema

Clues to Use

Understanding XML

With XML you can define your own tags. Consider the following very simple example:

```
<Tour>
<Tour_Title>Antarctica Marathon</Tour_Title>
     <Tour_Date>April 2 to April 20</Tour_Date>
     <Guides>
     <Guide_Name>Harriet Knutson</Guide_Name>
     </Guides>
</Tour>
```

This document contains five XML tags: Tour, Tour_Title, Tour_Date, Guides, and Guide_Name. The author of the XML document chose these tag names because they accurately describe the data they represent. These XML tags are defined in an XML schema attached to the document. Imagine that the document contains a list of 500 tours. After coding information about each tour with the appropriate tags, the author of the document could extract a list of tours, tour guides, or tour dates. Then, the extracted data could be used to update the database profiles of clients or users so a record of their preferences could be maintained, or a request could be sent to the tour operator for more information or for a reservation for a particular tour with choices of guide, tour location, etc. If this data is already included in a database, then extraction would be easy. XML provides users with the means of easily extracting data stored in documents so it can be used in other documents or in other applications without having to be rekeyed. You can handle an XML document in two ways. First, you can use a style sheet to display the content of an XML document in an Internet browser such as Explorer or Netscape and second, you can use a programming language such as JavaScript and Java to read and process the contents of an XML document, usually in a browser.

Managing XML Documents and Options

You have completed the first step in creating an XML document, which is to attach an XML schema to a document from which you want to extract specific information. The next step is to add tags from the XML schema that identify the information you want to be able to access. Once you have added XML tags from the XML schema to the Word document, you can save the document as an XML document. You can also modify XML options and work further with schemas in the Schema Library. 🎨🖌️ You add XML tags from the Book List schema to the Book List document, save the document as an XML document, then view XML options and the Schema Library.

STEPS

1. **Select from the line above Jonathon to the line below Sea Swept, click the check box next to List only child elements of current element in the XML Structure task pane to deselect it, then click Book in the Choose an element to apply to your current selection list box**

   The Book tag is inserted above and below the information relating to Jonathon Grant and his book called *Sea Swept*.

2. **Select Jonathon, click Author_First in the XML Structure task pane, select Grant, click Author_Last in the XML Structure task pane, select Sea Swept, scroll down and click Title in the Choose an element to apply to your current selection list box, then press [↓] once**

   The information related to Jonathon Grant and his book is tagged, as shown in Figure XML-3

3. **Repeats Steps 1 and 2 to apply the required XML tags shown in Figure XML-4 to the remaining text**

   Remember that you need to select the required text first and then select the tag. You start by selecting from the line above Emily to the line below Dragon Swindle and then selecting the Book tag.

4. **Click XML Options at the bottom of the XML Structure task pane**

   As shown in Figure XML-5, the XML Options dialog box contains options related to saving XML, applying Schema validation options, and changing XML view options. You accept the default setting, which is to validate the document against the attached schema. When this option is selected, a wavy pink line appears next to text that is tagged incorrectly. As you were applying tags to the document, the wavy pink line did appear. However, once the entire document is tagged as instructed, the wavy pink line that indicates violations no longer appears. From the XML Options dialog box you can also access options related to working with the Schema Library.

5. **Click Schema Library, then click Book List in the list of schemas**

   The options available for working with schemas appear. As you can see, you can choose to add another schema or you can delete the current schema. You can also change the name attached to the schema by selecting the Schema Settings button.

   QUICK TIP

   You should delete a schema when you share a computer with other users.

6. **Click Delete Schema, click OK to close the Schema Library dialog box, then click OK to close the XML Options dialog box**

7. **Click File on the menu bar, click Save As, click the Save as type list arrow, click XML Document, then click Save**

   The document is saved as Book List.xml.

8. **Press [Ctrl][End] to move to the bottom of the document, press [Enter], type your name, click File on the menu bar, click Print, click Options, click the check box next to XML tags to select it, click OK, then click OK**

   The document is printed along with the XML tags.

9. **Save and close the document, then exit Word**

FIGURE XML-3: Tags applied to Jonathon Grant information

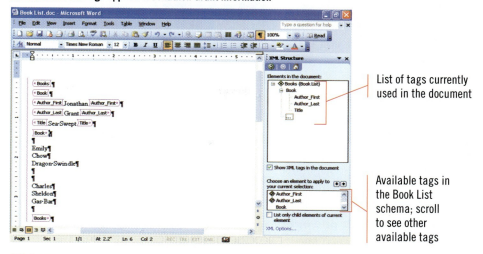

List of tags currently used in the document

Available tags in the Book List schema; scroll to see other available tags

FIGURE XML-4: Tags applied to Emily Chow and Charles Sheldon information

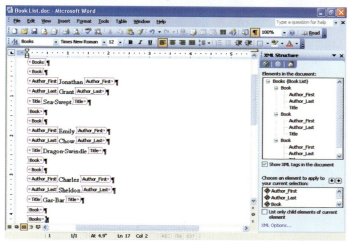

FIGURE XML-5: XML Options dialog box

Clues to Use

HTML and XML

XML is a meta-markup language; that is, a language that you use to create languages. As you have learned, you use XML to design your own tags. HTML is a markup language that you use to format data so that it can be displayed on the Internet. The HTML tags used to format the data are predefined. In other words, you must use the <b> and </b> HTML tags to indicate that selected text is to be displayed in bold. With XML, the focus is on content, *not* format. You can define your own tags that describe different types of data, depending on the nature of the information you wish to extract from a document. For example, you can define a tag called <author> and then create related children such as <authorfirst>, <authorlast>, etc. The fact that you can select your own names for XML tags makes XML an incredibly versatile language that you can use to process and share an almost limitless variety of information.

▼ SKILLS REVIEW

1. **Work with XML Schema.**
   a. Start Word, open the file WD XML-2.doc from the drive and folder where your Data Files are located, then save it as **Adventure Tours**.
   b. Show the XML Structure task pane.
   c. Open the Templates and Add-ins dialog box.
   d. Click Add Schema, navigate to the drive and folder containing your Data Files, then open AdventureTours_Schema.xsd.
   e. Type **Adventure Tours** for both the name and the alias of the schema, then attach the Adventure Tours schema to the document.
   f. Click Tours {Adventure Tours} in the XML Structure task pane, then click Apply to Entire Document.
   g. Deselect the text, then save the document.

2. **Manage XML documents and options.**
   a. Select from the line above Antarctica Marathon to the line below April 2 to April 20, then deselect the List only child elements of current element check box in the XML Structure task pane.
   b. Select the Tour tag.
   c. Apply the Tour_Title tag to Antarctica Marathon.
   d. Apply the Guide_Name tag to Harriet Knutson.
   e. Apply the Tour_Date tag to April 2 to April 20.
   f. Apply the Tour tag to the information about the Costa Rica Rainforest Odyssey tour.
   g. Apply the Tour_Title, Guide_Name and Tour_Date tags to the required information about the Rainforest tour.
   h. Open the XML Options dialog box.
   i. Open the Schema Library dialog box and click the Adventure Tours schema.
   j. Delete the Adventure Tours schema, then close the dialog boxes.
   k. Save the document as an XML document called **Adventure Tours**.
   l. Type your name at the bottom of the document, then print a copy of the document with the XML tags showing.
   m. Save and close the document, then exit Word

Glossary

Adjustment handle The yellow diamond that appears when certain AutoShapes are selected; used to change the shape, but not the size, of an AutoShape.

Alignment The position of text in a document relative to the margins.

Anchored The state of a floating graphic that moves with a paragraph or other item if the item is moved; an anchor symbol appears with the floating graphic when formatting marks are displayed.

Application *See* Program.

Area chart A chart similar to a line chart; however the space between the lines and the bottom of the chart is filled, and a different band of color represents each value.

Ascending order Lists data alphabetically or sequentially (from A to Z, 0 to 9, or earliest to latest).

Attribute In XML, extra information about an element that is stored in the start tag; for example, an assigned default value for the element is an attribute of that element.

AutoComplete A feature that automatically suggests text to insert.

AutoCorrect A feature that automatically detects and corrects typing errors, minor spelling errors, and capitalization, or inserts certain typographical symbols as you type.

Automatic page break A page break that is inserted automatically at the bottom of a page.

AutoShape A drawing object, such as a rectangle, oval, triangle, line, block arrow, or other shape that you create using the tools on the Drawing toolbar.

AutoText A feature that stores frequently used text and graphics so they can be easily inserted into a document.

Bar chart A chart that shows values as horizontal bars; Cylinder, Cone, and Pyramid charts can also show values in horizontal format, similar to the rectangles used in bar charts.

Bitmap graphic A graphic that is composed of a series of small dots called "pixels."

Boilerplate text Text that appears in every version of a merged document.

Bold Formatting applied to text to make it thicker and darker.

Bookmark Text that identifies a location or a selection of text in a document.

Border A line that can be added above, below, or to the sides of a paragraph, text, or a table cell; a line that divides the columns and rows of a table.

Browser A software program used to access and display Web pages.

Bullet A small graphic symbol used to identify items in a list.

Cell The box formed by the intersection of a table row and table column.

Cell reference A code that identifies a cell's position in a table; each cell reference contains a letter (A, B, C, and so on) to identify its column and a number (1, 2, 3, and so on) to identify its row.

Center Alignment in which an item is centered between the margins.

Character spacing Formatting that changes the width or scale of characters, expands or condenses the amount of space between characters, raises or lowers characters relative to the line of text, and adjusts kerning (the space between standard combinations of letters).

Character style A named set of character format settings that can be applied to text to format it all at once.

Chart A visual representation of numerical data, usually used to illustrate trends, patterns, or relationships.

Circular chart A chart that shows how values relate to each other as parts of a whole; a pie chart is an example of a circular chart.

Click and Type A feature that allows you to automatically apply the necessary paragraph formatting to a table, graphic, or text when you insert the item in a blank area of a document in Print Layout or Web Layout view.

Click and Type pointer A pointer used to move the insertion point and automatically apply the paragraph formatting necessary to insert text at that location in the document.

Clip A media file, such as a graphic, photograph, sound, movie, or animation, that can be inserted into a document.

Clip art A collection of graphic images that can be inserted into documents, presentations, Web pages, spreadsheets, and other Office files.

Clip Organizer A library of the clips that come with Word.

Clipboard A temporary storage area for items that are cut or copied from any Office file and are available for pasting. *See also* Office Clipboard and System Clipboard.

Column break A break that forces text following the break to begin at the top of the next column.

Column chart A chart that compares values side-by-side, usually over time; Cylinder, Cone, and Pyramid charts can also show values in vertical format, similar to the rectangles used in column charts.

Comment An embedded note or annotation that an author or a reviewer adds to a document; appears in a comment balloon when working in Page Layout view.

Copy To place a copy of an item on the Clipboard without removing it from a document.

Crop To trim away part of a graphic.

Cross-reference Text that electronically refers the reader to another part of the document.

Cut To remove an item from a document and place it on the Clipboard.

Cut and paste To move text or graphics using the Cut and Paste commands.

Cycle diagram A diagram that illustrates a process that has a continuous cycle.

Data field A category of information, such as last name, first name, street address, city, or postal code.

Data record A complete set of related information for a person or an item, such as a person's name and address.

Data source In mail merge, the file with the unique data for individual people or items; the data merged with a main document to produce multiple versions.

Datasheet A table grid that opens when a chart is inserted in Word.

Delete To permanently remove an item from a document.

Descending order Lists data in reverse alphabetical or sequential order (Z to A, 9 to 0, or latest to earliest).

Destination file The file to which data is copied.

Destination program The program to which the data is copied.

Digital certificate An attachment for a file that vouches for the authenticity of the file, provides secure encryption, or supplies a verifiable signature.

Digital signature An electronic stamp attached to a document to authenticate the document.

Document The electronic file you create using Word.

Document map A pane that shows all the headings and subheadings in a document.

Document properties Details about a file, such as author name or the date the file was created, that are used to organize and search for files.

Document window The workspace in the program window that displays the current document.

Drag and drop To move text or a graphic by dragging it to a new location using the mouse.

Drawing canvas A workspace for creating graphics; an area within which multiple shapes can be drawn and clip art or pictures inserted.

Drop cap A large dropped initial capital letter that is often used to set off the first paragraph of an article.

Dynamic Data Exchange (DDE) The connection between the source file and the destination file.

Element In XML, the unit of content that forms the basic structure of an XML document; an element consists of an element name and element content, and can also include the attributes (extra information) related to the element.

Embedded object An object contained in a source file and inserted into a destination file; an embedded object becomes part of the destination file that is no longer linked to the source file.

Endnote Text that provides additional information or acknowledges sources for text in a document and that appears at the end of a document.

Field A code that serves as a placeholder for data that changes in a document, such as a page number.

Field label A word or phrase that tells users the kind of information required for a given field.

Field name The name of a data field.

File An electronic collection of information that has a unique name, distinguishing it from other files.

Filename The name given to a document when it is saved.

Filename extension Three letters that follow the period in the filename; for example, .doc for a Word file and .xls for Excel files.

Filter In a mail merge, to pull out records that meet specific criteria and include only those records in the merge.

First line indent A type of indent in which the first line of a paragraph is indented more than the subsequent lines.

Floating graphic A graphic to which a text wrapping style has been applied, making the graphic independent of text and able to be moved anywhere on a page.

Font The typeface or design of a set of characters (letters, numbers, symbols, and punctuation marks).

Font effect Font formatting that applies a special effect to text, such as a shadow, an outline, small caps, or superscript.

Font size The size of characters, measured in points (pts).

Footer Information, such as text, a page number, or a graphic, that appears at the bottom of every page in a document or a section.

Footnote Text that provides additional information or acknowledges sources for text in a document and that appears at the bottom of the page on which the footnote reference appears.

Form field The location where the data associated with a field label is stored.

Form template A file that contains the structure of a form. Users create new forms from a form template; data entered into new forms based on a form template do not affect the structure of the template file.

Format Painter A feature used to copy the format settings applied to the selected text to other text you want to format the same way.

Formatting marks Nonprinting characters that appear on screen to indicate the ends of paragraphs, tabs, and other formatting elements.

Formatting toolbar A toolbar that contains buttons for frequently used formatting commands.

Frame A section of a Web page window in which a separate Web page is displayed.

Full screen view A view that shows only the document window on screen.

Getting Started task pane A task pane that contains shortcuts for opening documents, for creating new documents, and for accessing information on the Microsoft Web site.

Gridlines Nonprinting lines that show the boundaries of table cells.

Gutter Extra space left for a binding at the top, left, or inside margin of a document.

Hanging indent A type of indent in which the second and subsequent lines of a paragraph are indented more than the first.

Hard page break *See* Manual page break.

Header Information, such as text, a page number, or a graphic, that appears at the top of every page in a document or a section.

Header row The first row of a table that contains the column headings.

Highlighting Transparent color that can be applied to text to call attention to it.

Home page The main page of a Web site and the first Web page viewers see when they visit a site.

Horizontal ruler A ruler that appears at the top of the document window in Print Layout, Normal, and Web Layout view.

HTML (Hypertext Markup Language) The programming language used to code how each element of a Web page should appear when viewed with a browser.

Hyperlink Text or a graphic that opens a file, Web page, or other item when clicked. Also known as a link.

I-beam pointer The pointer used to move the insertion point and select text.

Indent The space between the edge of a line of text or a paragraph and the margin.

Indent marker A marker on the horizontal ruler that shows the indent settings for the active paragraph.

Index Text that lists many of the terms and topics in a document, along with the pages on which they appear.

Inline graphic A graphic that is part of a line of text in which it was inserted.

Insertion point The blinking vertical line that shows where text will appear when you type in a document.

Italic Formatting applied to text to make the characters slant to the right.

Justify Alignment in which an item is flush with both the left and right margins.

Keyboard shortcut A combination of keys or a function key that can be pressed to perform a command.

Label Text that describes the significance of a value in a chart.

Landscape orientation Page orientation in which the page is wider than it is tall.

Left indent A type of indent in which the left edge of a paragraph is moved in from the left margin.

Left-align Alignment in which the item is flush with the left margin.

Legend A chart element that identifies the patterns or colors that are assigned to the data series or categories in a chart.

Line spacing The amount of space between lines of text.

Line chart A chart that illustrates trends, where each value is connected to the next value by a line.

Linked object An object created in a source file and inserted into a destination file that maintains a connection between the 2 files; changes made to the data in the source file are reflected in the destination file.

List style A named set of format settings, such as indents and outline numbering, that can be applied to a list to format it all at once.

Macro A series of Word commands and instructions grouped together as a single command to accomplish a task automatically.

Mail Merge Combines a standard document, such as a form letter, with customized data, such as a set of names and addresses, to create a set of personalized documents.

Main document In a mail merge, the document with the standard text.

Manual page break A page break inserted to force the text following the break to begin at the top of the next page.

Margin The blank area between the edge of the text and the edge of a page.

Master document A Word document that contains links to two or more related documents called subdocuments.

Menu bar The bar beneath the title bar that contains the names of menus; clicking a menu name opens a menu of program commands.

Merge To combine adjacent cells into a single larger cell.

Merge field A placeholder that you insert in the main document to indicate where the data from each record should be inserted when you perform a mail merge.

Mirror margins Margins used in documents with facing pages, where the inside and outside margins are mirror images of each other.

Negative indent A type of indent in which the left edge of a paragraph is moved to the left of the left margin.

Nested table A table inserted in a cell of another table.

Normal style The paragraph style that is used by default to format text typed into a blank document.

Normal template The template that is loaded automatically when a new document is inserted in Word.

Normal view A view that shows a document without margins, headers and footers, or graphics.

Note reference mark A number or character that indicates additional information is contained in a footnote or endnote.

Nudge To move a graphic a small amount in one direction using the arrow keys.

Object Self-contained information that can be in the form of text, spreadsheet data, graphics, charts, tables, or sound and video clips.

Object Linking and Embedding (OLE) The ability to share information with other programs.

Office Assistant An animated character that offers tips and provides access to the program's Help system.

Office Clipboard A temporary storage area shared by all Office programs that can be used to cut, copy and paste multiple items within and between Office programs. The Office Clipboard can hold up to 24 items collected from any Office program. *See* Clipboard and System Clipboard.

Open To use one of the methods for opening a document to retrieve it and display it in the document window.

Organization chart A chart that illustrates a hierarchy, most often showing how functional areas in a company or organization relate to each other.

Outdent *See* Negative indent.

Outline view A view that shows the headings of a document organized as an outline.

Overtype mode A feature that allows you to overwrite existing text as you type.

Page border A graphical line that encloses one or more pages of a document.

Paragraph spacing The amount of space between paragraphs.

Paragraph style A named set of paragraph and character format settings that can be applied to a paragraph to format it all at once.

Paste To insert items stored on the Clipboard into a document.

Pixels Small dots that define color and intensity in a graphic.

Point The unit of measurement for text characters and the space between paragraphs and characters; 1/72 of an inch.

Point-to-point chart A chart used to identify patterns or to show values as clusters; the most commonly used type of point-to-point charts is the XY chart, also known as a Scatter chart.

Portrait orientation Page orientation in which the page is taller than it is wide.

Print Layout view A view that shows a document as it will look on a printed page.

Print Preview A view of a file as it will appear when printed.

Program Task-oriented software (such as Excel or Word) that enables you to perform a certain type of task such as data calculation or word processing.

Property A named attribute of a control set to define one of the control's attributes such as its size, its color, and its behavior in response to user input.

Pyramid diagram A diagram that illustrates a hierarchical relationship.

Radial diagram A diagram that illustrates the relationships of several related elements to a core element.

Reading Layout view A view that shows a document so that it is easy to read and annotate.

Right indent A type of indent in which the right edge of a paragraph is moved in from the right margin.

Right-align Alignment in which an item is flush with the right margin.

Sans serif font A font, such as Arial, whose characters do not include serifs, which are small strokes at the ends of letters.

Save To store a file permanently on a disk or to overwrite the copy of a file that is stored on a disk with the changes made to the file.

Save As Command used to save a file for the first time or to create a new file with a different filename, leaving the original file intact.

Scale To resize a graphic so that its height to width ratio remains the same.

ScreenTip A label that appears on the screen to identify a button or to provide information about a feature.

Scroll To use the scroll bars or the arrow keys to display different parts of a document in the document window.

Scroll arrows The arrows at the ends of the scroll bars that are clicked to scroll a document one line at a time.

Scroll bars The bars on the right edge (vertical scroll bar) and bottom edge (horizontal scroll bar) of the document window that are used to display different parts of the document in the document window.

Scroll box The box in a scroll bar that can be dragged to scroll a document.

Section A portion of a document that is separated from the rest of the document by section breaks.

Section break A formatting mark inserted to divide a document into sections.

Select To click or highlight an item in order to perform some action on it.

Serif font A font, such as Times New Roman, whose characters include serifs, which are small strokes at the ends of letters.

Shading A background color or pattern that can be applied to text, tables, or graphics.

Shortcut key *See* Keyboard shortcut.

Sizing handles The black squares or white circles that appear around a graphic when it is selected; used to change the size or shape of a graphic.

Smart tag A purple dotted line that appears under text that Word identifies as a date, name, address, or place.

Smart Tag Actions button The button that appears when you point to a smart tag.

Soft page break *See* Automatic page break.

Sort To organize data, such as table rows, items in a list, or records in a mail merge, in ascending or descending order.

Source file The file in which data is originally saved.

Source program The program in which data is originally created.

Split To divide a cell into two or more cells.

Standard toolbar A toolbar that contains buttons for frequently used operating and editing commands.

Status bar The bar at the bottom of the Word program window that shows the vertical position, section, and page number of the insertion point, the total number of pages in a document, and the on/off status of several Word features.

Style A named collection of character and/or paragraph formats that are stored together and can be applied to text to format it quickly.

Subdocument A document contained within a master document.

Subscript A font effect in which text is formatted in a smaller font size and placed below the line of text.

Superscript A font effect in which text is formatted in a smaller font size and placed above the line of text.

Symbols Special characters that can be inserted into a document using the Symbol command.

System Clipboard A clipboard that stores only the last item cut or copied from a document. *See* Clipboard and Office Clipboard.

Tab *See* Tab stop.

Tab leader A line that appears in front of tabbed text.

Tab stop A location on the horizontal ruler that indicates where to align text.

Table A grid made up of rows and columns of cells that you can fill with text and graphics.

Table style A named set of table format settings that can be applied to a table to format it all at once.

Tags HTML codes placed around the elements of a Web page to describe how each element should appear when viewed with a browser.

Target diagram A diagram that illustrates steps toward a goal.

Task pane An area of the Word program window that contains shortcuts to Word formatting, editing, research, Help, clip art, mail merge, and other features.

Template A formatted document that contains placeholder text you can replace with your own text; a file that contains the basic structure of a document.

Text box A container that you can fill with text and graphics.

Text form field A location in a form where users enter text.

Theme A set of complementary design elements that you can apply to Web pages, e-mail messages, and other documents that are viewed on screen.

Thumbnail Smaller version of a page that appears in the Thumbnails pane to the left of the document window when you select thumbnails on the View menu.

Title bar The bar at the top of the program window that indicates the program name and the name of the current file.

Toggle button A button that turns a feature on and off.

Toolbar A bar that contains buttons that you can click to perform commands.

Tracked change A mark that shows where an insertion, deletion, or formatting change has been made in a document.

Type a question for help box The list box at the right end of the menu bar that is used to query the Help system.

Undo To reverse a change by using the Undo button or command.

URL (Uniform Resource Locator) A Web address.

User template Any template created by the user.

Value A number in a chart.

Venn diagram A diagram that illustrates areas of overlap between two or more elements.

Vertex The point where two straight lines meet or the highest point in a curve.

Vertical alignment The position of text in a document relative to the top and bottom margins.

Vertical ruler A ruler that appears on the left side of the document window in Print Layout view.

View A way of displaying a document in the document window; each view provides features useful for editing and formatting different types of documents.

View buttons Buttons to the left of the horizontal scroll bar that are used to change views.

Watermark A picture or other type of graphics object that appears lightly shaded behind text in a document.

Web Layout view A view that shows a document as it will look when viewed with a Web browser.

Web page A document that can be stored on a computer called a Web server and viewed on the World Wide Web or on an intranet using a browser.

Web site A group of associated Web pages that are linked together with hyperlinks.

Wizard An interactive set of dialog boxes that guides you through a task.

Word processing program A software program that includes tools for entering, editing, and formatting text and graphics.

Word program window The window that contains the Word program elements, including the document window, toolbars, menu bar, and status bar.

Word-wrap A feature that automatically moves the insertion point to the next line as you type.

WordArt A drawing object that contains text formatted with special shapes, patterns, and orientations.

Workgroup Templates Templates created for distribution to others.

X-axis The horizontal axis in a two-dimensional chart.

XML Acronym that stands for eXtensible Markup Language, which is a language used to structure, store, and send information.

XML Schema A formal specification that is written in XML code and then attached to an XML document to define the structure of the document.

Y-axis The vertical axis in a two-dimensional chart.

Index